D0880926

KEATS' CRAFTSMANSHIP

A STUDY IN POETIC DEVELOPMENT

KEATS' CRAFTSMANSHIP

A STUDY IN POETIC DEVELOPMENT

By

M. R. RIDLEY

Fellow of Balliol College, Oxford
Hon. L.H.D. Bowdoin College, U.S.A.

OXFORD
AT THE CLARENDON PRESS
1933

OXFORD
UNIVERSITY PRESS
AMEN HOUSE, E.C. 4
London Edinburgh Glasgow
Leipzig New York Toronto
Melbourne Capetown Bombay
Calcutta Madras Shanghai
HUMPHREY MILFORD
PUBLISHER TO THE
UNIVERSITY

PRINTED IN GREAT BRITAIN

PREFACE

IT is always pleasant to say 'thank you', and I take this opportunity of expressing my gratitude to various people who have directly or indirectly helped in the production of this book.

First to my wife, whose book it largely is, without whose criticism and patient assistance over vexatious details it would have been a great deal more imperfect, and without whose earlier work on the subject it would hardly have taken shape at all. Whatever is here of value in regard to Keats' 'sources' was lying inaccessibly interred in an unpublished thesis of hers—pyramidally but not otherwise extant—and she urged me to open the pyramid and rifle the tomb.

Secondly, not only to the Boards of Trustees and Overseers, and to the President, of Bowdoin College, U.S.A., whose appointment of me to, and arrangement of my duties during my year's tenure of, the Tallman Visiting Professorship, gave me a period of comparative leisure, unexpected and invaluable; but also to the whole faculty of the College, and especially to the Department of English, for a welcome which made the stranger within the gates almost forget that he was a stranger, and allowed him to occupy his leisure in an atmosphere at once so kindly and so stimulating.

I have also to thank the Marquess of Crewe for allowing me free access to much valuable material; Dr. G. P. Winship of the Widener Library at Harvard for allowing me to examine all the Keats MSS. in the Amy Lowell collection and providing me with all the many photostats that I needed; and Miss Belle da Costa Greene, the librarian of the Pierpont Morgan Library in New York, for providing me with a photostat of some interesting notes by Woodhouse. And I am much indebted to Mr. H. W. Garrod for his benignant and critical interest, and to him and Mr. C. Bailey for saving me from several bad blunders.

I am of course throughout indebted to editors and critics of Keats, notably to H. Buxton Forman and Professor E. de Sélincourt. It will not, I hope, be supposed, because I have questioned certain isolated points of transcription or interpretation, that I am any the less conscious of the debt. And I hope that in correcting errors of transcription I shall not be too often convicted of throwing stones from a greenhouse. All the transcriptions in the book are made, wherever the original is accessible, either from the original or from a photostat of the original, and I have done my best to present students of Keats with transcriptions as accurate as I can make them. But no one can be more conscious than I am of the wisdom of the temperate remark of that most exact and almost impeccable of editors, H. Buxton Forman, 'we are only mortals—the printers and I'.

M. R. R.

NOTE

The facsimile between pp. 162 and 163 is a reproduction of a page of the holograph MS. of *The Eve of St. Agnes*. I am much indebted to the Librarian of the Widener Library at Harvard University for his courtesy in permitting the reproduction and in providing the photograph from which the illustration was made.

CONTENTS

LIST OF THE PRINCIPAL WORKS REFERRED TO WITH ABBREVIATION USED

HBF =*The Complete Works of John Keats*, edited by H. Buxton Forman, 5 vols., Gowans & Gray, 1900.

de S =*The Poetical Works of John Keats*, edited by E. de Sélincourt, 5th ed., Methuen, 1926.

MBF =*The Letters of John Keats*, edited by M. Buxton Forman, 2 vols., Oxford University Press, 1931.

(This is by far the most complete and accurate edition of the letters, and all references are to this edition, with the number of the letter, and the page in brackets. But for the convenience of those who are using either of the other editions (by Sir Sidney Colvin or H. Buxton Forman) a table is appended giving the corresponding numbers of the letters referred to.)

SC =*John Keats, his Life and Poetry*, by Sidney Colvin, 3rd ed., Macmillan, 1920.

AL =*John Keats*, by Amy Lowell, 2 vols., Jonathan Cape, 1924.

MV =*Keats Memorial Volume*, John Lane, 1921.

The quotations from Mrs. Radcliffe's Novels are taken from the following editions; the abbreviations used in the notes are prefixed:

SR =*A Sicilian Romance*, 2 vols., 1790.
RF =*The Romance of the Forest*, 3 vols., 1791.
AD =*The Castles of Athlin and Dunbayne*, 1 vol., 1793.
MU =*The Mysteries of Udolpho*, 4 vols., 1794.
It =*The Italian*, 3 vols., 1797.

There are modern reprints by Routledge of *The Romance of the Forest* and *The Mysteries of Udolpho*. References to these are given in brackets.

LETTERS

MBF	*SC*	*HBF*	*MBF*	*SC*	*HBF*
12	VIII	IX	75	LXII	LXVII
14	X	XI	76	LXIII	LXVIII
18	XIV	XV	77	LXIV	LXIX
19	XV	XVI	82	LXIX	LXXIV
29	XXII	XXV	88	LXXVI	LXXX
30	XXIV	XXVI	89	LXXIII	LXXXI
38	XXX	XXXIII	93	LXXX	LXXXV
39	XXXII	XXXIV	104	—	XCVI
41	XXXIV	XXXVI	105	XCI	XCVII
45	XXXVII	XXXIX	107	—	XCIX
48	XXXIX	XLII	108	XCIV	C
51	XLII	XLV	113	XCIX	CV
55	XLVI	XLIX	114	XCII	CVI
56	XLVII	L	125	—	CXVII
59	L	LIII	128	CVIII	CXX
60	LI	LIV	130	—	CXXII
61	LII	LV	133	CX	CXXV
63	LIII	LVII	140	CXV	CXXXI
67	—	—	142	CXVII	CXXXIII
68	—	—	143	—	—
69	LVI	LXI	144	CXVIII	CXXXIV
71	LVIII	LXIII	147	CXVI	CXXXVII
72	LX	LXIV	206	CXLVIII	CXCVI

I. INTRODUCTION

THERE are various angles from which the work of any literary artist may be studied. We may study it biographically, seeing it formed by and reflecting the events of his own life; or historically, seeing it influenced by and reflecting the events and thought of his age. We may subject it rather to an 'absolute' criticism, deliberately neglecting its relation to its age or country, or even to its author and his life, trying to estimate simply its artistic merits. Or again we may try to trace in it the development of the artist's 'philosophy of life', and his 'message', if we think that he had one. Each of those methods of approach is illuminating, and we can hardly suppose ourselves to have made an honest attempt to understand and appreciate a writer's work, to gain from him what he has to give, until we have used them all. But there is another way of studying an artist, another line of approach which we should not neglect, less ambitious perhaps, but within its limits not less illuminating. We can study his craftsmanship, watch his imagination at work on its materials, see what he was trying to do and how far he succeeded, watch him make his blunders and learn from them, as he finds out by degrees how to use his tools, and so approaches nearer and nearer to the ideal that still eludes him. And sometimes, when we are lucky, we can surprise him in the act of creation, seeing not only the finished statue but also the strokes of the chisel. In the following chapters an attempt will be made to apply this method to a great English poet, in the study of whom the method is not only peculiarly illuminating, but also, from an unusual variety and wealth of material, peculiarly applicable. In the brief three and a half years of his creative poetic life Keats developed with startling rapidity from a blundering apprentice into a very finished craftsman; and for the last eighteen months of that period we have left to us evidence which enables us to study his methods and watch his development with unusual precision.

When a critic is trying to follow the steps of a creative artist's development, to watch how his mind works, and to discover his aims and the methods by which he moved towards their achievement, it is as well that he should be wisely cautious in relying upon his own conjectures and inferences until he has taken the trouble to find out what the artist has to say about himself and his art. Keats, as we shall find, has a great deal to tell us about his aims and his methods. But before we come to examine what he has to say we shall perhaps be prudent to recollect that artists, however honest in intention, are not always wholly to be trusted when they are talking about themselves, and to inquire how much credence we can attach to what Keats tells us.

The calm sanity of Keats' critical judgements on his own work (and for the matter of that on the work of others) has been so often pointed out that there is no need to illustrate or elaborate a commonplace. But it has not, I think, been so frequently nor so emphatically pointed out that his judgements on his own character and on the processes of his own mind (and for that matter on those of others) are at least equally calm and sane, and have besides something rarer than calmness and sanity, a power of penetrating analysis quite uncommon. Keats indeed knew a hundred years ago as much as most of us to-day about the 'New' Psychology (much of which is no more than scientifically applied common sense, and as old as the Delphic *γνῶθι σεαυτόν*), and could express himself much more lucidly, because he had not learned a terminology which he did not understand. As early, for example, as February of 1818 he ends a letter to Reynolds by expatiating on the advantages of idleness:

> 'Now it is more noble to sit like Jove than to fly like Mercury —let us not therefore go hurrying about and collecting honey, bee-like buzzing here and there impatiently from a knowledge of what is to be aimed at; but let us open our leaves like a flower and be passive and receptive—budding patiently under the eye of Apollo and taking hints from every noble insect that favours

> us with a visit—sap will be given us for meat and dew for drink. I was led into these thoughts, my dear Reynolds, by the beauty of the morning operating on a sense of Idleness—I have not read any Books—the Morning said I was right—I had no idea but of the morning, and the thrush said I was right—seeming to say, [here follows the Sonnet 'O thou whose face, . . .].'[1]

And at the end of this superb and penetrating vindication of indolence, a poet's 'Apology for Idlers', he appends the wise qualification, which yet he does not in the misguided enthusiasm of the *volte-face* overstate, 'Now I am sensible all this is a mere sophistication (however it may neighbour to any truths), to excuse my own indolence'. He knows, that is, that he has been conducting what we may call, if we like technicalities, a 'rationalization'; but he also knows, what the psychologists sometimes forget, that a rationalization need not be all false.

Here he is in a straightforward rather than analytical mood: 'I am three and twenty, with little knowledge and middling intellect. It is true that in the height of enthusiasm I have been cheated into some fine passages; but that is not the thing.'[2] And here in an amusing though analytical triviality: 'In my walk to-day I stoop'd under a railing that lay across my path, and ask'd myself "Why I did not get over". "Because", answered I, "no one wanted to force you under".'[3] In the same kind of way, with the same insight, in his comments on Burns he describes a 'defence-mechanism'; 'how sad it is when a luxurious imagination is obliged, in self-defence, to deaden its delicacy in vulgarity and in things attainable, that it may not have leisure to go mad after things which are not';[4] and in his comments on parsons[5] the simplest type of what we now elaborately call a repression.

Most significant of all perhaps is the passage in which he is discussing his aversion from women. 'I must absolutely get over this—but how? The only way is to find the root of evil, and so cure it "with backward mutters of

[1] MBF, 45 (112). [2] MBF, 107 (308). [3] MBF, 142 (420).
[4] MBF, 71 (187). [5] MBF, 114 (322).

dissevering Power"—that is a difficult thing; for an obstinate Prejudice can seldom be produced but from a gordian complication of feelings, which must take time to unravell and care to keep unravelled.'[1] One could hardly wish for a clearer brief definition of a 'complex' and the methods of its resolution.

Even these few instances may, I hope, encourage us to suppose that whatever Keats tells us about himself merits our very serious attention, and probably our acceptance. And the more one studies Keats' letters the more, I think, one becomes convinced that the critics who are not too proud to accept Keats' self-analysis are wiser than those who, prompted by a serene vanity and a misplaced confidence in their own analytical powers, present us with a Keats in their own image.

Let us then begin our study of the processes of Keats' creative imagination by trying to discover all we can, from what he says in his own letters, about himself, about his notions of Poetry, and about the relations between the two.

In the first place then we are dealing with a man who relied on and lived by his 'imagination' rather than his reason—which does not at all mean, as the most superficial examination of Keats' use of the word will reveal, a man who lived in a world of inconsequent fantasies. But it is upon imagination that he relies for his findings, those findings by which life has to be conducted. 'What the imagination seizes as Beauty must be truth—whether it existed before or not.'[2] A detailed examination of this and similar passages has often been made, and to traverse the ground again would not be relevant to our present inquiry, important though it is to the complete comprehension of Keats; but I would suggest in passing that if in most places where Keats uses the word 'truth' (with its connotation of 'correspondence') we substitute the word 'reality', we are likely to come nearer to his meaning. In

[1] MBF, 75 (210). [2] MBF, 29 (72).

this passage, for example, the connexion of 'whether it existed before or not' becomes much clearer. He is not prepared to deny that reality may be arrived at by the processes of the reason; but yet he cannot see how it can be so arrived at; and at any rate it is not the road for him. 'I have never yet been able to perceive how anything can be known for truth by consequitive reasoning—and yet it must be.'[1] But this passage needs to be checked by, and read in the light of, a later passage in a letter to Taylor, in which he is speaking of the first draft of a passage in *Endymion*. 'The whole thing must I think have appeared to you, who are a consequitive Man, as a thing almost of mere words—but I assure you that when I wrote it it was a regular stepping of the Imagination towards a Truth.'[2] This indicates that in the earlier passage the emphasis is rather on 'reason' than on 'consequitive'. Keats' advance to a 'Truth' is not at all a haphazard fluttering; it is as ordered a progress as that of the reasoner; but the steps of the progress are those of Imagination, not of Logic. In the same way Keats' test for an axiom is not reason but experience; 'axioms in philosophy are not axioms until they are proved upon our pulses'.[3] But it is worth noticing that he subjects the products of the imagination to the same test; 'we read fine things, but never feel them to the full until we have gone the same steps as the Author'.[3] And his test for a 'truth' is whether he can or cannot gain a clear perception of its beauty: 'I never can feel certain of any truth but from a clear perception of its Beauty.'[4]

If any justification is needed for this recapitulation, brief though it is, of what has so often been said before, it lies in this, that in any study of Keats, in any of his aspects, as poet, as thinker (if we are rash enough to try that unpromising line), as lover, we inevitably go wandering off on the wrong road, and find ourselves in brakes and thickets, with Keats' ghost cheerfully laughing at us from a cloud, if we do not realize, and keep on realizing, that

[1] MBF, 29 (73). [2] MBF, 39 (98). [3] MBF, 61 (154)
[4] MBF, 93 (281).

to Keats the 'real' world, the world that matters, is that of men and women and things, the world apprehended by the senses and the feelings, where the imagination has its unfettered scope, and not the world of the reason. In that world of 'things' the mind finds its material; and to that world it must bring back its products for verification, since in Keats' view the mind cannot guarantee the validity of its own creations. To say that a thing was 'true' because it was reasonable would have been to Keats merely foolish. If a thing was reasonable, it was reasonable, and no more; its truth was a matter to be settled in another court, where the reason was not the judge but was itself on trial.

In the second place, we are dealing with a man who thought for the most part (except, that is, when Milton, if we agree with Mr. Murry, had temporarily ousted Shakespeare) that the essence of the poetic character was what he called in an odd and famous phrase, 'Negative Capability'; that is, as he defines it, 'when a man is capable of being in uncertainties, mysteries, doubts, without any irritable reaching after fact and reason'.[1] This is the man who can be content to make up his mind about nothing, to let his mind be a thoroughfare for all thoughts;[2] who can enter into all other bodies, and not only human ones[3] (even, according to Woodhouse, a billiard ball), who can feel the 'intellect' of a waterfall,[4] and pick about the gravel with the sparrow.[5] The poet, in Keats' view, which he draws from his experience of himself, is the least poetical of beings,[6] because he has no identity, is infinitely capacious of external impressions and reacts to all external stimuli, unhampered and unrestricted by the dominance of an intellect which consciously or unconsciously selects its material for easy coordination into an intended logical scheme. When a man is endowed with this negative capability he need do nothing but remain passive to set his imagination free

[1] MBF, 30 (77). [2] MBF, 147 (466). [3] MBF, 88 (245).
[4] MBF, 67 (170), 68 (171). [5] MBF, 29 (74). [6] MBF, 88 (245).

to wander where it chooses, and there are no limits to its range.

> 'I feel more and more', says Keats, 'every day, as my imagination strengthens, that I do not live in this world alone but in a thousand worlds. No sooner am I alone than shapes of epic greatness are stationed around me, and serve my Spirit the office which is equivalent to a King's body guard—then "Tragedy with scepter'd pall, comes sweeping by". According to my state of mind I am with Achilles shouting in the Trenches, or with Theocritus in the Vales of Sicily. Or I throw my whole being into Troilus, and repeating those lines, "I wander, like a lost Soul upon the Stygian Banks staying for waftage", I melt into the air with a voluptuousness so delicate that I am content to be alone.'[1]

So much for the nature of the poet, as Keats saw it. What of the poetry? Keats' first demand, in poetry as in every other art, is 'intensity'. 'It [West's *Death on the Pale Horse*] is a wonderful picture, when West's age is considered; but there is nothing to be intense upon, no women one feels mad to kiss, no face swelling into reality. The excellence of every art is its intensity, capable of making all disagreeables evaporate from their being in close relationship with Beauty and Truth.'[2] A few months later Keats is going to illustrate his own dictum in *Isabella*. But along with intensity Keats demands another quality which may at first sight appear incompatible, namely 'unobtrusiveness'. 'Poetry should be great and unobtrusive, a thing which enters into one's soul, and does not startle it or amaze it with itself, but with its subject.'[3] If we are not to mistake Keats it is important to take that sentence as a whole, and not stop at 'unobtrusive'. Keats is not saying that in reading great poetry we should not be startled and amazed; we should (and he himself elsewhere insists on this element of surprise), but not by the 'poetry' in the narrower sense of the technical vehicle of presentation. We are to be startled and amazed by the tragic figure of Lear, not by

[1] MBF, 89 (261). [2] MBF, 30 (76). [3] MBF, 41 (103).

the dramatic and poetic skill with which Shakespeare presents him. And the more we become aware of the poet's design, even if it is artistic, and still more if it is didactic, the worse does the poetry become. 'We hate poetry that has a palpable design upon us, and if we do not agree, seems to put its hand in its breeches pocket.'[1] It appears from the context that Keats was experiencing at the moment that reaction to much of Wordsworth[2] with which most of us are familiar; when we are docile (or lazy) we call Wordsworth a great poet; when we are independent (or rebellious) we are tempted to call him a didactic egotist. But whatever was the immediate cause of his remark, there is no reason to suppose that Keats would ever have thought otherwise about the detestability of a palpable design. And though he illustrates his point by a contrast between Jacques 'under an oak' and 'Matthew with a bough of wilding in his hand', we may substitute Keats himself for Shakespeare in the contrast. For all that Keats is in some ways the most 'personal' of poets, yet in all his great work nothing is more remarkable than the way in which he stands aside, and allows, for example, the Nightingale to work her own way with us; we forget to admire the artistry in the beauty. There is the embalmed darkness, there is the song of the nightingale, and there are we; but Keats has withdrawn to watch his magic working. Whereas Wordsworth, and other poets like him, will too often not be content to allow us just to observe as we will, and to gain from our observation results which are no doubt limited by our capacities, but are at least our own; we must observe just in the way in which *they* want us to observe, and draw the conclusions which *they* want us to draw. The trouble with Wordsworth in this mood is not that he puts his hand in his breeches pocket but that he puts it all too firmly in our button-holes. But the true poetry to Keats, as he read it, and with very few excep-

[1] MBF, ib.

[2] Keats felt, and expressed, very real admiration for some of Wordsworth's work, notably *The Excursion* (see MBF, 33 (85)); and he had not seen *The Prelude*.

tions as he wrote it, is removed as far as may be from this assertive pedagogy. 'Man should not dispute or assert but whisper results to his neighbour and thus'—and then he launches out on a vision of the power of the interaction between human minds of which this great and unobtrusive poetry is part—'by every germ of spirit sucking the sap from mould ethereal every human might become great, and Humanity instead of being a wide heath of Furze and Briars with here and there a remote Oak or Pine, would become a grand democracy of Forest Trees!'[1] And in another letter of a few days later he repeats as one of his poetic 'axioms' this idea of the necessity for combining intensity in the effect with unobtrusiveness in the means. 'I think Poetry should surprise by a fine excess and not by Singularity—it should strike the Reader as a wording of his own highest thoughts, and appear almost a Remembrance.'[2] It is noteworthy that the element of surprise is again insisted on, but the sudden flash is to be one of vivid and delighted recollection, not of astonishment at the artistry. There is all the difference in the world between the critical comment 'What a remarkable and striking phrase' and the excited welcome 'Yes, what I have always felt, but I never could say it'. I do not think that of all his critics and expositors Keats would have approved of any, at least in this regard, more highly than of Mr. E. M. Forster, whose boy in *The Celestial Omnibus* says about the sonnet to Homer 'Yes—and look further on. "Aye on the shores of darkness there is light, And precipices show untrodden green." It *is* so, sir. All those things are true. . . . There is light upon the shores of darkness. I have seen it coming.'

And finally, poetry, for all its intensity, should so present its beauty that it leaves the reader in the end content and not restlessly excited and dissatisfied. 'Its [Poetry's] touches of Beauty should never be halfway thereby making the reader breathless instead of content: the rise, the progress, the setting of imagery should like

[1] MBF, 45 (112). [2] MBF, 48 (116).

the sun come natural to him—shine over him and set soberly although in magnificence leaving him in the Luxury of twilight.'[1]

How then does the poet, or perhaps we should now say specifically Keats, produce this poetry that is to be at once intense and unobtrusive, that is to surprise by a fine excess, and leave the reader not breathless but content?

In the first place the 'poetical Character', of Keats's own type, as 'distinguished from the wordsworthian or egotistical sublime', 'lives in gusto, be it foul or fair, high or low, rich or poor, mean or elevated—It has as much delight in conceiving an Iago as an Imogen. What shocks the virtuous philosopher, delights the camelion Poet.'[2]

In the second place everything is material for this intensely living spirit from which to create realities of a higher order than the concrete realities from which they are created. The poet looks 'upon the Sun, the Moon, the Stars, the Earth and its contents, as materials to form greater things—that is to say ethereal things',[3] and though he half apologizes for this at the moment, saying 'but here I am talking like a Madman,—greater things than our Creator himself made!!', yet he held to this belief always, that the most real things, and the stuff of which great poetry is made, are the creations of the imagination working upon the things of sense.

But there is no need for much in the way of material if the originating spirit is vigorous and sensitive. If it is 'ripe' enough, very little suffices to start it on its voyaging. There is a significant passage in a letter to Reynolds of February 1818 which in any study of Keats one needs to bear in mind.

> 'I had an idea that a Man might pass a very pleasant life in this manner—let him on a certain day read a certain Page of full Poesy or distilled Prose, and let him wander with it, and muse upon it, and reflect upon it, and bring home to it, and prophesy upon it, and dream upon it, until it becomes stale—but when will it do so? Never. When Man has arrived at a certain ripeness

[1] MBF, ib. [2] MBF, 88 (245). [3] MBF, 14 (31).

> in intellect any one grand and spiritual passage serves him as a starting-post towards all "the two-and-thirty Palaces". How happy is such a voyage of conception, what delicious diligent Indolence! A doze upon a sofa does not hinder it, and a nap upon Clover engenders ethereal finger-pointings—the prattle of a child gives it wings, and the converse of middle-age a strength to beat them—a strain of music conducts to "an odd angle of the Isle", and when the leaves whisper it puts a girdle round the earth. . . . Now it appears to me that almost any Man may like the spider spin from his own inwards his own airy Citadel—the points of leaves and twigs on which the spider begins her work are few, and she fills the air with a beautiful circuiting. Man should be content with as few points to tip with the fine Web of his Soul, and weave a tapestry empyrean full of symbols for his spiritual eye, of softness for his spiritual touch, of space for his wandering, of distinctness for his luxury.'[1]

And now what of the way in which the 'tapestry empyrean' is woven? What can we learn of Keats' actual methods of work, either from what he says himself or from what his friends record? The accounts are somewhat contradictory, but not so contradictory as at first sight they appear. The well-known remark that if poetry comes not as naturally as leaves to a tree it had better not come at all[2] suggests a careless ease of writing, a lisping in numbers; and this seems to be borne out by part at least of Bailey's description of Keats at work on *Endymion*: 'He wrote with as much regularity and apparently with as much ease as he wrote his letters',[3] and by Keats' own comment on the *Ode to Psyche*, 'the first and the only poem with which I have taken even moderate pains. I have for the most part dash'd off my lines in a hurry.'[4] As against this we find him 'reading and writing eight hours a day';[5] he insists that the road for him lies through application study and thought;[6] and though the composition of *Endymion* is noteworthy as an example of 'regularity', an output of 50 lines a day is hardly the rate of production of a man writing with the 'ease' with which he writes his letters.

[1] MBF, 45 (111).
[2] MBF, 48 (116).
[3] MBF, 18 (40) note.
[4] MBF, 114 (367).
[5] MBF, 14 (30).
[6] MBF, 59 (146).

And we have only to look at early drafts of Keats' poems, where we have them, to see that at all periods of his life there were at least passages on which he expended considerable pains. But what I conceive Keats to have meant when he said that if poetry does not come as naturally as leaves to a tree it had better not come at all is that the poetic *mood* will not come to order, and that any attempt to force it is much worse than useless. Even in his letters he waits for the right mood to come, and says to Bailey, 'I cannot force my letters in a hot bed. I could not feel comfortable in making sentences for you';[1] and *a fortiori* he will not force himself in poetry. And we know from himself that he had periods of inactivity, of a kind of spiritual lethargy. He tells Bailey that he 'sometimes feels not the influence of a Passion or affection during a whole week';[2] he finds himself in a temper 'that if I were under Water I would scarcely kick to come to the top';[3] and later the week has lengthened, 'my sensations are sometimes deadened for weeks together'.[4] But then comes the reaction and he cannot exist without poetry—eternal poetry—half the day will not do—the whole of it; when he becomes all of a tremble from not having written anything of late, and the writing of a sonnet does him some good and lets him sleep;[5] or when he feels that a change has taken place in his intellect and he 'cannot bear to be uninterested or unemployed, I, who for so long a time have been addicted to passiveness';[6] or when scenery makes him feel that he is going to a tournament.[7]

The picture presented is sufficiently coherent; Keats was wise enough to recognize that in him what we are pleased to call 'inspiration' was intermittent, and he was willing, if not content, to accept the periods of lying fallow, those periods when he knew that he was incapable of 'the innumerable compositions and decompositions which take place between the intellect and its thousand

[1] MBF, 63 (160). [2] MBF, 29 (75). [3] MBF, 63 (160).
[4] MBF, 72 (193). [5] MBF, 12 (21). [6] MBF, 38 (95).
[7] MBF, 69 (176).

materials before it arrives at that trembling delicate and snail-horn perception of beauty'.[1] Then suddenly the poetic mood would come to him, and when it came, then no exertion of energy was too much. But I think that it is true that, though at all periods of his life he was prepared to take pains, whether with isolated passages, or with a whole poem like *The Eve of St. Agnes*, it was not till the end of his career, not indeed, if we accept his own words, and I see no reason why we should not, until about the period of the *Ode to Psyche*, that he learned to take *leisurely* pains. *Endymion* after all was a kind of task which he had set himself, and though his determination did not falter it is clear from his comments that long before it was finished he was eager to be done with it and go on to the next stage of his poetic advance. Even the *Eve of St. Agnes*, for all the zealous pains it shows in correcting and re-correcting, shows also the clearest evidence of rapid, sometimes of hurried and impatient, composition and correction. But from this time onwards he became, as we shall see, more and more capable of maintaining at once a high imaginative intensity and that craftsman's exigence which demands 'a brighter word than bright, a fairer word than fair';[2] and often by some miracle found it.

We can round out our picture of Keats' methods of work by the account which Woodhouse gives of them:

> 'These lines give some insight into Keats's mode of writing Poetry. He has repeatedly said in conversation that he never sits down to write, unless he is full of ideas, and then thoughts come about him in troops, as tho' soliciting to be accepted and he selects—one of his maxims is that if Poetry does not come naturally it had better not come at all—the moment he feels any dearth he discontinues writing and waits for a happier moment.' [So far, it will be observed, this exactly bears out what we have seen reason to suppose that Keats meant in regard to the poetic mood.] 'He is generally more troubled by a redundancy than by a poverty of images, and he culls what appears to him at the time the best.—He never corrects, unless perhaps a word here or there should occur to him as preferable to an

[1] MBF, 56 (139). [2] MBF, 125 (382).

expression he has already used—He is impatient of correcting and says he would rather burn the piece in question and write another or something else—"My judgment, (he says) is as active while I am actually writing as my imagination. In fact all my faculties are strongly excited, and in their full play—And shall I afterwards, when my imagination is idle, and the heat in which I wrote has gone off, sit down coldly to criticise when in Possession of only one faculty, what I have written, when almost inspired". —This fact explains the reason of the Perfectness, fullness, richness and completion of most that comes from him—He has said that he has often not been aware of the beauty of some thought or expression until after he had composed and written it down—It has then struck him with astonishment and seemed rather the production of another person than his own—He has wondered how he came to hit upon it. This was the case with the description of Apollo in the 3rd book of Hyperion 79 etc. . . . It seemed to come by chance or magic—to be as it were something given to him.'[1]

There are two main points in this account of Keats' methods. The second of the two, the 'unconsciousness' with which he sometimes produced his best effects, is borne out by a passage in a letter of Keats' own to Haydon. Writing in May of 1817 he says: 'I remember your saying that you had notions of a good Genius presiding over you. I have of late had the same thought, for things which I do half at Random are afterwards confirmed by my judgment in a dozen features of Propriety. Is it too daring to fancy Shakespeare this Presider?'[2] The first point is at first sight more difficult to accept. When we look at Keats' manuscripts, and find them full of erasures, and substitutions, and castings back to the first attempt, and so on, it seems absurd that Woodhouse should say that Keats never corrected except perhaps a word here or there. But I do not think that either Keats or Woodhouse is talking about that kind of correction, made *currente calamo*, which is incidental to the actual process of composition. What Keats meant by correction, and repudiated, is a later process, the coming back in cold

[1] AL, i, 501, 502; *and see Note A* (*page* 291). [2] MBF, 14 (30).

blood to tinker with something which was composed in hot blood. But that repudiation has no relevance to the corrections in the manuscripts. It is quite clear from an examination of these corrections that the great bulk of them were made in the moment of composition; a word is discarded before it is even completely written, or the first two lines of a stanza are written and immediately deleted and a new start made, or, as in one notable case which we shall examine later, almost a whole stanza is written, altered, resolved into its elements, and recast. All these corrections, that is, are made during the period when he is 'actually writing', when, as he told Woodhouse, 'his judgement was as active as his imagination'. It would be hard I think to produce evidence of any extensive corrections, corrections more than Woodhouse's 'word here and there', which were made at an interval after composition. There are insertions of complete new passages; and there are omissions of complete passages, which are in key with Keats' remark that he would rather burn than correct; but there are extremely few instances of later recastings; and what there are are usually unhappy. And we may notice further that Woodhouse does not imply that Keats wrote out his poems as they were to stand, as though he never blotted a line. He implies rather that when the period of composition was over, whatever in the way of correction may have been involved in that period, then, apart from minor points, the poem had to stand or fall as it was. The picture given by Woodhouse, by Keats as reported by Woodhouse, and by the manuscripts, is surely perfectly clear and perfectly congruent. Keats composed with all his faculties in action, the creative, sometimes even too fertile, imagination, and the selecting and shaping judgement; during that period he corrected with the most unsparing freedom and the most secure skill, leaving for our examination a fascinating and often obscure collection of *membra, disiecta* and otherwise. But he knew also that when the ardour of composition had subsided, and imagination was dormant again, his judgement was no longer to be trusted, and that any attempt to exercise it was liable to damage rather than improve.

There are then three distinct aspects of Keats' art which are worth study, which may be called very briefly 'sources', 'materials', and 'workmanship'; or, in other words, the 'points of attachment', the stuff of the web, and the artistry of its spinning.

There are first the 'points of attachment' for the 'empyrean tapestry', or the starting-points for the journey to the two and thirty palaces, the direct suggestions in his reading or his observation which he so gloriously expanded, as in *Lamia*, or transmuted, as in *Isabella*, or filled with significance, as in the *Ode to a Nightingale*.

Secondly, there is the stuff of the web; he is spinning, in his own phrase, from his own inwards; but, with a nature of so ready a receptivity, it is interesting to see where we can why the inwards were what they were, or, to take the picture of Woodhouse's account, whence came the redundance of images from which the selecting judgement made its choice. This we shall study most easily in *The Eve of St. Agnes*, or as we watch the process whereby various passages in his own early work are made to yield their concentrated essence in the Odes.

Finally, there is the actual spinning of the web, the 'mere' craftsmanship; the development in metrical skill from the fumblings of *Isabella*, through the brilliant imitativeness of *Hyperion*, to the original creation of the stanza of the Odes; the growth in power of presentation, from the 'weak-sided'[1] *Isabella*, through the strength of *Hyperion* to the 'fire'[2] of *Lamia*; the increasing security in the rejection and choice of verbal expression from the errors of *Isabella* through the felicities of the *Eve of St. Agnes* to the magic of the *Nightingale* and the serene perfection of *To Autumn*.

No attempt is here made to trace the whole of Keats'

[1] MBF, 143 (426). [2] MBF, 147 (439).

development from the outset of his career to the end. The choice of the 1820 volume (and not even all the poems in that)[1] excludes on the one hand his more immature efforts and *Endymion* and on the other two at least of his most notable achievements (*La Belle Dame sans Merci* and *The Eve of St. Mark*), his experiments in drama, and *The Cap and Bells*. But the kind of examination that I propose grows no more illuminating from being extended over too wide a field, and further, being of necessity detailed, is apt to grow wearisome. And the poems selected are those which offer the most significant and richest material for such examination, and are, I hope, enough to illustrate adequately Keats' methods and the development of his genius and his craftsmanship during that period in which with a rapidity so astonishing he grew from poetic adolescence to poetic maturity.[2]

[1] *The Fall of Hyperion* is, from its close connexion with *Hyperion*, difficult to omit, and is inconsistently included.

[2] *See Note B* (*page* 293).

II. *ISABELLA*

ISABELLA was begun in the early part of 1818 and was certainly finished by April of that year.[1] It thus precedes by at least seven or eight months the opening of Keats' great creative period, and is in many respects both of temper and technique more closely linked with *Endymion* than with the poems of the 1820 volume among which it ultimately appeared. But just for that reason, as a document illustrative of Keats' development, as the stones by which he crossed, not too securely, into the promised land, it repays a more detailed and more critical study than it sometimes receives.

When *Endymion* was finished Keats projected with Reynolds a versification of some tales of Boccaccio, and as his contribution to the joint venture he took[2] a translation of the *Decameron* printed in London in 1684,[3] selected the fifth tale of the fourth day, and got to work on his transmutation. But the alchemist is still only an apprentice at his difficult trade, and the transmutation is only partially successful. In the result we have a few pieces of the purest gold, as flawless as any that Keats at the very height of his power ever achieved; but we have also a considerable mass of a nondescript alloy, to which in the opinion of most readers the plain silver of Boccaccio is preferable.

In the first place Keats made an infelicitous choice of a metrical crucible. Usually, as we shall see, he showed himself a master in the choice, or modification, or sometimes the creation, of metres suitable for his purpose; but here, probably from mere lack of technical experience, he almost certainly blundered. He chose *ottava rima*. The instinct was undoubtedly right which led him to prefer, for a story so short as that which he projected, a stanzaic

1 MBF, 60 (149).

2 Woodhouse notes that this was the translation used.

3 *The Novels and Tales of the renowned John Boccacio: the Fifth Edition, much Corrected and Amended.* London, printed for Awnsham Churchill, 1684.

form rather than the loose heroic couplet of *Endymion*; and he was probably also right in feeling that for a story so simple and quiet in tone he needed a stanzaic form less elaborate than the Spenserian stanza.

But there are certain difficulties inherent in the metre which Keats was as yet hardly craftsman enough continuously to overcome, and also certain qualities which render it indeed uniquely suitable for a certain tone of writing, but recalcitrant for adaptation to another tone. In the first place there is the mere mechanical difficulty of the two triplets of rhyming words which the first six lines require. That no doubt to the practised craftsman is a trivial difficulty, but we shall find Keats again and again displaying an inefficient impatience with the requirement. In the second place the *ottava rima* stanza falls naturally into two parts, a sestet and a couplet. Now this peculiarity admits, and indeed invites, the production of a particular effect. It allows the poet to make the sestet a mere prelude to a sort of clinching 'snap' in the couplet, and it invites him to make the clinch even more vigorous by a change of tone between the sestet and the couplet. It produces, that is, in an expanded form, the effect of Dryden's satiric couplet at its best, when the first line and a half are no more than the prelude to the crashing blow in the end of the second line.

> *Shadwell* alone of all my Sons is he
> Who stands confirm'd in full stupidity.

Byron, for once, and unusually, happy in his choice of metre, exploited this quality of *ottava rima* with brilliant effect in both *Beppo* and *Don Juan*. It allowed him the freest scope for that street-arab's trick in which he took such delight, the turning round in the couplet to jeer at the readers whom he has for the moment deluded into thinking him serious:

> But still there is unto a patriot nation,
> Which loves so well its country and its King,
> A subject of sublimest exultation—
> Bear it, ye Muses, on your brightest wing!

Howe'er the mighty locust, Desolation,
  Strip your green fields, and to your harvests cling,
Gaunt famine never shall approach the throne—
Though Ireland starve, great George weighs twenty stone.

The metre had of course been used earlier, and used for serious narrative, notably by Fairfax in his translation of Tasso, which Keats possessed and presumably read, and on which it is generally supposed that he modelled the versification of *Isabella*. Fairfax used the metre competently, but he cannot avoid showing its difficulties for his purpose. And if Fairfax was Keats' model, it is interesting to see the attempts he made at modification. Here are three typical stanzas from Fairfax:

O heavenly Muse, that not with fading baies
Deckest thy brow by th' Heliconian spring,
But sittest crownd with stars immortall raies
In heaven where legions of bright Angels sing,
Inspire life in my wit, my thoughts upraise,
My verse ennoble, and forgive the thing,
  If fictions light I mixe with truth divine,
  And fill these lines with others praise then thine.

. . . .

And with such care his busie work he plied,
That to nought els his acting thoughts he bent,
In yong *Rinaldo* fierce desires he spied,
And noble hart, of rest impatient,
To wealth or soveraigne powre he nought applied
His wits, but all to vertue excellent,
  Patternes and rules of skill and courage bolde
  He took from *Guelpho*, and his fathers olde.

. . . .

Thither he gallopt fast, and drawing nere
Rambaldo knew the knight, and lowdly cride,
Whence comes yong *Eustace*, and what seekes he here?
I come (quoth he) to serve the Queene *Armide*,
If she accept me, would we all were there
Where my good-will and faith might best be tride.
  Who (quoth the other) chuseth thee to prove
  This hie exploit of hers? he answered, love.

The characteristics are obvious, the heavy end-stopping, and the tendency for the final couplet to stand away in awkward isolation from the rest of the stanza. Now it is clear that Keats took steps to modify both these characteristics. In the first place the proportion of end-stopped lines, which in a representative sixty stanzas of Fairfax is 80 per cent., drops in *Isabella* to 70 per cent., and in the central section of twenty stanzas (which are, one may observe, the most purely 'narrative') as low as 60 per cent. He also seriously tackled the problem of the couplet. Fairfax had made some attempt to deal with the difficulty by avoiding too heavy a pause at the end of the sixth line of the stanza. In just one-quarter of the sixty stanzas is the stop at the end of the sixth line heavier than a comma. But he cannot screw his courage to the sticking place of running on between the sixth and seventh lines, and of the remaining forty-five stanzas only one runs on at that point. Further, there is in all the sixty stanzas only one in which the couplet itself is broken at the end of the seventh line by a stop heavier than a comma. The result is neither one thing nor the other. The couplet remains a couplet, but is rather loosely attached to the rest of the stanza, and a measure of continuity is secured at the price of a slack monotony. Keats is a much bolder experimenter. In the first place he grasps the nettle, and in rather more than half his stanzas he breaks at the end of the sixth line with a heavy stop. If we are to have a couplet, at least let it be strong and unmistakable. So we get a stanza like the forty-eighth:

> That old nurse stood beside her wondering
>   Until her heart felt pity to the core
> At sight of such a dismal labouring;
>   And so she kneeled with her Locks all hoar
> And put her lean hands to the horrid thing:
>   Three hours were they at this travel sore.
> At last they felt the kernel of the grave,
> And Isabella did not stamp and rave.

That at least is firm and decisive. And he is almost as

decisive in the other direction. In fourteen stanzas there is a definite run on with no stop at all between the sixth and seventh lines, and in three more the stop at the end of the seventh is stronger than that at the end of the sixth. That is to say, in more than a quarter of his stanzas he deliberately secures that the couplet cannot be read or felt as a couplet. We get stanzas of this type:

XXXII

In the mid days of Autumn, on their eves,
  The Breath of Winter comes from far away,
And the sick west continually bereaves
  Of some gold tinge, and plays a roundelay
Of death among the Bushes and the leaves,—
  To make all bare before he dares to stray
From his north cavern: so sweet Isabel
By gradual decay from beauty fell—

XLIV

See as they creep along the river side
  How she doth whisper to that aged dame;
And after looking round the campaign wide
  Shows her a knife. What feverous hectic flame
Burns in thee child? What good can thee betide
  That thou dost smile again? The Evening came,
And they had found Lorenzo's earthy bed:
The flint was there, the berries at his head.

But effective within their limits though these modifications are, and sure though the instinct was that guided them, they are no more than modifications, and the limits of their effectiveness are narrow. By no loppings and pullings on the Procrustean bed can *ottava rima* be made a suitable metre in English for narrative verse, and the energy expended upon the levers is so much waste energy. Part of the business of the poetic craftsman is the selection of a metre which will help him to produce the effect he desires, and make it also easier for his reader to apprehend that effect. He is perversely hampering himself if he condemns himself in advance to a perpetual contention with the natural genius of his metre.

However, wisely or unwisely, *ottava rima* was the metre

which Keats chose in which to retell the story of Boccaccio, and it is time to examine how he handled his material. The narrative in Boccaccio starts as follows:

> 'In *Messina* there dwelt three young men, Brethren, and Merchants by their common Profession, who becoming very Rich by the death of their Father, lived in very good fame and repute. Their Father was of *San Gemignano*, and that (for 'they') had a Sister named *Isabella*, young, beautiful, and well condition'd; who upon some occasion, as yet remained unmarryed. A proper youth, being a Gentleman born in *Pisa*, and named *Lorenzo*, as a trusty Factor or Servant, had the managing of the Brethrens business and affairs. This *Lorenzo* being of comely personage, affable, and excellent in his behaviour, grew so gracious in the Eyes of *Isabella*, that she afforded him many respective looks, yea kindnesses of no common quality. Which *Lorenzo* taking notice of, and observing by degrees from time to time, gave over all Beauties in the City, which might allure any Affection from him, and only fixed his Heart on her, so that their love grew to a mutual embracing, both equally respecting one another, and entertaining kindnesses, as occasion gave leave.
>
> Long time continued this Amorous League of Love, yet not so cunnin(g)ly concealed, but at length the secret meeting of *Lorenzo* and *Isabella*, to ease their poor Souls of Loves oppressions, was discovered by the Eldest of the Brethren, unknown to them who were thus betrayed.'

That is a piece of plain, concise, and forthright narration. The caste of characters is given, and their relations to one another precisely defined. To Boccaccio, with his story-teller's instinct, the love of Isabella and Lorenzo is of importance solely because from it springs the pitiful story which is to follow; he wants to make it explicit, and then without loss of time get on with his narration. Not so Keats. He takes this brief introduction, which occupies not quite a seventh of Boccaccio's whole narrative, and expands it into a not very satisfactory love idyll which occupies twenty of his sixty-three stanzas.

The version of *Isabella* here given is that which is contained in Keats' own writing in George Keats' book of transcripts now in the British Museum, since this is the nearest approach we can make to the poem as Keats left it after his completion of it in 1818; and as we are attempting a study of Keats' poetic development it is important to examine the poem as nearly as possible as he wrote it, and not as he made it by revision eighteen months later. The probable degree of coincidence between this version and the poem in its original state is discussed in the notes.[1]

I

Fair Isabel, poor simple Isabel:
  Lorenzo a young Palmer in Love's eye
They could not in the selfsame mansion dwell
  Without some stir of heart, some Malady
They could not sit at Meals but feel how well
  It soothed each to be each other by
They could not sure beneath the same roof sleep
But to each other dream, and nightly weep.

II

With every morn their love grew tenderer;
  With every eve deeper and tenderer still:
He might not in house field or garden stir,
  But her full shape would all his seeing fill;
And his continual voice was pleasanter
  To her than noise of trees or hidden rill:
Her Lute string gave an echo of his name
She spoilt her half done broidery with the same.

III

He knew whose gentle hand was at the latch
  Before the door had given her to his eyes;
And from her Chamber window he would catch
  Her Beauty farther than the Faulcon spies;
And constant as her vespers would he watch
  Because her face was turn'd to the same skies,
And with sick longing all the night outwear
To hear her morning step upon the stair.

IV

A whole long Month of May in this sad plight
  Made their cheeks paler by the break of June.
'To morrow will I bow to my delight
  To morrow will I ask my Lady's boon'

[1] *See Note C (page 296).*

'O may I never see another night
  Lorenzo if thy tongue speak not Love's tune'!
So spake they to their Pillows, but alas!
Honeyless days and days did he let pass.

V

Until sweet Isabella's untouch'd cheek
  Fell sick within the Roses just domain,
Fell thin as a young Mother's who doth seek
  By every lull to cool her infant's pain.
'How ill she is' said he 'I may not speak—
  And yet I will, and tell my love all plain:
If Looks speak Love-laws I will drink her tears,
And at the worst 'twill startle off her cares.

VI

So said he one fair morning and all day
  His heart beat awfully against his side;
And to his heart he inwardly did pray
  For power to speak; but still the ruddy tide
Stifled his voice and pulsed resolve away—
  Fever'd his high conceit of such a Bride,
Yet brought him to the meekness of a child.
Alas, when Passion is both meek and wild.

VII

So once more had he waked and anguished
  A dreary night of Love and misery,
If Isabel's quick eye had not been wed
  To every symbol on his forehead high:
She saw it waxing very pale and dead,
  And straight all flush'd: so lisped tenderly,
'Lorenzo, I would clip my ringlet hair
To make thee laugh again and debonair!'

(VII *a*)

'Then should I be' said he 'full deified;
  And yet I would not have it, clip it not;
For Lady I do love it where 'tis tied
  About the Neck I dote on; and that spot
That anxious dimple it doth take a pride
  To play about—Aye Lady I have got
Its shadow in my heart and ev'ry sweet
Its Mistress owns there summed all complete.'

VIII

'O Isabella I can half perceive
That I may speak my grief into thine ear:
If thou didst ever any thing believe,
Believe how I love thee—believe how near
My Soul is to its doom—I would not grieve
Thine hand by unwelcome pressing; would not fear
Those eyes by gazing: but I cannot Live
Another night and not my passion shrive'

IX

'Love! thou a[r]t leading me from wintry cold!
Lady, thou leadest me to summer clime!
And I must taste the blossoms that unfold
In its ripe warmth this gracious morning time.'
So said, his erewhile timid lips grew bold,
And poesied with hers in dewy rhyme:
Great Bliss was with them; and great happiness
Grew, like a Lusty flower in June's caress.

X

Parting they seem'd to tread upon the air,
Twin Roses by the Zephyr blown apart,
Only to meet again all close and share
The inward fragrance of each other's heart.
She, to her chamber gone, a ditty fair
Sung of delicious Love and honied dart;
He with light steps went up a western hill
And bade the Sun farewell, and joy'd his fill.

XI

All close they met again before the dusk
Had taken from the stars its pleasant veil;
All close they met all eves before the dusk
Had taken from the stars its pleasant veil;
Close in a Bower of hyacinth and Musk
Unknown of any, free from whispring tale.
Ah! better had it been for ever so
Than idle ears should pleasure in their woe.

XII

Were they unhappy then? It cannot be.
Too many tears for Lovers have been shed;
Too many sighs give we to them in fee;
Too much of pity after they are dead;

Too many doleful stories do we see
  Whose Matter in bright gold were best be read:
Except in such a page where Theseus' spouse
Over the pathless waves towards him bows.

XIII

But for the general award of Love,
  The little sweet doth kill much bitterness:
Though Dido silent is in undergrove
  And Isabella's was a great distress;
Though young Lorenzo in warm indian clove
  Was not embalm'd, the truth is not the less.
Even Bees, the little Almsmen of spring bowers,
Know there is richest juice in poison flowers.

Now whatever may be the beauties of those stanzas there is a number of flaws. In the first place there are several downright obscurities, which are the last things one wants in the telling of a simple story. We are, for example, hardly into the poem at all before we have either to read inattentively or to stop and reflect what is meant. Lorenzo may be a palmer because of the play which Romeo and Juliet make with that image,[1] but what is he doing *in Love's eye*? What in the third stanza is he watching? Presumably, judging from the next line, the skies; but the first picture that suggests itself is that he is watching her lit window. What does *bow to my delight* mean? If his delight is Isabella the phrase is clumsy. If he means that he will yield to his desire, and *delight* is merely a concession to rhyme, then the phrase does not represent the situation, since his trouble is not to refrain from speech but to nerve himself to speaking. Consider the last two lines of the fifth stanza. What does *If looks speak love-laws* mean? and even if they do, why should the apodosis to this odd condition be that he will drink her tears? and the even more curious alternative of the last line is not improved by ending with a false rhyme. And in stanza VII, however high his forehead has to be in order to rhyme with misery, and however many symbols it unexpectedly dis-

[1] I. v. 97–105.

plays, why this *mésalliance* of Isabella's quick eye to the symbols? Of minor flaws, there are too many words which we feel uneasily are where they are not because Keats wanted their sense but because he needed their sound, notably *fear*, *shrive*, and *in fee*; and there are a few mere feeblenesses, such as *with the same* in stanza II, *all plain* in stanza V, and the concluding words of stanza VII. Worst of all are some sadly unsuccessful conceits, *the rose's just domain*, *taste the blossoms*, and above all *And poesied with hers in dewy rhyme*, which, apart from conveying a sensation of somewhat tasteless lusciousness, seems to convey as little meaning as is possible for seven English words arranged in a grammatical clause.

In the balance against these weaknesses one has, of course, to set certain beauties to which not the most critical reader can be insensitive, the sestet of the second stanza, the opening of the eighth, and almost all of the eleventh and thirteenth, even though the one has an unsuccessful repetition and the other a certain obscurity of meaning. And above all there is, no doubt, about the whole passage a freshness and delicate sweetness which seldom declines into sentimentality. It may be held that we should rest content with this general impression of loveliness, and not allow ourselves to be troubled with flaws of detail. But it is surely a poor poem that can only be read with pleasure if it is also read with inattention. And even if we do so content ourselves, where, at the end of fourteen stanzas of ostensible narrative, have we arrived? We know nothing whatever of Isabella except that she has a full shape, that Lorenzo thinks her beautiful, that she embroiders, and that she is deeply in love. We know nothing whatever of Lorenzo except that Isabella thinks that he has a pleasant voice, that he also is deeply in love, though painfully diffident about saying so, and that he is not going to be embalmed in Indian clove. He has leisure (in a cancelled stanza) for hunting, and (in the text) for wandering up a western hill to admire the sunset. But as to what his position is, why he dwells in the selfsame mansion as Isabella and meets her at meals, and whether his diffidence is due to natural timidity, or to inferiority in rank, or to what, we have no inkling. Surely this is no way at all to tell a story, and no wealth of incidental beauties should delude us into thinking that it is.

At the opening of the fourteenth stanza Keats seems for the moment to make up his mind to be more explicit, and we are introduced to the other actors, in the shape of Isabella's two brothers (Boccaccio's unnecessary third being wisely discarded). But Boccaccio's concisely adequate sketch of them in five lines is expanded into six stanzas, containing some vivid description, but contributing nothing relevant to the actual story.

XIV

With her two Brothers, this fair Lady dwelt,
  Enriched from ancestral Merchandise;
And for them many a weary hand did swelt
  In torched Mines and noisy factories;
And many once proud quiverd loins did melt
  In blood from stinging whip; with hollow eyes
Many all day in dazzling river stood
To take the rich-ored driftings of the flood.

XV

For them the Ceylon diver held his breath
  And went all naked to the hungry shark;
For them his ears gush'd blood: for them in death
  The Seal on the cold ice with piteous bark
Lay full of darts; for them alone did seath
  A thousand Men in troubles wide and dark:
Half ignorant they turn'd an easy wheel
That set sharp Racks at work to pinch and peal.

XVI

Why were they proud? Because their marble founts
  Gush'd with more pride than do a Wretches tears?
Why were they proud? because fair orange Mounts
  Were of more soft ascent than Lazar stairs?
Why were they proud? Because red lin'd accounts
  Were richer than the songs of grecian years?
Why were they proud? again we ask aloud;
Why in the name of glory were they proud?

XVII

Yet were these Florentines as self retired,
In hungry pride and gainful cowardice,
As two close Hebrews, in that land inspired,
Paled in and vinyarded from beggar spies.
The Hawks of Shipmast forests; the untir'd
And pannier'd Mules for ducats and old lies:
Quick catspaws on the generous stray away;
Great Wits in Spanish Tuscan and Malay.

(XVII *a*)

Two young Orlandos far away they seem'd,
But on a near inspect their vapid Miens—
Very alike,—at once themselves redeem'd
From all suspicion of Romantic spleens—
No fault of theirs, for their good Mother dream'd
In the longing time of Units in their teens
Of proudly-bas'd addition and of net—
And both their backs were mark'd with tare and tret.

This last stanza is cancelled in the holograph, but it is worth a moment's observation as showing what Keats was capable of, even as early as the original composition of *Isabella*, in the satirico-comic Byronic vein, to which, even though he was never happy in it, he reverted in *The Cap and Bells*, and of which, as we shall see, there were touches at one stage even of *The Eve of St. Agnes.*

XVIII

How was it these same Ledger Men could spy
Fair Isabella in her downy nest?
How could they find out in Lorenzo's eye
A straying from his toil? Hot Egypt's pest
Into their vision covetous and sly!
How could these moneybags see east and west
Yet so they did; and every dealer fair
Must see behind as doth a hunted hare.

This is a most interesting passage, for more than one reason. Technically it is a great improvement on what has preceded it. There are a few awkwardnesses due to the exigences of rhyme, such as *seath* and *peal*; there are one or two obscurities such as *orange Mounts*, and *dealer fair;*

and the whole of stanza XVII needs more attention for the deciphering of its metaphorical pictures than we are naturally, in so smooth-flowing a narrative, inclined to spare. But in general there is an ease and security of movement which was certainly absent from the opening stanzas. There is secondly the provoking problem of sources. The reminiscence of Dryden's *Annus Mirabilis*[1] in the opening of stanza XV has been pointed out, and doubtless justly, by more than one critic. But the significant details of the three pictures are not in Dryden, and the dazzling river, and the bleeding ears, and the seal's bark come, one can hardly doubt, from some books or other of travel which Keats had been reading. But the most remarkable thing about this passage is surely the complete difference in tone between it and the rest of the poem. It stands out in much the same way as does the ecclesiastical 'interlude' in *Lycidas*. There is a power and vigour, amounting almost to bitterness, about this biting contrast between the wealth of the few at ease and the misery of the thousand who toil to gain the wealth, and between the wealth when gained and the things which matter which it cannot buy, whose value cannot be estimated in terms of money. One is almost tempted to wonder whether Keats when he wrote it was fresh from a more than ordinarily exasperating interview with Mr. Abbey and the shades of the counting-house. But whatever prompted it, Keats is aware that it is out of harmony, and he turns to Boccaccio (as Milton to Alpheus) with an apology.

XIX

O Eloquent Boccace of green Arno!
  Of thee we now should ask forgiving boon;
And of thy spicy myrtles as they blow;
  And of thy roses amorous of the Moon;
And of thy lillies that do paler grow
  Now they can no more hear thy guittern's tune
For venturing one word unseemly mean
In such a place on such a daring theme.

[1] Stanza 3.

XX

Grant thou a pardon here, and then the tale
  Shall move on soberly, as it is meet:
There is no other crime; no mad assail
  To make old prose in modern rhyme more sweet,
But it is done, succeed the verse or fail,
  To honour thee and thy gone Spirit greet
To stead thee as a verse in english tongue
An echo of thee in the north wind sung.

After this Keats turns again to Boccaccio and finds the narrative proceed as follows:

He (the eldest brother) being a man of great discretion, although this sight was highly displeasing to him: yet notwithstanding he kept it to himself till the next morning, labouring his brain what might best be done in so urgent a case. When day was come, he resorted to his Brethren, and told them what he had seen in the time past, between their Sister and *Lorenzo.*

Many deliberations passed on in this case; but after all, thus they concluded together, to let it proceed on with patient supportance, that no scandal might ensue to them or their Sister, no evil Act being (as yet) committed. And seeming as if they knew not of their Love, had a wary Eye still upon her secret walks, awaiting for some convenient time, when without their own prejudice, or *Isabellaes* knowledge, they might safely break off this stolen Love, which was altogether against their liking. So, shewing no worse Countenance to *Lorenzo*, than formerly they had done, but employing and conversing with him in kind manner; it fortuned, that riding (all three) to recreate themselves out of the City, they took *Lorenzo*, in their company, and when they came to a solitary place, such as suited best with their vile purpose: they ran suddenly upon *Lorenzo*, slew him, and afterward enterr'd his Body, where hardly it could be discover'd by any one. Then they returned back to *Messina*, and gave it forth (as a credible Report) that they had sent him abroad about their Affairs, as formerly they were wont to do: which every one verily believed, because they knew no reason why they should conceit any otherwise.

Now in this section the contrast between Keats and Boccaccio is a signally different contrast from that which was presented in the two introductions. There is a kind of nervelessness about Boccaccio's narrative. The brothers are displeased, but we are not told specifically why they are displeased; and anyway they can think of nothing better to do than to wait inactively till chance throws some opportunity in their way, and we are left to conjecture whether they propose to terminate the situation which they dislike by murder or by less violent means. In the end they seize the accident of a casual ride to kill Lorenzo. But the progress in Keats' narrative is orderly and strong. Quite apart from any adornments, his story-telling, simply as such, is the better of the two. In stanza XXI the brothers discover the truth; in XXII they confer, and decide both on murder and the method of it; in XXIII and XXIV they proceed to action. Stanzas XXV and XXVI are devoted to an interlude, which, whatever it may be in execution, is highly effective in conception, the ironically happy and careless farewell of the lovers. In stanza XXVII they ride to the selected place, and by the end of the first line of XXVIII Lorenzo is dead and buried. Here is Keats' narrative:

XXI

These Brethren having found, by many signs,
  What Love Lorenzo for their sister had
And how she lov'd him too, each unconfines
  His bitter thoughts to other, well nigh mad
That he, the servant of their trade designs
  Should in their Sister's Love be blythe and glad:
When 'twas their plan to coax her by degrees
To some high noble and his olive trees.

XXII

And many a jealous conference had they,
  And many times they bit their lips alone;
Before they fix'd upon a surest way
  To make the youngster for his crime atone;
And at the last these Men of cruel clay
  Cut Mercy with a sharp Knife to the Bone:
For they resolved in some forest dim
To kill Lorenzo and there bury him.

XXIII

So on a pleasant morning, as he leant
  Into the Sunrise o'er the Ballustrade
Of the garden terrace, towards him they bent
  Their footing through the dews, and to him said;
'You seem there in the quiet of content
  Lorenzo, and we are most loath to invade
Calm Speculation; but if you are wise,
Bestride your Steed while cold is in the skies.

XXIV

'To-day we purpose, aye, this hour we mount
  To spur three Leagues towards the Appenine:
Come down we pry' thee ere the hot sun count
  His dewy rosary on the eglantine
Lorenzo, courteous, as he was wont
  Bow'd a fair greeting to these Serpents' whine,
And went in haste to get in readiness
With belt and Spur and bracing Huntsman's dress.

XXV

And as he to the court yard pass'd along
  Each third step did he pause and listend oft
If he could hear his Lady's matin-song,
  Or the light whisper of her footsteps soft;
And as he thus over his passion hung
  He heard a laugh full musical aloft,
And looking up he saw her smiling through
A little indoor Lattice

XXVI

Love Isabel said he, I was in pain
  Lest I should miss to bid thee a good morrow
Ah, what if I should lose thee! when so fain
  I am to stifle all the heavy sorrow
Of a poor three hours absence—but we'll gain
  Out of the amorous dark what day doth borrow:
Good bye! I soon be back—'Good bye, said she;
And as he went, she chaunted merily—

XXVII

So the two Brothers and their murder'd Man
  Rode past fair Florence, to where Arno's stream
Gurgles through straighten'd banks, and still doth fan
  Itself with dancing bullrush;—and the Bream

Keeps head against the freshe(s)ts. Sick and wan
  The Brothers faces in the ford did seem:
Lorenzo's flush with Love. They pass'd the Water
Into a forest quiet for the slaughter.

XXVIII

There was Lorenzo slain and buried in:
  There in that forest did his great Love cease.
Ah, when a soul doth thus its freedom win
  It aches in loneliness; is ill a peace
As the break-covert bloodhounds of such sin.
  They dipt their swords in the River and did tease
Their Horses homeward with convulsed spur
Each richer by his being a Murderer.

XXIX

They told their Sister, how, with sudden speed
  Lorenzo had ta'en ship for foreign Lands,
Because of some great urgency and need
  In their affairs, requiring trusty hands;
Poor Girl put on thy stifling widow's weed
  And 'scape at once from hopes ac[c]ursed bands:
To day thou wilt not see him, nor tomorrow;
And the next day will be a day of sorrow.

There are still plenty of flaws. There are awkward inversions for the sake of metre or rhyme, like

What Love Lorenzo for their sister had

or

And many a jealous conference had they,

There are feeble duplications of epithets like *blythe and glad* or *sick and wan* (though that itself is an improvement on the first attempt *pale and wan*). There are still words which seem to be demanded by rhyme rather than selected for sense. *Well nigh mad* is a piece of febrile emphasis, *by degrees* is flaccid prose, and the olive-trees a most irrelevant piece of forestry. *Cruel clay* is awkward, and the cutting of Mercy to the bone hardly redeemed by the Chaucerian reminiscence of 'My throot is kut unto the nekke boon'.[1] In stanza XXIII there is no question of

[1] *Prioress's Tale*, B. 1839.

Lorenzo being *wise*; he is doing what his masters tell him to do; and in the next stanza there is a piece of ophiology as remarkable as it is unnecessary; since there could be few descriptions less fitly applicable to the brothers' address than a whine, by whatever creature probably or improbably produced. But here again Keats is finding himself mastered by the metre which ought to be his servant. The 'youngster' of stanza XXII reminds us that Keats has still not wholly emancipated himself from the worst of Leigh Hunt's influence; so does the *amorous dark* (even though he found *amorous* in Boccaccio); and so, worst of all, does the lamentable *Good bye! I soon be back*, where the attempt at simplicity achieves only a tasteless triviality. And what in the world is the middle of stanza XXVIII about? Why is the soul that is freed by murder more lonely than one released by a more normal death;[1] and in any case what has the loneliness to do with the restlessness and the bloodhound trailing of the murderers? And at the end of this stanza, as though it were not awkward enough already, Keats reverts with even less than usual felicity to a favourite earlier word;[2] and the two desperate brothers, for all that they use a convulsed spur, are no more drastic with their horses than to *tease* them homewards.

And yet, in spite of all the obvious flaws, while we are actually reading we forget to cavil. After the limp introduction Keats has tightened his grip on the story and on us, and he never again wholly relaxes it. And I think that the turning-point in the poem, the moment at which we are aware that Keats has put a lock on our imaginations,

[1] Mr. C. Bailey has pointed out to me that a note on *Aeneid* vi. 435 in Norden's edition implies a traditional belief that the souls not only of suicides, but of all who met an untimely death, had to wander 'staying for waftage' until they had accomplished their normal tale of days. And this may be what was in Keats' mind.

[2] Keats uses the word twice in the early poems; 'How vain for me the niggard Muse to tease' (*Epistle to GFM*, 73); 'my spirit teaze' (*Sleep and Poetry*, 82): and five times in *Endymion*; 'the solitary breeze Bluster'd, and slept, and its wild self did teaze' (I. 686); 'would I so teaze My pleasant days' (ib. 745); 'for vexing Mars had teaz'd Me even to tears' (ii. 558); 'Streams subterranean teaze their granite beds' (ib. 602); 'teaze me not With syren words' (ib. 954).

from which no turnings and twistings of rebellious criticism can free us, is the famous opening of stanza XXVII. From the moment when the brothers make their discovery and begin their plotting till the moment when Lorenzo goes off to make ready, the tension has been increasing. Then comes the lighter interlude of farewell, of which not even the deplorable execution can ruin the ironic effectiveness; and then we read

So the two Brothers and their murder'd Man

The proleptic epithet in that line has been celebrated or censured by all critics since Lamb; but I am not sure that the full force of it has been as universally observed. It is much more than a daring use of a rhetorical trick, a matter of 'wit' appreciable by the intellect; it carries compressed in it a strong appeal to the dramatic imagination. As Lorenzo turns from his careless farewell to Isabella at the window, leaves her happily singing, and joins the brothers, he signs his death-warrant; from that instant, though there is the temporal respite of the ride, from that instant he is a dead man and she his maiden widow. From the dramatic point of view indeed that stanza is the high-water mark of the poem, ending as it does with another brilliant touch.

Into a forest quiet for the slaughter.

There is the stage set, the three figures on it, the audience expectant. We wait for the details of the crime; but Keats knew better than Boccaccio. The curtain falls; and when it rises there are only two figures, and a grave.

Lorenzo being dead and the brothers returned to Florence, Keats reverts to his original and begins the second half of his story. Here is Boccaccio:

> *Isabella*, living in expectation of his return, and perceiving his stay to her was so offensive long: made many demands to her Brethren, into what parts they had sent him, that his tarrying was so quite from all wonted course. Such was her importunate speeches to them, that they taking it very discontentedly, one of them returned her this frowning Answer. What is your meaning

Sister, by so many questionings after *Lorenzo*? What urgent Affairs have you with him, that makes you so impatient upon his Absence? If hereafter you make any more Demands for him, we shall shape you such a Reply, as will be but little to your liking. At these harsh words *Isabella* fell into abundance of Tears, where-among she mingled many Sighs and Groans, such as were able to overthrow a far greater constitution: so that being full of fear and dismay, yet no way distrusting her Brethrens so wicked and hainous a cruel deed; she durst not question any more after him.

In the silence of dark Night, as she lay afflicted in her Bed, oftentimes would she call for *Lorenzo*, entreating his speedy return to her. And then again, as if he had been present with her, she checkt and reproved him for his long Absence.

Here again Keats improves upon his original. He shows the development of Isabella's state of mind from sorrow at her own loneliness through anxiety for Lorenzo to a desolation which wastes her. And he avoids the unnatural stupidity both of the brother's harsh answer and Isabella's unsuspecting acceptance of it. We could well spare the superior moral tone of the opening of stanza XXXI, and even better the over-elaboration of XXXII, not to mention the sudden intrusion of 'Himmon'; but at least where Boccaccio's narrative is jumbled Keats' is orderly; and we can well put up with a flat moment or two when we are just about to watch the performance of a miracle.

XXX

She wept alone for Pleasures not to be;
Sorely she wept untill the night came on:
And then, instead of Love, O Misery!
She brooded o'er the Luxury alone:
His image in the dusk she seem'd to see
And to the silence made a gentle moan;
Spreading her perfect Arms upon the Air
And on her Couch, low murmuring where Oh where!

XXXI

But Selfishness Love's cousin held not Long
Its fiery vigil in her single Breast;
She fretted for the golden hour and hung
Upon the time with feverish unrest—

Not long—for soon into her heart a throng
  Of higher occupants—a richer Zest,
Came tragic. Passion not to be subdued,
And sorrow for her Love in travels rude.

XXXII

In the mid days of Autumn, on their eves,
  The Breath of Winter comes from far away,
And the sick west continually bereaves
  Of some gold tinge, and plays a roundelay
Of death among the Bushes and the leaves,—
  To make all bare before he dares to stray
From his north cavern: so sweet Isabel
By gradual decay from beauty fell—

XXXIII

Because Lorenzo came not; oftentimes
  She ask'd her Brothers, with an eye all pale,
Striving to be itself, what dongeon climes
  Could keep him off so long. They spake a tale
Month after Month to quiet her: their Crimes
  Came on them like a Smoke from Himmon's vale,
And every night, in dreams, they groan'd aloud
To see their sister in her snowy shroud.

And now for Boccaccio again:

One Night among the rest, she being grown almost hopeless, of ever seeing him again, having a long while wept and grievously lamented; her senses and faculties utterly spent and tyred, that she could not utter any more Complaints, she fell into a Trance or Sleep, and dreamed that the Ghost of *Lorenzo* appeared unto her, in torn and unbefitting Garments, his looks pale, meager, and starving, and (as she thought) thus spake to her. My dear Love *Isabella*, thou dost nothing but torment thy self, with calling on me, accusing me for overlong tarrying from thee: I am come therefore to let thee know, that thou canst not enjoy my Company any more, because the very same day when last thou sawest me, thy Brethren most bloodily murther'd me. And acquainting her with the place where they had buryed his mangled body, he strictly charged her not to call him at any time afterward, and so vanished away.

And here is Keats dealing with the material:

XXXIV

And she had died in drowsy ignorance
  But for a thing more deadly dark than all:
It came like a fierce potion, drank by chance,
  Which saves a sick man from the feather'd pall
For some few gasping moments; like a lance
  Waking an Indian from his cloudy Hall
With cruel pierce, and bringing him again
Sense of the gnawing fire at heart and brain.

XXXV

It was a Vision. In the drowsy gloom,
  The dull of Midnight, at her Couches' foot
Lorenzo stood, and wept. The forest tomb
  Had marr'd his glossy hair that once could shoot
Lustre into the Sun; and put cold doom
  Upon his Lips, and taken the soft Lute
From his lorn voice, and past his loamed ears
Had made a miry channel for his tears.

XXXVI

Strange sound it was when the poor Shadow spake
  For there was striving in its piteous tongue
To speak as when on Earth it was awake,
  And Isabella on its Music hung.
Langour there was in it and tremulous shake
  As in a palsied Druid's harp unstrung:
And th[r]ough it moan'd a ghostly undersong
Like hoarse night gusts sepulchral briars among.

XXXVII

Its eyes though wild were still all dewy bright
  With Love, and kept all phantom fear aloof
From the poor Girl by Magic of their light;
  The while it did unthread the horrid woof
Of the late darken'd time; the murdrous spite
  Of Pride and Avarice; the dark pine roof
In the forest and the sodden turfed dell
Where without any word from stabs he fell.

XXXVIII

Saying moreover 'Isabel my sweet,!
  Red wortle berries droop above my head
And a large flint stone weighs upon my feet:
  Around me Beeches and high chesnuts shed
Their leaves and prickly nuts; a sheepfold bleat
  Comes from beyond the river to my bed
Go shed a tear upon my hether bloom
And I shall turn a diamond in the tomb.

XXXIX

I am a Shadow now, Alas Alas!
  Upon the Skirts of human nature dwelling;
Alone, I chaunt alone the holy Mass
  While little sounds of life are round me knelling,
While glossy Bees at noon do fieldward pass
  And many a chapel bell the hour is telling,
Paining me through; those sounds grow strange to me
And thou art distant in Humanity.

In this passage stanza XXXIV whether in key or not is in itself brilliantly effective, and the slight obscurity of it is pretty certainly due to a vigorous compression of some description which Keats had read of opium smokers or eaters together with a reminiscence of Southey.[1] And then follow five stanzas which are the most marvellous piece of transmutation in the poem. It is no longer a question of whether Keats is telling the story better or worse than Boccaccio, or whether he is better in some aspects and worse in others. This passage is in a different realm of creative art from anything that was ever within Boccaccio's range. There are still flaws, and we do a poor service to a great poet by closing our eyes to them; we had better observe them and dismiss them. The glossy hair has unfortunate associations; we may feel uneasy about lustre being shot into the sun, and not too happy, though for diverse

[1] Opposite this stanza in Woodhouse's transcript ('Poems II' in the Houghton-Crewe collection) there is pencilled in shorthand, 'Keats had been reading Southey's poems again at the time he wrote this stanza'. In the earlier books of *The Curse of Kehama* the 'fire in heart and brain' which occurs first as part of the curse (ii. 14) recurs as a kind of refrain (iii. 10; v. 2; ix. 10).

reasons, about the cold doom and the lute. We may resent the intrusion of the Druid, and wonder whether, if he suffered from the double disadvantage of his own palsy and an unstrung harp, he could produce even tremulous music. But I do not know that there is anything else in those five stanzas which jars even in the slightest degree. And on the positive side, what an achievement! The precision and economy of detail with which the ghost is depicted are beyond praise; and they are something new in Keats' work; and there are precision and economy no less admirable in the description of the place of the death and burial. But the real problem which this section of the tale presents is one which Boccaccio deals with by the easy road of avoiding it. The general tone must be pathetic rather than horrible; and so all that Boccaccio ventures on in the way of description of the ghost of a murdered man is to say that his garments are torn and unbefitting and his looks pale, meagre, and starving. But Keats will not be content with this easy evasion. He is determined that he will not flinch from the realistic description and yet that he will somehow make the whole effect one of beauty and not of terror. And he achieves this difficult task in the first three lines of XXXVII in which the spiritual so triumphantly transcends the physical. And the whole passage culminates in that line which for richness of content and beauty of music is surpassed by few others that even Keats ever wrote.

And thou art distant in Humanity.

After this, as though exhausted, as well it might be, by the effort, the inspiration seems for two stanzas to flag, XL being a vague anticlimax after XXXIX, and XLI vivid but unnecessary.

XL

I know what was, I feel full well what is,
    And I should rage if spirits could go mad:
Though I forget the heaven of a kiss,
    That paleness warms my grave as though I had

A Seraph chosen from the bright abyss
  To be my spouse—Thy paleness makes me glad
Thy Beauty grows upon me and I feel
A greater love through all my essence steal'

XLI

The Spirit mourn'd adieu, dissolv'd and left
  The Atom darkness in a slow turmoil
As when of healthful midnight sleep bereft,
  Thinking on rugged hours and fruitless toil,
We put our eyes into a pillowy cleft
  And see the spangly gloom froth up and boil;
It made sad Isabella's eyelids ache,
And in the dawn she started up awake.

Boccaccio's account of the next episode is:

The Young Damosel awaking, and giving some credit to her Vision, sighed and wept exceedingly; and after she was risen in the Morning, not daring to say anything to her Brethren, she resolutely determined to go see the place formerly appointed her, only to make tryal, if that which she seemed to see in her Sleep, should carry any likely-hood of Truth. Having obtained favour of her Brethren, to ride a days journey from the City, in company of her trusty Nurse, who long time had attended on her in the house, and knew the secret passages of her Love: they rode directly to the designed place, which being covered with some store of dryed leaves, and more deeply sunk than any other part of the Ground thereabout, they digged not far, but they found the body of the murthered *Lorenzo*, as yet very little corrupted or impaired, and then perceived the truth of her Vision.

Wisdom and government so much prevailed with her, as to instruct her soul, that her tears spent there, were meerly fruitless and in vain, neither did the time require any long tarrying there. Gladly would she have carryed the whole body with her, secretly to bestow honourable Enterment on it, but yet exceeded the compass of her Ability. Wherefore, in regard she could not have all, yet she would be possessed of a part, and having brought a keen Razor with her, by help of the Nurse, she divided the Head from the Body, wrapped it up in a Napkin, which the Nurse conveyed into her Lap, and then laid the Body in the Ground again. Thus being undiscovered by any, they departed thence, and arrived at home in convenient time, where being alone by themselves in the Chamber: she washed the Head over and over with her tears, and bestowed infinite kisses thereon.

Keats is considerably less happy with his adaptation of this. He starts with a rather unnecessary stanza:

XLII

'Ha! ha!' said she, 'I knew not this hard Life
  I thought the worst was simple misery,
I thought some fate with pleasure or with strife
  Portion'd us, happy days or else to die:
But there is crime, a Brothers Bloody Knife!
  Sweet spirit thou has schooled my infancy;
I'll visit thee for this and kiss thine eyes,
And greet thee morn and even in the Skies'

One could wish that the instinct for erasure had been more actively at work. As an example of how not to do it this could hardly be improved upon. It opens badly and continues worse. Is *Ha! ha!* ironic, or hysteric, or what? The reversion to the moralizing vein of stanza XXXI is bad enough, but is made even less acceptable both by the forced and rhyme-enforced contrast of pleasure and strife, which is so ill-adjusted an introduction of the perfectly normal contrast of happy days and death, and by the penny-dreadful capitalization in line 5. *For this*: for what? to get more schooling or in requital for the schooling? Why are the eyes in particular to be kissed except that they rhyme? And if they, as one must assume, are the eyes of the dead body, what kind of greeting is to be given to what kind of *thee* in the skies?

XLIII

When the full morning came she had devis'd
  How she might secret to the forest hie;
How she might find the clay so dearly priz'd
  And sing to it one latest lullaby;
How her short absence might be unsurmiz'd
  While she the inmost of the dream would try
Resolv'd: she took with her an aged Nurse,
And went into that dismal forest herse.

XLIV

See as they creep along the river side
  How she doth whisper to that aged dame;
And after looking round the campaign wide
  Shows her a knife. What feverous hectic flame
Burns in thee child? What good can thee betide
  That thou dost smile again? The Evening came,
And they had found Lorenzo's earthy bed:
The flint was there, the berries at his head.

XLV

Who hath not loiter'd in a green Churchyard,
  And let his Spirit, like a demon-mole,
Work through the clayey soil and gravel hard,
  To see Skull, coffin'd bones and funeral stole;
Pitying each form that hungry death hath marr'd
  And filling it once more with human soul
Ah, that is holiday to what was felt
When Isabella by Lorenzo knelt.

Keats' grip is for the moment slackened and confusion and awkwardness result. The third and fourth lines of stanza XLIII imply an acceptance of the truth of the vision, but the two following lines imply a doubt. *Hearse* is a poor metaphor for a place of burial. And the *short absence* of XLIII is incongruous with the *Evening* of XLIV. Then follows a stanza of which the sestet is powerful, even though its compressed elaborateness is a little out of key, but in which the weakness of the couplet wrecks the total effect. Even apart from the use of *holiday*, which misses the ironic effect that was intended, it is astonishing that Keats, at a moment when the attention needs to be concentrated upon Isabella, should permit himself the weak passive *was felt.*

After this period of becalmment the wind of inspiration returns, though hardly in full strength, and the sails fill again.

XLVI

She gaz'd into the fresh thrown mould as though
  One glance did fully all its secrets tell;
Clearly she saw as other eyes would know
  Pale Limbs at bottom of a crystal well:

Upon the murdrous spot she seem'd to grow
  Like to a native lilly of the dell:
Then with her knife, all sudden, she began
To dig more fervently than misers can.

XLVII

Soon she turn'd up a soiled glove, whereon
  Her silk had play'd in purple phantasies:
She kist it with a Lip more chill than stone,
  And put it in her Bosom where it dries
And freezes utterly unto the Bone
  Those da[i]nties made to still an infant's cries.
Then 'gan she work again nor staid her care
But to throw back at times her veiling hair.

XLVIII

That old nurse stood beside her wondering
  Until her heart felt pity to the core
At sight of such a dismal labouring;
  And so she kneeled with her Locks all hoar
And put her lean hands to the horrid thing:
  Three hours were they at this travel sore.
At last they felt the kernel of the grave,
And Isabella did not stamp and rave.

The first of these three stanzas is as good an example as one need wish of the inequalities of the poem, and of the way in which the conception is perpetually outrunning the execution. About the first four lines no reader, I suppose, has any doubts, though there is a touch of awkwardness about *other eyes would know*, as though Pegasus pecked and recovered. Opinions will differ about the next two lines; is the contrast between Isabella's sweet beauty and the murderous spot worth making, and, if it is, does the slightly 'conceited' parallel with the native lily make it? The conception of the last couplet is admirable, the abrupt transition from lily-like repose to feverish activity, and the parallel in action accentuated by difference in motive. But the whole effect is spoiled by one word. There is no question of how misers *can* dig, as though they were being defeated in a digging competition; it is a matter of how they *do* dig, but the demands of rhyme will not allow Keats to say so. Opinions have differed, and will differ, even more acutely about the first six lines of the next stanza. The discovery of the glove is a vivid touch, and the rest of the conception, picking up, as it does, an idea from stanza v and elaborating it, seems to me one of the most perfectly and suggestively moving things in the whole moving poem. But surely the false Leigh-Huntian 'delicacy' of the word *dainties* is intolerably jarring. Isabella is in a region of passionate experience far beyond such prettinesses, and so should the poet and his readers be. The last line again is a master-stroke. Nothing could set before our eyes the kneeling figure so vividly as this indirect comment. After the next stanza, with its unfortunate conclusion, where a positive statement would have been so much more effective, there is a curious interlude:

XLIX

Ah, wherefore all this wormy circumstance?
  Why linger at the yawning tomb so long?
O for the gentleness of old Romance,
  The simple plaining of a Minstrell's song!
Fair Reader at the old tale take a glance;
  For here in truth it doth not well belong
To speak: O turn thee to the very tale
And taste the Music of that Vision pale.

What is the relevance of this? What, indeed, is its meaning? When Keats expresses a wish for the gentleness of old Romance he may be alluding to Boccaccio; but it is very hard to suppose that the prose of Boccaccio can be alluded to as a minstrel's song. Does Keats then mean that he would like the way in which the tale might have been handled by some mediaeval troubadour? But in the next line the invitation to take a glance at the old tale seems to imply something that we have or may have in front of us; and then comes the final problem of the last line. What in the world is the music of a pale vision that we shall taste if we turn to the very tale? The only vision in Boccaccio is that of Lorenzo's ghost, and we are in the narrative long past that. The description of the scene at the graveside is in Boccaccio the briefest possible, and though it is undoubtedly devoid of wormy circumstance it is even more signally devoid of either music or a vision.

L

With duller sliver than the persean sword
  They cut away no foul Medusa's head;
But one's whose gentleness did well accord
  With death as Life. The ancient Harps have said
Love never dies, but lives immortal Lord.
  If ever any piece of Love was dead
Pale Isabella kist it, and low moan'd
'Twas Love cold dead indeed, but not dethron'd

LI

In anxious secrecy they took it home
  And then the prize was all for Isabel:
She calm'd its wild [h]air with a golden comb,
  And all around each eye's sepulchral cell
Pointed each single lash: the smeared loam
  With tears as chilly as a dripping well
She drench'd away; and still she comb'd and kept
Sighing all day and still she kiss'd and wept.

The first of the two stanzas is not satisfactory. There seems little significance in the steel being duller than Perseus' sword; nor much in the mention of Medusa.[1] The rest of the stanza is an attempt to express a fine but rather difficult idea, and the attempt is only partly successful. But in the second of the two stanzas Keats, at home again in the world of concrete imagery rather than of abstract idea, achieves for the second time the same

[1] These two lines are an interesting instance of the perils of correction. Though there seems no very special reason for the introduction of Perseus and Medusa, the lines as they stand do at least hang together; and there is perhaps, if one is determined to justify them, some kind of effective and ironic contrast between the clean dismemberment of Medusa by Harpe, and the more mangling dismemberment of Lorenzo by Isabella's blunter knife. But in the final revision Medusa disappears and her place is taken by a 'formless monster' which does not even suggest a Gorgon. And so 'Persean', though its quantity has been corrected, has no relevance at all.

miracle, even though this time the conditions are harder. Earlier he was dealing with a vision; here he must of necessity deal with the actual head that has been cut from the body. But somehow he succeeds; he divests the horrible of its repulsiveness and leaves it beautiful, without any evasive attempt to pretend that it is not horrible.

And now back to Boccaccio:

> Not long after, the Nurse having brought her a large Earthen Pot, such as we use to set Basile, Marjoram, Flowers, or other sweet Hearbs in; and shrowding the Head in a Silken Scarf, putting it into the Pot, covering it with Earth, and planting divers Roots of excellent Basile therein, which she never watered but either with her Tears, Rose-water, or water distilled from the Flowers of Oranges. This Pot she used continually to sit by, either in her Chamber, or any where else: for she carryed it always with her, sighing and breathing forth sad Complaints thereto, even as if they had been utter'd to her *Lorenzo*, and day by day this was her continual Exercise, to the no mean admiration of her Brethren, and many other Friends that beheld her.
>
> So long she held on in this mourning manner, that, what by the continual watering of the Basile, and putrefaction of the Head, so buried in the Pot of Earth; it grew very flourishing, and most odoriferous to such as scented it, that as no other Basile could possibly yield so sweet a savour. The Neighbours noting this behaviour in her, observing the long continuance thereof, how much her bright Beauty was defaced, and the Eyes sunk into her Head by incessant weeping, made many kind and friendly motions, to understand the reason of her so violent oppressions; but could not by any means prevail with her, or win any discovery by her Nurse, so faithful was she in secresie to her.

To this passage of Boccaccio Keats devotes six stanzas, three of description, in which he follows his original more closely than usual, and three of a kind of interlude. And the first three of these stanzas are the most entirely satisfactory piece of transmutation in the poem. The achievement is not so brilliant as the passage on the vision, since the task is easier. We are not aware of that slight sense of strain which a *tour de force* always produces. The material in this case is much more readily susceptible of the change; Keats is the serenely competent alchemist, and the good plain prose of Boccaccio and his translator is transmuted, as it were without losing its shape, into the purest gold of poetry.

LII

Then in a silken Scarf, sweet with the dews
  Of precious flowers pluck'd in Araby,
And divine liquids come with odorous ooze
  Th[r]ough the cold serpent pipe refreshfully,
She wrapp'd it up and for its tomb did choose
  A Garden pot wherein she laid it by,
And cover'd it with mould, and o'er it set
Sweet Basil, which her tears kept ever wet.

LIII

And she forgot the stars, the Moon, the Sun;
  And she forgot the blue above the trees;
And she forgot the dells where waters run;
  And she forgot the chilly Autumn breeze;
She had no knowledge when the day was done,
  And the new morn she saw not; but in peace
Hung over her sweet Basil evermore,
And moistened it with tears unto the core.

LIV

And so she ever fed it with thin tears;
  Whence thick and green and beautiful it grew,
So that it smelt more balmy than its peers
  Of Basil-tufts in Florence: for it drew
Nurture besides and Life from human fears,
  From the fast mouldring head there shut from view,
So that the jewel safely casketed
Came forth and in perfumed leafits spread.

The next two stanzas are pure interlude, leading us back to the narrative at the end of the second. And the first at least has such a perfection of grave beauty that we could ill spare it; but yet we feel uneasily that they halt the narrative unduly, and also that they strike an incongruously deep note. The Muse of Tragedy with her sceptred pall is too majestical for this setting.

LV

O Melancholy linger here awhile,
  O Music Music breathe despondingly!
O Echo, Echo, from some sombre isle
  Unknow[n]—lethean—sigh to us—O sigh!
Spirits in Grief lift up your heads and smile!
  Lift up your heads sweet spirits heavily,
And make a pale light in your cypress glooms,
Tinting with silver wan your marble tombs.

LVI

Moan hither all ye syllables of woe
  From the deep throat of sad Melpomene;
Through bronzed lyre in tragic order go,
  And touch the strings into a mystery:—
Sound mournfully upon the winds and low,
  For simple Isabel is soon to be
Among the dead: she withers like a palm
Cut by an Indian for its juicy balm

LVII

O leave the Palm to wither by itself,
  Let not quick Winter chill its dying hour:
It may not be—those Baalites of Pelf
  Her Brethren, noted the continual shower
Of her dead eyes, and many a curious elf
  Among her kindred, wonderd that such dower
Of youth and beauty should be thrown aside
By one mark'd out to be a noble's bride.

And now we move on to the conclusion. Here is Boccaccio:

Her Brethren also waxed weary of this cariage in her; and having veryoften reprov'd her for it, without any other alteration in her: at length, they closely stole away the Pot of Basile from her, for which she made infinite woful lamentations, earnestly entreating to have it restor'd again, avouching that she could not live without it.

Perceiving that she could not have the Pot again, she fell into an extreme Sickness, occasioned only by her ceaseless weeping; and never urged she to have any thing, but the restoring of the

Basile-Pot. Her Brethren grew greatly amazed thereat, because she never called for aught else beside; and thereupon were very desirous to ransack the Pot to the very bottom. Having emptyed out all the Earth, they found the Scarf of Silk, wherein the Head of *Lorenzo* was wrapped; which was (as yet) not so much consumed, but by the Locks of Hair, they knew it to be *Lorenzo's* Head, whereat they became confounded with Amazement.

Fearing lest their offence might come to open publication, they buried it very secretly; and before any could take notice thereof, they departed from *Messina*, and went to dwell at *Naples*, *Isabella* crying and calling still for her Pot of Basile, being unable to give over Mourning, dyed within a few days after.

Thus have you heard the hard fate of poor *Lorenzo* and *Isabella*. Within no long while after, when this Accident came to be publickly known, an excellent Ditty was composed thereof, beginning thus:

Cruel and unkind was the Christian,
That rob'd me of my Basiles bliss, &c.

And here is Keats, adhering quite closely to his model:

LVIII

And furthermore her brethren wondered much
Why she sat drooping by the Basil green,
And why it flourished as by magic touch;
Greatly they wonder'd what the thing might mean;
They could not surely give belief that such
A very nothing would have power to wean
Her from her own fair youth and pleasures gay
And even remembrance of her Love's delay.

LIX

Therefore they watch'd a time when they might sift
This hidden whim, and long they watch'd in vain;
For seldom did she go to chapel shrift,
And seldom felt she any hunger pain
And when she left she hurried back as swift
As Bird on wing to breast its eggs again;
And patient as a hen-bird sat her there
Beside the basil weeping through her hair.

LX

Yet they contrived to steal the Basil pot,
  And to examine it in secret place.
The thing was vile with green and livid spot,
  And yet they knew it was Lorenzo's face
The guerdon of their murder they had got,
  And so left Florence in a Moments space—
Never to turn again away they went
With blood upon their heads to Banishment.

LXI

O Melancholy turn thine eyes away!
  O Music, Music breathe despondingly!
O Echo, Echo on some other day
  From isles Lethean sigh to us O sigh!
Spirits of Grief sing not you well a way,
  For Isabel, sweet Isabel will die,
Will die a death too lone and incomplete
Now they have ta'en away her Basil sweet.

LXII

Piteous she look'd at dead and senseless things
  Asking for her lost Basil amourously;
And with melodious chuckle in the strings
  Of her lorn voice, she oftentimes would cry
After the Pilgrim in his wanderings
  To ask him where her Basil was and why
'Twas hid from her for cruel 'tis said she
To steal my Basil-pot away from me.

LXIII

And so she pin'd and so she died forlorn,
  Imploring for her Basil to the last.
No heart was there in Florence but did mourn
  At pity of her Love so overcast;
And a sad ditty, of this story born,
  From mouth to mouth through all the country past;
Still is the Burden sung—'O Cruelty
To steal my Basil-pot away from me.'

It has been assumed hitherto that the only translation of Boccaccio which Keats used was that mentioned by Woodhouse. It is true that it is more or less out of the question that he read Boccaccio in the original, since even some time later we find him making very slow progress with Ariosto.[1] But he had a very reasonable facility with French, as is witnessed not only by his translation from Ronsard,[2] but by his beginning to compose a sonnet in 'french of Ronsard'.[3] And it is at least a tempting conjecture that he had read another translation of the *Pot of Basil*, described as a *traduction libre*, by Mirabeau, published in Paris in 1802.[4] The conjecture is no more than a conjecture; its probability is increased if an old French translation of Boccaccio's *Il Filocolo* is accepted as one of the many sources of *The Eve of St. Agnes*, but there are in *Isabella* fewer direct parallels than those which in the case of *The Eve of St. Agnes* seem to me to raise conjecture to somewhere near certainty. Nevertheless there are certain points which are worth observing where both Keats and Mirabeau, with a greater or less degree of mutual resemblance, differ from the original. In the first place there is a certain number of resemblances of detail. In Mirabeau's introduction the phrase 'il n'avoit pu la voir sans l'aimer' recalls 'They could not in the self-same mansion dwell Without some stir of heart'. The elder brother in Mirabeau and the brothers in Keats are both much more deeply stirred by the discovery of the love between Isabella and Lorenzo than the elder brother is in Boccaccio. He finds the discovery 'highly displeasing'; but in Mirabeau he is 'brûlant de se venger' and in Keats the brothers are 'well nigh mad'. As to Lorenzo's head, in Boccaccio, quite concretely, as she cannot have the whole body, she 'would be possessed of a part'. But Mirabeau's description of her desire 'emporter avec elle un gage funeste et précieux de son amour' is much closer both in idea and in diction to 'And then the prize was all for Isabel'. The conception of the pot as a 'tomb' is common to both Mirabeau and Keats, and absent from Boccaccio ('ce

[1] MBF, 147 (465).
[2] *Nature withheld Cassandra* . . .; see MBF, 83 (239). [3] MBF, 143 (423).
[4] *Nouvelles de Jean Boccace*, *Traduction libre*, par Mirabeau. 2 vols. Paris, 1802.

monument funèbre' and 'arroser de ses larmes le tombeau qu'elle avoit su donner à son amant'). Mirabeau's description of Isabella's pining is again nearer to Keats: 'car elle dépérissoit sensiblement, et sa langueur, ses traits défigurés l'avertissoient assez que le terme de ses malheurs approchoit'. We look in vain in Boccaccio for remorse or (till the final discovery) of fear in the brothers; but in Keats they 'groan aloud To see their sister in her snowy shroud', and in Mirabeau they are 'dechirés de remords et de crainte'. In Boccaccio, again with the characteristic concreteness, they want to 'ransack the *pot* to the very bottom'; in Keats they want to 'sift this whim', and in Mirabeau 'éclaircir ce mystère'. In Boccaccio after the discovery of the head they depart with no more hurry than is represented by 'before any could take notice thereof', in Mirabeau 'ils quittèrent à l'instant Messine', and in Keats they 'left Florence in a moment's space'.

In the second place there are certain general resemblances between Keats and Mirabeau which are interesting. One of the most salient differences between Keats and Boccaccio in the general structure of the poem is the 'interludes' in Keats. I do not know that he required any hint to prompt these other than his poetic instinct; but if he did, he could find it in Mirabeau, in whose introductory passage we read: '. . . ils furent heureux. Hélas! ils ne devoient pas l'être long-temps. Mais un des bienfaits de l'amour est de bannir aisément les soucis de l'avenir. Aucune passion ne sait de même s'emparer de tous les instans de notre courte durée, et saisir le présent, ce bien si précieux et si méconnu, le seul sur lequel le sort et la fortune ne sauroient exercer leur caprices et leur tyrannie.' This is like in tone though not in verbal expression to Keats' interlude on Love in stanzas XII and XIII, and there is no sign of it in Boccaccio's direct narrative. Similarly Mirabeau comments on the brothers' attitude towards the love they have discovered. 'Un éclat pouvoit les déshonorer. . . . Comme si le déshonneur consistoit plutôt dans une mésalliance que dans la vile cupidité qui fait mettre à prix sa fille ou sa sœur, et sacrifier son bonheur à plus ou moins d'or!' Which is strongly reminiscent of Keats' attitude towards the brothers, their wealth, and the high noble and his olive trees.

I do not think that these parallels amount at all to evidence that Keats had read Mirabeau's translation, but they seem to me to establish a possibility, even perhaps a probability, too interesting to be passed over in silence. Nor do I think that so detailed a study of *Isabella* is, when we are examining the development of Keats' craftsmanship, a waste of time. It is a poem of transition. In many ways it is, in its brief compass, oddly like *Endymion*. Both are unequal, the beauties of both, exquisite though they are, are of parts rather than of the whole. In neither are the horses of the sun under full control; but at least in *Isabella* there are fewer of those dizzying plunges almost to destruction, fewer of those erratic wheelings and divagations that make the reader of *Endymion* sometimes feel that the poet is not only incapable of holding his team on their course, but almost careless of what the course should be. In *Isabella* the course is known, the control is being learned, and from now onwards Apollo can hand the reins to Phaethon with no apprehension of disaster.

We should not leave *Isabella* without reminding ourselves of Keats' own opinion of it, as sane and discriminating as are all his judgements on his own work:

> 'I will give you a few reasons why I shall persist in not publishing The Pot of Basil. It is too smokeable. I can get it smoak'd at the Carpenters shaving chimney much more cheaply. There is too much inexperience of live [life], and simplicity of knowledge in it. . . . It is possible to write fine things which cannot be laugh'd at in any way. Isabella is what I should call were I a reviewer 'A weak-sided Poem' with an amusing sober-sadness about it. . . . If I may so say, in my dramatic capacity I enter fully into the feeling: but in Propria Persona I should be apt to quiz it myself. There is no objection of this kind to Lamia—A good deal to St. Agnes Eve—only not so glaring.'[1]

[1] MBF, 143 (425, 6).

III. *HYPERION*

THE dates of the composition of *Hyperion* are difficult to determine with any degree of certainty. Lord Houghton recorded on the authority of Brown that it was begun after Tom Keats' death. But Keats had had the subject in mind for six months at least before that, since he says in a letter to George and Georgiana Keats of December 1818 that they knew before they left England (in June) that his next subject would be the Fall of Hyperion; and in the same passage he says 'I went on a little with it last night, but it will take some time to get into the vein again'.[1] This clearly implies that he had started the poem previously, and even that he had at one time been 'in the vein'. His accounts of his work during Tom's illness are somewhat conflicting, since he says on the one hand, in September, that he is obliged to write and plunge into abstract images to ease himself of Tom's countenance and voice and feebleness,[2] and on the other that during Tom's illness he was not able to write and since his death the task of beginning has been a hindrance;[3] while at the end of October he says to Reynolds 'Might I not at that very instant have been cogitating on the Characters of Saturn and Ops?',[4] which seems to imply quite clearly that he was at least meditating *Hyperion*. But later in the letter of December his large poem is 'scarce began'.[5] The most probable conjecture seems to be that the subject had been in his mind for some time, and that when he returned from the Scotch tour in August, fresh from his reading of Cary's *Dante* which he took with him,[6] he made a beginning on the writing of it, but that the increasing claims of his attendance on Tom more and more precluded any creative work except as an intermittent escape, that no effective start was made until December, after Tom's death, and that even then it was laborious and against the grain. In February 1819 he records that he has not gone

[1] MBF, 93 (274). [2] MBF, 82 (236). [3] MBF, 93 (266, 7).
[4] MBF, 88 (245). [5] MBF, 93 (280). [6] MBF, 75 (212).

on with *Hyperion*,[1] and on the 15th of April he is 'still at a stand in versifying—I cannot do it yet with any pleasure'.[2] But in the same month Woodhouse records that Keats lent him the fragment of *Hyperion* '2 books and ½—(abt 900 lines in all)'. Since the end of January was, as we shall see, occupied with *The Eve of St. Agnes*, it looks as though *Hyperion* must have been written in a continuous burst of reluctant creation in the last three weeks of December and the first three of January. It seems to me hard to believe that any of *Hyperion* was written in the most un-Miltonic four months which open with *The Eve of St. Agnes*, and include the beginning of *The Eve of St. Mark*, *La Belle Dame*, and the Odes, and much easier to believe that after carrying *Hyperion* to the point where it now ends Keats broke off a task which, however great and however brilliantly executed, did not 'set his genius', and turned with relief into that other atmosphere in which he was so freely and securely at home. But it was characteristic of his courage and determination that he was not content to leave a piece of work incomplete, and some time during the summer he reverted to it, and tried not so much to recast it, as the process is often described, as to use what he had already written, and put it, with little alteration, into a new setting, as part of a poem of quite different scope and aim. Brown tells us that he was at work on this new poem at the same time that he was working on *The Cap and Bells*, in the winter of 1819, and apart from Brown's evidence, which there is no reason to doubt, there is at least one small but interesting piece of internal evidence which tends to confirm this.[3] But it is equally certain that a good deal of the resetting was done in the summer of that year. It began, I think, as early as July. On the 25th Keats writes to Fanny Brawne, 'I have been all day employ'd in a very abstract Poem'.[4] There is surely no work of Keats which merits that description except considerable passages of *The Fall of Hyperion*.

[1] MBF, 114 (322).
[2] MBF, 114 (345).
[3] *See Note D* (*page* 298).
[4] MBF, 130 (392).

Certainly neither *Hyperion* nor *Lamia* with their strong concrete narration can be so described. At all events in the middle of August he reports to Bailey that he has been writing parts of his *Hyperion*;[1] as he does not say 're-writing', and as Woodhouse had the original *Hyperion*, as complete as it was ever to be, in April, this is presumably the new *Hyperion*. By the end of September this new attempt had also been given up, since he writes to Reynolds on the 21st 'I have given up Hyperion—there were too many Miltonic inversions in it—Miltonic verse cannot be written but in an artful or rather artist's humour. I wish to give myself up to other sensations.'[2] But it was not given up before a considerable proportion of the new poem had been written, since in the 'lost' letter to Woodhouse[3] of the same date he quotes not only the first 11 lines of canto I, and lines 61–86 of the same canto, but also the opening lines of canto II. Now as the rest of canto II, with the exception of four lines, is no more than a revision of a passage in the original *Hyperion* the natural inference is that a great part of the new *Hyperion* had been completed by September. A determination of dates is here of more importance than questions of chronology often are, since if the bulk of the new *Hyperion* was completed before the end of September it belongs to the end of Keats' great creative period which culminated with *To Autumn*, and we are automatically saved from a prejudice which has, I think, vitiated a good deal of the criticism of *The Fall of Hyperion*. If we attribute it to the winter of 1819, then we expect to find in it evidence of flagging powers, the work of a man physically debilitated by disease, and spiritually exhausted by hopeless passion; and we naturally find what we expect to find. But if it is to be dated earlier, then we have to start with no such presupposition, and with clearer eyes; and we may find ourselves, as I hope to show, being drawn towards a different critical conclusion.

I do not propose in this book to attempt any complete

[1] MBF, 133 (399). [2] MBF, 142 (419). [3] MBF, 143 (422–4).

examination of either the sources or the workmanship of *Hyperion*, or of the relations between it and *The Fall of Hyperion*, partly because such an examination would extend to a disproportionate length and partly because I do not wish inadequately to anticipate the complete examination for which I understand students of Keats will have to thank Professor Livingston Lowes, and which if conducted by him will be both adequate and masterly. All I propose here is to examine one or two of the many sources, the importance of one at least of which has not, I think, been sufficiently recognized; to watch Keats at work on some of the more famous passages; and to suggest certain considerations in regard to the relations of the two *Hyperions*.

First as to the 'sources'. There was for long a kind of conspiracy of the critics, originating no doubt from a remark of Cowden Clarke's, to persuade us that Keats drew all or most of his classical knowledge from Lemprière's *Classical Dictionary*. It is on the face of it improbable that any man of Keats' temper of mind was willing to stifle himself with the dusty entries of Lemprière if he could breathe the freer air of Chapman and other Elizabethan translators; any reader who will take the trouble to compare the descriptions in *Endymion* of the figures of classical mythology with the particulars given of them in Lemprière will, I think, be convinced that Keats' debt to Lemprière is negligible, that to Spence's *Polymetis* considerable,[1] and that to other more 'literary' sources more extensive still; and so far as *Hyperion* is concerned it is to be hoped that Professor de Sélincourt[2] has once for all exploded the Lemprière myth by showing that there is almost nothing of the classical material in *Hyperion* which Keats could not have found elsewhere than in Lemprière, whether in Chapman's translation of Hesiod's *Works and Days*, Cooke's translation of Hesiod's *Theogony*, or Sandys's translation of Ovid's *Metamorphoses*, not to mention more casual allu-

[1] *See Note E* (*page* 299). [2] de S, 485, 6.

sions, scattered all up and down Elizabethan and other literature, to the Titans and their war with the Olympians. He would for example find Tethys frequently in Spenser, and half a dozen miscellaneous giants (including two not mentioned by Hesiod) in an Ode of Ronsard[1] to which Woodhouse refers us. But the trouble with all these allusions is that, with the exception of those in the *Theogony*, they are scattered, and each deals with only a few of the figures in *Hyperion*; while the list in the *Theogony*, though concentrated, is incomplete when we compare it with *Hyperion*. Of the two dozen or so figures in the great catalogue at the opening of the second book of *Hyperion* the following are not mentioned in the *Theogony*: Cybele, Dolor, Porphyrion, Caf, Tellus, Enceladus, Ops (the discrepancy is partly of course because Keats on the whole uses the Latin aliases). And one cannot help wishing that one could find some source which gave a reasonably complete list and included at least some of those missing from the *Theogony*. And there is such a list, in a book which we know Keats to have possessed, and which has, I think, though mentioned by Sir Sidney Colvin in another context,[2] been unduly neglected by critics. This is the *Pantheon* of 'E. Baldwin' (i.e. William Godwin).[3] I have an idea that one reason for its neglect is that any one who has glanced at Tooke's *Pantheon*, which Keats is also supposed to have used, and has been repelled by its aridity, will naturally regard *Pantheon* as an ominous title. But in fact Baldwin's book is as far removed as may be from the spirit of either Lemprière or Tooke. It is, as Sir Sidney Colvin describes it, a 'well-felt and well-written little primer of mythology'. It is no more than a primer, but it is written by one who really cares for what he is writing about, and it is thoroughly readable. And Baldwin gives us Tellus, tells us that

[1] *A Michel de l'Hospital*; see de S, 579, 580.
[2] SC, 228, 231.
[3] *The Pantheon; or Ancient History of the Gods of Greece and Rome. For the use of schools, and young persons of both sexes*; by E. Baldwin, London, 1806 (also 1809, 1810, and 1814).

Saturn married Ops, otherwise called Cybele, gives a list of the Titans, and in the list of the giants includes both Enceladus and Porphyrion.[1] We are left with Dolor and the most unclassical Caf to account for. Professor de Sélincourt, pursuing a hint of Sir Sidney Colvin's, has settled the provenance of Dolor.[2] He comes from Hyginus, who says 'ex Aethere et Terra, Dolor, Dolus, Ira . . .'. Caf is more mysterious. The same critic suggested[3] that she comes from the *Arabian Nights*, with which, as we shall see when we come to examine *The Eve of St. Agnes*, Keats was almost certainly familiar; and the suggestion is probable enough. But I should hazard a conjecture that his later suggestion[4] is right and that she comes from *Vathek*. There is a great deal about Caf (which Beckford identifies with Caucasus) in *Vathek*,[5] and the notion of Caucasus as the child of Earth's painful labour on the one hand, and the parent of Asia on the other, is natural enough.

[1] He also gives Thea the unusual spelling of 'Theia', which may account for the perpetual difficulty which Keats had with spelling her.

[2] de S, 506.

[3] de S, 507. But the quotation from Burton is irrelevant, since Burton was not born till 1821, and I have not in fact found Caf in any editions of the *Arabian Nights* which it seems likely that Keats might have read, though I should not be prepared to deny her existence in them.

[4] de S, 581.

[5] It is clear that Keats had read *Vathek*, from the allusion in a letter of July 1818 (MBF, 72 (192)), 'I should like to employ Caliph Vatheck to kick him'; cf. 'The rage of Vathek exceeded all bounds on finding . . . his guards lying lifeless around him. In the paroxism of his passion he fell furiously on the poor carcases, and kicked them till evening without intermission.' And indeed see *Vathek* passim for kicking. As to Caf, Beckford says: 'This mountain, which, in reality, is no other than Caucasus, was supposed to surround the earth. . . . The fabulous historians of the East affirm, that this mountain was founded upon a stone. . . . It is added, that whenever God would excite an earthquake, he commands the stone to move one of its fibres, and, that being moved, the part of the earth connected with it, quakes, is convulsed . . .' (*Vathek*; 3rd edition revised and corrected, London, 1816). And when we read in *Hyperion* of the domes and the vaults and the diamond-paved arcades, and Hyperion sitting on his orbed fire, and then turn to *Vathek*, and find, in the description of the subterranean palace, a lofty dome, columns and arcades, a vaulted ceiling, a pavement strewn with gold dust, and finally the formidable Eblis who sat upon a globe of fire, it is hard to resist the conviction that Keats has used his reading of *Vathek*. But as some at least of the more significant parallels are to passages in *The Eve of St. Agnes* and *The Fall of Hyperion* the detailed examination of them can be deferred.

But after all, the list of the Titans and giants, their relationships and their wars, are no more than the raw material, whencesoever derived, and Keats deals with it in a way of which there is no hint at all in any of the accounts which we have hitherto discussed. In all of these, though there are considerable discrepancies, notably as to the side on which the giants are fighting, the picture is that of a straightforward epic war *à outrance* between the Titans and the Olympians. Whereas the picture in *Hyperion* is wholly different. Even Saturn himself is not fighting for revenge, but for freedom to show his love. He feels himself

> smother'd up,
> And buried from all godlike exercise
> Of influence benign on planets pale,
> Of admonitions to the winds and seas,
> Of peaceful sway above man's harvesting,
> And all those acts which Deity supreme
> Doth ease its heart of love in. (i. 106–12.)

and he desires a 'golden victory' after which there will be

> trumpets blown
> Of triumph calm, and hymns of festival
> Upon the gold clouds metropolitan,
> Voices of soft proclaim, and silver stir
> Of strings in hollow shells; and there shall be
> Beautiful things made new, for the surprise
> Of the sky-children; (i. 127–33.)

There are those whose sentence is for open war, with Hyperion and Enceladus as their leaders; but the key-note of the poem is surely struck in the great speech of Oceanus in the second book, in which he tells his fellow Titans that as they fall

> by course of Nature's law, not force
> Of thunder, or of Jove. (ii. 181, 2.)

they must be content to stoop. They are only a stage in a great onward progress. As Chaos and blank darkness yielded to Heaven and Earth, and Heaven and Earth were succeeded by the Titans, so

> on our heels a fresh perfection treads,
> A power more strong in beauty, born of us
> And fated to excel us, as we pass
> In glory that old Darkness: nor are we
> Thereby more conquer'd, than by us the rule
> Of shapeless Chaos. (ii. 212–17.)

And so strongly has he himself felt the power of this fresh perfection that he has, however sadly, without waiting to be conquered, given place of his own will to his successor.

> Have ye beheld the young God of the Seas,
> My dispossessor? Have ye seen his face?
> Have ye beheld his chariot, foam'd along
> By noble winged creatures he hath made?
> I saw him on the calmed waters scud,
> With such a glow of beauty in his eyes,
> That it enforc'd me to bid sad farewell
> To all my empire: (ii. 232–9.)

Now Keats owned a book, the oddest possible farrago of curious learning, dubious philology, and unbridled conjecture, compiled by one Edward Davies, and published in 1804 with the title *Celtic Researches, on the Origin, Traditions & Language, of the Ancient Britons.* Few titles could sound less relevant to the classical subject of *Hyperion*; but if Keats began to read the book with his new poem in his mind, he would soon find himself among familiar names and encouraged to proceed. He would find a preliminary reference to Hesiod and the Titans on page 33 and to the war in which the Gods and the sons of the Gods scattered the giants on page 74. But later on, when Davies becomes interested in the origins of the Celtae, he becomes also much more fully interested in the Titans:

'Long before *Troy* had acquired celebrity, *Iapetus* married, or took possession of *Asia*, where he generated a race of *Titans*, and those *Titans*, progenitors of *Thracians* and *Celtae*, contested with *Javan's* posterity the possession of these countries; raising

> the mountains, that is, their inhabitants, against the *Greeks*, or, in poetical description, against their *Gods*. Such of them as became partizans for the cause of *Jupiter*, were led by *Cottus*, *Briareus*, and *Gyges*—names which are evidently connected with a *Cimmerian*, or *Celtic race*. . . . The *Titans*, or *Giants*, were, after a long struggle, vanquished, and were driven to the *West*, into the *regions* of *Pluto*, the acknowledged progenitor of the *Gauls*. Thither they were attended by *Cottus*, *Briareus*, and *Gyges*, to whose charge they were committed; that is, their chiefs, or their tribes, retained their names.'[1]

And earlier we have been told that 'These Titans, the sons of the Heaven and the Earth, or of the Climate and the Country, and the parents of the Celtae, according to Hesiod's account, were driven into the *lower part* of the *Earth*, into a land already inhabited by some of their brethren'.[2] Also that Atlas, the chief of the Titans, and General of the Titan army against Jupiter, was a Hyperborean.[3] But the most significant passage in Davies is, I think, the concluding paragraph of his first section, since though no doubt as worded it expected the answer 'No', it appears to contain in it something like the germ of the central idea of *Hyperion*. 'Can it be imagined that the Gods and the Sons of the Gods who vanquished and dispersed the rebellious giants, and those giants themselves, were not only one and the same people, but frequently the same individuals; and that, by being thus self-vanquished and self-destroyed, the same giants became Lords of the world?'[4] And when we later find Davies identifying Apollo with 'Titan' and saying that he was an accredited Hyperborean,[5] he seems to be admitting the identity on which he here throws doubt. Other points of interest in Davies, notably the Druids and the Egyptians, will come under review in connexion with particular passages in the poem.

And now it is time to turn to the poem itself, to see what kind of a thing it is, what advance it marks, and how

[1] Davies, pp. 205, 6.
[2] Davies, p. 132.
[3] Davies, p. 130 (note) and p. 187.
[4] Davies, p. 116.
[5] Davies, pp. 169, 182.

some passages in it came to be what they are. And in the first place let us try to imagine that we are reading it for the first time, and reading it not as the last printed work of a writer whom we know as the poet of *St. Agnes' Eve*, and *Lamia* and the Odes, but as we might have read it in January 1819, or as Woodhouse, if he had not in the interval seen *The Eve of St. Agnes*, did read it in April of that year. We know Keats as the poet of the 1817 volume, the poet that is of some pleasant trivialities, of one great and a number of mediocre sonnets, of some pleasant enough light verse letters much in the manner of Leigh Hunt, and of two more thoughtful poems; we know him as the poet of *Endymion*, a long verse narrative, full of exquisite but spasmodic and apparently often accidental beauties, and immature, with a luscious and unpruned exuberance; and we know him as the poet of *Isabella*, an unequal though often lovely handling of a delicate romantic theme, with one or two moments of perfect achievement, but on the whole with that 'softness' about its beauty which made Keats himself call it 'weak-sided'. Since *Isabella*, now nearly a year ago, there has been some pleasant versification, but almost nothing that can be called full poetry or even that has had the promise of it. Has Keats written himself out? If not, what is the new poem like? Is it *Endymion* over again, easily flowing and facile in its beauties, though, we hope, stiffened in structure and pruned in expression? And with a kind of apprehensive eagerness we take up the first of the great folio pages on which Keats has written it out. And before we have read four lines we catch our breath, and know that *Endymion* is far behind, that even if the promised land is not yet conquered the trumpets have blown round the walls of Jericho.

> Deep in the shady Sadness of a Vale,
> Far sunken from the healthy breath of Morn,
> Far from the fiery noon, and Eve's one star,
> Sat grey hair'd Saturn quiet as a Stone,
> Still as the Silence round about his Lair.

Forest on forest hung above his head
Like Cloud on Cloud. No stir of air was there;
Not so much life as on a Summer's day
Robs not at all the dandelions fleece:
But where the dead leaf fell, there did it rest.
A Stream went voiceless by, still deadened more
By reason of his fallen divinity
Spreading a shade: the Naiad mid her reeds
Press'd her cold finger closer to her lips.

This is very certainly no Keats that we have known before. What has happened? The answer no doubt is that Milton has happened, both directly and through the medium of Cary's *Dante*, which Keats took with him on the Scotch tour. There is nothing here of the dancing ripple of 1817 and of *Endymion*, which seemed for the most part to pause when it chose and go on when it thought about it. This has not indeed the full harmonics of Milton, nor is it the work of a mere imitator; but it has a considerable measure of that grave, ordered progress, never hurrying, and halting only by deliberate design, that relentless march of the legions, of which Milton alone among English poets knew the secret.

And now let us make an attempt to see how the passage was arrived at. So far as watching the craftsman at work is concerned the manuscript of *Hyperion* stands between that of *Isabella*, where we can hardly watch him at all, and that of *The Eve of St. Agnes*, where we can if we choose watch him throughout. The manuscript of *Hyperion*[1] was clearly intended for a fair copy, and large portions of it are written out with no more than an occasional verbal correction. But there is a certain number of passages, and among them several of the finest, which evidently did not satisfy Keats as they stood in the first draft, and which he works over as he writes the intended fair copy. For this opening passage his material we may suppose was a passage

[1] Now in the British Museum. A facsimile of this, together with a transliteration of Woodhouse's transcript of *The Fall of Hyperion*, was published in 1905 by the Clarendon Press with an introduction and notes by Professor de Sélincourt.

in the *Iliad* (probably in Chapman's translation) in which Zeus says of Cronos

> where endless night confounds
> Japhet and my dejected sire, who sit so far beneath
> They never see the flying sun, nor hear the winds that breathe.[1]

together with a number of Miltonic reminiscences, the shady vale from *Paradise Regained*,[2] the morn-noon-eve sequence perhaps from the fall of Mulciber,[3] the blaze of noon from *Samson Agonistes*,[4] and the breath of morn pretty certainly from the speech of Eve in the fourth book of *Paradise Lost*.[5] And nothing occurs to Keats that he wants to correct in his first draft till the seventh line. Here he first writes

> Like Clouds that

then scratches out *that* and writes *whose bosoms* and then scratches out *bosoms* and writes *thundrous bosoms*. The instance is a trivial one in itself, but it is so characteristic of Keats' methods of composing in a hurry that it is worth giving, since it is the first time we have met them and we shall see much of them later. In his earlier work at any rate he did a great deal of his composing on paper, not working out the line in his head and then writing it down, but writing down his false starts and tentative experiments and deleting them. Finally, in the instance before us, he deletes all that he has written, and starts a new line, contenting himself with

> Like Cloud on Cloud

Then he copies down the next two lines and a half:

> No stir of air was there;
> Not so much Life as what an eagle's wing
> Would spread upon a field of green ear'd corn

He is now engaged on a task which always interested him, from the time that he wrote

> A little noiseless noise among the leaves,
> Born of the very sigh that silence heaves[6]

[1] Chapman's *Homer*, *Iliad*, viii. 421-3, and cf. *Hyp.* ii. 80.
[2] *P.R.* i. 304.
[3] *P.L.* i. 742, 3.
[4] *S.A.* 80.
[5] *P.L.* iv. 641.
[6] '*I stood tiptoe . . .*', 11, 12.

the task namely of describing silence and stillness. And what he has written is not in the least satisfactory. As it stands it seems almost meaningless, or at best a very complicated way of saying 'no life', since the beat of an eagle's wings can by no possibility affect the corn far below. One might think that Keats had in mind the sudden cessation of all animate life under the shadow of a bird of prey, were it not that the stress is on the stir of air or the absence of it. The next attempt is

> Not so much Life as a young vulture's wing

but this if anything makes matters worse. However, either then, or perhaps before beginning operations on the two lines at all, he went on to at least the end of the paragraph, since the next attempt is written in the margin. In this he discards the bird altogether, greatly to the improvement of the image, and writes

> Not so much life as on a Summer's day
> Robs not at all the dandelions fleece.[1]

And so for the moment he left it, much improved, but still waiting for the final touch, which probably did not come till he was writing the new *Hyperion* six months or more later.

The scene is now set, and it is interesting to notice the emergence of that strong dramatic instinct, that sense indeed of 'theatre', which was so conspicuously wanting in the opening of *Isabella*, but which is to be so effective in *The Eve of St. Agnes* and in all his later work. One wonders indeed whether he had at the back of his mind

[1] It is clear that this is connected with Keats' note in *Troilus and Cressida*, and I wish one could be certain when that note was made. See n. B, p. 293, to Chapter I. I think that there is not much doubt that the note precedes the passage in *Hyperion*, partly because it is clear in the note that Keats wrote *despoils* and then deleted it and wrote *Robs*. On the other hand, the words in the note begin with a capital letter, as though Keats was transcribing a line of verse which he knew. Is it possible that the words in the note are a line which Keats is quoting from somewhere, and not his own composition?

that setting of a similar and specifically theatrical scene in the fourth book of *Paradise Lost*:

> over head up grew
> Insuperable highth of loftiest shade,
> Cedar, and Pine, and Firr, and branching Palm
> A Silvan Scene, and as the ranks ascend
> Shade above shade, a woodie Theatre
> Of stateliest view.[1]

At any rate the curtain has risen, and it remains to define more particularly the figure which so far has been no more than indicated. The passage was, judging from the fact that the corrections have to be crowded in between the lines, written out in full from the draft before he went back to emend it.

> Along the margin sand large footmarks went
> No further than to where his feet had stay'd,
> And slept without a motion since that time.
> His old right hand lay nerveless on the ground
> Unsceepter'd; and his white browd eyes were clos'd;
> While his bow'd head seem'd listning to the Earth
> The Ancient Mother for some comfort yet.

The main trouble here is manifestly the third and fourth lines; they both end feebly, and *without a motion* barely escapes being redundant. The first change is to get rid of *since that time*, put a colon after *motion* and transfer *on the ground* to the line above; the second of the two lines can then be completed by two more adjectives for hand, and the lines read

> And slept without a motion: on the ground
> His old right hand lay nerveless dead supine,

That, amongst other things, has vastly improved the rhythm. But the weak *without a motion* is still there, and if the other line is to end with three adjectives, as a matter of both sound and sense the emphatic and heavy monosyllable should come at the end, as in a cadence which he learned perhaps from his much admired Chatterton

[1] *P.L.* iv. 137–42.

(*withered, forwynd, dead*),[1] had used in *Endymion* (*lovelorn, silent, wan*),[2] and used later in *The Eve of St. Agnes* (*meagre, barefoot, wan*).[3] So the two lines are further altered to read

> And slept there since: upon the sodden ground
> His old right hand lay nerveless listless, dead

where *dead* is made even more emphatic by the similarity of accent and sound in the two preceding words. Next, in the sixth line of the passage, *bow'd* is deleted because of the assonance with *white brow'd*, but before anything is substituted the cancellation has drawn attention to the weakness of *white brow'd* itself, an adjective of mere description following one (*unscepter'd*) so fully charged with significance. First Keats tries *ancient*, which is at least not merely visual; but it will not serve, because of *ancient* two lines lower; and then it occurs to him that if the hand is unsceptered the just balance will be secured if the eyes are also deprived of what they once had, and the inspiration comes that gives the crowning touch to the whole passage, and the eyes shall be *realmless*; the visual *bow'd* is now thoroughly in place and is restored, and with the change which makes the Ancient Mother personal rather than general the passage is complete:

> Along the margin sand large footmarks went
> No further than to where his feet had stay'd,
> And slept there since: upon the sodden ground
> His old right hand lay nerveless listless, dead
> Unsceepter'd; and his realmless eyes were clos'd;
> While his bow'd head seem'd listning to the Earth
> His Ancient Mother for some comfort yet.

There follow four lines which do not appear in the printed version and are worth recording, since they show how uncertain Keats yet was in his judgement. They almost achieve the impossible of destroying the grandeur of what has preceded them, and the Keats of six months later

[1] *Excellent Ballad of Charitie*, st. IV (de S. quotes with 'sapless', which is the gloss, not Chatterton's word).

[2] *End.* iv. 764.

[3] *The Eve of St. Agnes*, st. II.

could hardly have written them, let alone allowed them even temporarily to stand:

> Thus the old Eagle drowsy with great grief
> Sat moulting his weak Plumage never more
> To be restored or soar against the Sun,
> While his three Sons upon Olympus stood—

After this, however, Keats recovers himself and returns to the earlier level with the entry upon this still and silent scene of the second actor. In the fifty lines which describe the entry and speech of Thea there is hardly a correction, and little else to comment on. One correction is of interest; Keats first wrote (26–8):

> She was a Goddess of the infant world;
> Placed by her side, the tallest Amazon
> Had stood a little child:

He is using of course the common Miltonic device for giving the impression of great size more effectively than by inadequate direct description:

> His Spear, to equal which the tallest Pine
> Hewn on *Norwegian* hills, to be the Mast
> Of some high Ammiral, were but a wand,[1]

But he decides that he wants to make it more Miltonic, and he remembers in the same book of *Paradise Lost* 'that small infantry'[2] and the other passage in which the specific name is given, 'that Pigmean Race',[3] and he rewrites his lines

> By her in stature the tall Amazon
> Had stood a Pigmy's height:

The point is worth noticing as being the first instance of Keats' desire in *Hyperion* to increase the Miltonic effect, whereas in *The Fall of Hyperion*, as we shall see, he is conducting exactly the opposite process, and de-Miltonizing his earlier work.

The other noteworthy passage is lines 31–3:

> Her face was large as that of Memphian Sphinx
> Pedestal'd haply in a Palace court
> When Sages look'd to Egypt for their lore.

[1] *P.L.* i. 292–4. [2] *P.L.* i. 575. [3] *P.L.* i. 780.

Miss Helen Darbishire has pointed out in a most interesting paper[1] how much Egyptian atmosphere and description there is in *Hyperion*. And she suggests, with every probability, that when Keats wrote these lines he was remembering what he had read in the *Annals of the Fine Arts* for April 1818 of the colossal statue found 'In one of the courts of the Palace of Memnon'. There can at least be no doubt that Keats is using in *Hyperion* the knowledge of Egypt and its buildings and statues which had come to him from reading and more directly from seeing the Egyptian collection in the British Museum, in particular the new accessions of January 1818, and notably among them the famous head of 'Memnon'.

This whole passage of the entry and speech of Thea gives an odd impression of conflict. Keats is not yet happy in his Miltonic singing robes. He writes a few lines like those on the tall Amazon that have the desired ring; he makes his first experiment with the Miltonic repetition or 'turn', in the lines

> How beautiful, if sorrow had not made
> Sorrow more beautiful than beauty's self

but, lovely though the lines are, the turn is Keats', not Milton's, and it is not till later in the poem that he really learns the trick. He writes three superbly Miltonic lines on the clouds and their stored thunder and follows them with three more that are as un-Miltonic as they can well be. In general the natural Keats is always breaking in, and writing his own characteristically lighter music.

But immediately upon the speech of Thea comes that famous passage which is not indeed an imitation of Milton but which could hardly have been written without his influence, in which the music is slowed and solemnized and weighted so that each stroke of the picture has time to tell, and in which Keats achieved, not without labour,

[1] 'Keats and Egypt', *The Review of English Studies*, vol. iii, No. 9, January, 1927. The paper is full of interest with regard to other passages, notably the pyramids and bronzed obelisks of Hyperion's palace, and the winged orb of fire.

a simile which, different in spirit though it is, takes rank with any of the great similes of Milton. It first stood thus:

> As when upon a tranced summer night
> Those green rob'd Senators of mighty woods
> The Oaks, stand charmed by the earnest Stars:
> And thus all night without a stir they rest
> Save from one sudden momentary gust
> Which comes upon the silence and dies off
> As if the Sea of Air had but one wave:

The first two lines were good enough to satisfy any one, and they are not touched; but then corrections begin. The first alteration was probably the minor one of *remain* for *they rest.* The stages of the remaining alterations are not too clear. It first I think occurred to him that it would be much better if the verb was held up till the second of the two lines, and that in any case *stand* is a colourless word for a passage so highly charged and so vivid with personification. So he deleted *stand,* leaving the gap to be considered later, and altered the second line to

> Dream and all night without a stir remain.

But this fades away feebly, so cut out the weak verb and repeat the strong one,

> Dream and so dream all night without a stir

And now for the other line. The substitute for *stand* is hard to decipher, but I think that the first attempt was, with deletion of *The*

> Oaks, drowsily-charmed

But this is an awkward rhythm, and *drowsily* presses the personification to almost absurd lengths. And then come the two touches which so clearly define the visual picture and make the oaks trees while still leaving them senators,

> Tall Oaks, branch-charmed by the earnest Stars

Finally, the momentary gust becomes much more effectively *solitary*, and the picture of the Sea of Air is retained but made fuller of suggestion by becoming the *ebbing Air*. And so the passage was left

> As when upon a tranced summer night
> Those green rob'd Senators of mighty woods
> Tall Oaks, branch-charmed by the earnest Stars
> Dream and so dream all night without a stir
> Save from one sudden solitary gust
> Which comes upon the silence and dies off
> As if the ebbing Air had but one wave.

The voice may have some at least of the accents of Milton, but the imagination is the imagination of Shakespeare and of Keats.

The passage which follows this magnificent opening is hardly up to its level. From the narrative and dramatic point of view it is well enough, with the month's statuesque stillness, the waking of Saturn and his speech to Thea, which includes the preparation for the entry of Hyperion. But the movement is uneasy; it seems unable to settle down into either one temper or one tempo, and it is not till the end, in lines 126–33, that it 'finds itself'. And it is in those lines that it becomes most avowedly Miltonic. *Voices of soft proclaim* has the true Miltonic ring, and the *gold clouds metropolitan* is the typical Miltonic elaboration of the inversion. And if it were not that Keats' instinct for the excision of weak growth is working strongly the central section of the passage would be even less satisfactory than it is. Lines 111 and 112 originally read thus:

> And all those acts which Deity supreme
> ~~Must do to ease itself lest two hot grown~~
> Doth ease its heart of Love in just as tears
> Leave a calm pleasure in the human breast.
> O Thea I must burn—my Spirit gasps

But the last two and a half lines, feeble in themselves, and the first part of them dramatically quite unsuitable to Saturn, are cut out, and the strong phrase *Doth ease its heart of Love in* left standing out.

In the passage which follows (135–58) there is little to remark upon except one surprising phrase. Why in the world should the locks of a primitive Greek (or Roman) deity be *Druid* locks? I think that the answer is Davies' *Celtic Researches*. There is a hint as early as *Isabella* that Keats was interested in Druids, in the 'palsied Druid's harp unstrung', and the fact that the locks of Saturn which here shake are 'Druid's' may be due simply to a combination of the phrase in *Isabella* with another in *Endymion*, 'By old Saturnus' forelock, by his head Shook with eternal palsy', where there is an obvious link in the word 'palsy'. But Davies is not only full of discussions of the Druids, which in a work on his subject was inevitable, but also in a number of places connects the Druids with Greece and Rome, with Jupiter, with Apollo, and with Greek mythology in general. The point is of minor importance and the details will be found in the notes.[1]

By now we have had enough, and perhaps more than enough, of Saturn and Thea. The poem shows signs of flagging, and there is need of a change of scene, and still more imperative need of action, if it is not to lose its hold on the attention. And the change and the action both come. With the entry of

Blazing Hyperion on his orbed fire

the poem, like Milton's noble and puissant nation, rouses itself like a strong man after sleep and shakes its invincible locks. Through two hundred lines, to the end of the first book, there is hardly a moment's slackening in the sustained power of its movement and the swelling flood of its harmonies. Again and again the ear catches the inexorable rhythms, the 'majestic instancy' of *Paradise Lost*, the clang of the hammers on Cyclopean anvils. Here is a

[1] *See Note F* (*page* 299).

passage which leaves no doubt what master Keats had determined to acknowledge:

> His palace bright
> Bastioned with pyramids of glowing gold,
> And touch'd with Shade of bronsed Obelisks,
> Glared a blood red through all its thousand Courts
> Arches and Domes and fiery Galleries;
> And all its curtains of aurorian clouds
> Flush'd angerly: (176–82.)

This time both voice and imagination are Miltonic. And, as we should expect, the reminiscences of Milton, both verbally and in idiom, are frequent. It is perhaps worth while examining these in some detail, since there is sometimes a temptation to under-estimate the Miltonic element in *Hyperion*. Keats is far too strong and original an artist to suffer from a study of what happens when for a time, and for a specific purpose, he subdues his own genius to an alien influence. At the opening of the passage Keats specifically confesses himself to be in the same difficulty as that which was inherent in the subject of *Paradise Lost*, though the difficulty for him is less extreme; the sorrow and woe of the Titans,

> Too huge for mortal tongue or Pen of scribe,

are still more within the range of description than the 'Almightie works' to recount which

> What words or tongue of Seraph can suffice?[1]

Hyperion on his orbed fire is perhaps a reminiscence of Satan and his orbed shield,[2] and his snuffing of the incense is suggestive of the meager shadow who snuff'd the smell of mortal change.[3] The *omens drear* which fright and *perplex* recall the eclipse which 'with fear of change Perplexes Monarchs'.[4] The use of the verb *jar* twice within thirty lines ('*jar* their battlements and towers'[5] and '*Jarr'd* his own golden region') suggests that Keats had

[1] *P.L.* vii. 113.
[2] Ib. vi. 543.
[3] Ib. x. 272.
[4] Ib. i. 598.
[5] A Miltonism later than the MS.

been observing Milton's effective use of this word ('*Jarr'd* against natures chime' in *At a Solemn Musick*,[1] and the 'impetuous recoile and *jarring* sound' of the infernal doors).[2] The use of *slope* in line 204 ('came *slope* upon the threshold of the west') is Miltonic ('Bore him *slope* downward').[3] The question of Hyperion,

> Am I to leave this haven of my rest,
> This cradle of my Glory? This soft clime
> This calm luxuriance of blissful light,
> These crystalline Pavillions, and pure fanes
> Of all my Lucent Empire?

irresistibly recalls, both in general tone, in the repeated *this*, and in the use of *clime*, the speech of Satan:

> Is this the Region, this the Soil, the Clime,
> Said then the lost Arch Angel, this the seat
> That we must change for Heav'n, this mournful gloom
> For that celestial light?[4]

In line 248

> I will advance a terrible right arm

the use of *advance* is rather Shakespearean than Miltonic, but the terrible right arm recalls the 'terrour of this Arm'[5] and the *right hand* that grasped ten thousand thunders.[6] And the *colure* and the *zenith* of the description of the orb of fire (ll. 273–7) are both characteristically Miltonic.[7] And in two of the passages the Miltonisms are later and deliberate introductions. Lines 235–9 at first read

> Am I to leave this haven of my rest,
> This cradle of my Glory? It is left
> Deserted. . . .

Then comes the addition on the opposite page

> This soft clime
> ~~Unknow[n] elsewhere but~~
> This calm luxuriance of blissful light,
> These crystalline Pavillions, and pure fanes
> Of all my Lucent Empire?

[1] *At a Solemn Musick*, l. 20.
[2] *P.L.* ii. 880. [3] Ib. iv. 591. [4] Ib. i. 242–5.
[5] Ib. i. 113. [6] Ib. vi. 836. [7] Ib. i. 745, x. 329, ix. 66.

And the whole passage about the orb is full of interest. The first two lines show no alterations:

> The planet orb of fire whereon he rode
> Each day from east to west the heavens through

The next line was first

> Spun at his round in blackest curtaining

then *blackest* was changed to *darkest*, and then both were deleted and the line completed with *of clouds*, and Keats went on

> Not therefore hidden up and muffled quite
> But
> ~~For~~ ever and anon the glancing spheres
> ~~Shot through~~ Glow'd through and still upon the sable shroud

Then he tried *within their sable shroud* and finally *about the sable shroud* and went on

> Made sweet shap'd lightning: wings this splendent orb
> Possessd for glory. . . .

and then the whole thing from *Spun round* to *lightning* was deleted, and an extended version worked at on the opposite page. It will be noticed that so far there is little specifically Miltonic except *muffled quite*,[1] though the subject invites Miltonic treatment.

> Spun round in sable curtaining of clouds
> Not therefore veiled quite, blindfold and dusk

but *dusk* does not please him, and he tries successively *dim* and *veil'd* before arriving at *hid.*

> But ever and anon the glancing spheres,

so far as in the other version, but they will be the better for being more exactly defined, so

> Circles and Arcs and zones

zones is Miltonic, but the rhythm is getting monotonous;

[1] e.g. 'extinguish'd quite' (*Samson Agonistes*, 168).

so why not at the same time be yet more Miltonic, more technical, and also cure the rhythm?

> Circles and Arcs and broad belting colure,

In the next line Keats first tries to retain both the rejected and accepted reading of the first version, but he cannot reconcile himself to *shot* and it goes out again as soon as written,

> Glowd through and ~~shot~~ struck throughout the muffling black

Then he tries something else which I cannot decipher for *black*[1] and finally writes *dark*. But he is still not happy about the *struck through*, and alters it to the far more effective *wrought upon*. Now he completes the passage and brings in the Miltonic *Zenith* from which Mulciber fell.[2]

> Sweet shaped Lightnings, from the nadir deep
> Up to the Zenith;

One can see in this passage a characteristic habit of Keats, which we shall meet again in the 'casement' passage in *The Eve of St. Agnes*, the habit of using much of the material of a rejected passage in different combinations in the new passage. Here for example *sable* is removed from one of its Miltonic nouns, *shroud*,[3] and attached to the other, *cloud*,[4] whereas *muffled* is used to complete the phrase which takes the place of the *sable shroud*. The passage is then completed, with one or two minor experiments and corrections, as it stands in print.

So much for the Miltonic vocabulary of the last half of the first book. But more significant than vocabulary is the idiom. There is an almost tedious use of Miltonic inversion; *omens drear*, *palace bright*, *metal sick*, *rest divine*, *fragrance soft*, *Phantoms pale*, *nadir deep*, *remnants huge*, *marble swart*, *plumes immense*, *porches wide*, *radiance faint*, *palpitations sweet*, and *pleasures soft*. Then there is a

[1] *black* itself is not certain; HBF reads *blind*, having mistaken for the dot of the *i* part of the deleting stroke. It looks more like *blast* or *blust* than anything; and might be *blank*. The other word looks like *grand*. And I am fairly clear that Keats' final notion of the line was to end it with *muffle* (not *muffling*) and an adjective, since the *ng* is deleted and the *i* altered to an *e*.

[2] *P.L.* i. 745.

[3] *Lycidas*, 22.

[4] *Comus*, 221.

number of instances of the Miltonic repetition, amounting in several cases to the full 'turn':

> while sometimes eagle's wings
> Unseen before by Gods or wondring Men
> Darkened the place; and neighing Steeds were heard
> Not heard before by Gods or wondring Men. (182–5)

> Two wings this orb
> Possessd for glory, two fair argent wings (283–4)

> Awaiting for Hyperion's command.
> Fain would he have commanded. . . . (289–90)

> And the bright Titan phrensied with new woes,
> Unused to bend, by hard compulsion bent
> His spirit. . . . (299–301)

and a curious one, which is Miltonic in form, but completely un-Miltonic in cadence and feeling:

> My Life is but the Life of Winds and tides
> No more than Winds and tides can I avail. (341–2)

There are also two similes, of which the first is Miltonic throughout, and the second starts with the Miltonic ring and then falls:

> His winged minions, in close clusters stood
> Amaz'd and full of fear, like anxious men
> Who on wide plains gather in panting troops
> When an Earthquake hath shook their city towers. (197–200)

> For as in Theatres of crowded men
> Hubbub increases more they call out hush! (253–4)

But however carefully we notice, and ought to notice, the strong Miltonic influence, it would be uncritical not to notice also the readiness with which Keats as it were slips out of the groove in which he has elected to move, and becomes Elizabethan, or (which indeed is perhaps the same thing) becomes himself. The passage which follows the last of the repetitions instanced above is purely Elizabethan:

> Be thou therefore in the van
> Of Circumstance; yea seize the Arrow's barb
> Before the tense string murmurs— (343–5)

and there is one of the famous lines of the poem to which any reader who follows Keats' own directions will inevitably find himself putting the mark || as a passage which shows the 'true voice of feeling', rather than the × which is to indicate 'the false beauty proceeding from art'.[1] And it is the more interesting since it comes in a passage which has at least a hint of the Miltonic repetition.

> Hyperion arose and on the stars
> Lifted his curved Lids, and kept them wide
> Until it ceas'd; and still he kept them wide.
> And still they were the same bright patient Stars. (350–3)

There is a number of other instances in this first book which show Keats the craftsman at work, but, as we shall be examining his craftsmanship in detail and at length when we come to *The Eve of St. Agnes*, the study of them may be omitted. Readers who are interested will find the material for such study in H. Buxton Forman's[2] and Professor de Sélincourt's editions, and best of all in the facsimile of the *Hyperion* MS. edited by the latter critic. They will find also in the notes some comments on passages in which it seems to me that these two editors have misread the text.[3]

The second book is the counterpart in *Hyperion* of the description of the fallen angels and the great debate in Hell of the second book of *Paradise Lost*; and as one would expect the Miltonic influence is still strong. Here is a typical passage:

> still upon the flint
> He ground severe his skull, with open Mouth
> And eyes at horrid working. Nearest him
> Asia, born of most enormous Caf,
> Who cost her Mother Tellus keener pangs
> Though feminine, than any of her Sons: (50–5)

where *ground severe* and the parenthetic *though feminine* are in Milton's manner, and also we catch a reminiscence

[1] MBF 142 (419).
[2] In this case the Oxford *Keats*.
[3] *See Note G* (*page* 300).

of 'which cost *Ceres* all that pain'.[1] If again we look at a passage in the fourth book of *Paradise Lost*

> So farwel Hope, and with Hope farwel Fear,
> Farwel Remorse: . . .
> Thus while he spake, each passion dimm'd his face
> Thrice chang'd with pale, ire, envie and despair,[2]

one can hardly doubt that it was in Keats' mind when he wrote

> (She) sidelong fix'd her eyes on Saturn's face:
> There saw she direst strife—the supreme God
> At war with all the frailty of grief
> Of Rage, of fear, Anxiety, Revenge
> Remorse, Spleen, Hope but most of all Despair. (91–5)

There are in the book four 'turns', and a number of phrases in the Miltonic idiom, such as *uncertain where* (9), *all prostrate else* (65), besides the ordinary inversions. But I do not think that one can escape the feeling that from the moment that Oceanus begins to speak, about half-way through the book, the Miltonic influence becomes less dominant, or at least that Keats finds the surrender to it less easy. And the reason for this, if it is a fact, is clear. Up to this point Keats has been engaged primarily on description, and superb description it has been; but because it has been only description, because Keats has been writing externally, not from his heart, not, in his own phrase, from his inwards, he has found it comparatively easy to write 'in an artful or rather an artist's humour'. And even so, in all the grandeur of description which at first reading blinds one to defects, there is something lacking, something that for all its inequalities and imperfections was present in *Isabella*, and is going to be present without the imperfections in *The Eve of St. Agnes*. That something is, briefly, reality. The figures are described with a wealth of detail that ought to make them live before us; and yet for the most part they remain lay figures dressed in gorgeous robes; they are not fully 'felt'; they are verbally vivid, but not spiritually vivid. The truth is, I suppose,

[1] *P.L.* iv. 271. [2] Ib. 108–15.

that no creative artist's imagination can have its own 'unfettered scope' when it is working in another artist's medium; Milton's imagination naturally expressed itself in the Miltonic idiom, and the figures of *Paradise Lost* have an unsurpassed vitality. Keats could adopt the alien idiom, but only by sacrificing the freedom of his imagination; he could write in it masterfully, but not feel in it truly. And so with the speech of Oceanus a change comes over the poem. Keats is no longer content to describe; he has come to the point where it is urgent that he should say what he feels, and he can only do that as Keats, not as Milton. And when one's ears are open it is almost comic to watch how Keats, when he has something that he wants to say, says it in his own voice; and when it is said reverts to the skilled ventriloquist. The speech of Oceanus, which is in some ways the kernel of the poem, grows more and more un-Miltonic as it proceeds, and rises in a kind of exultant consciousness of increasing freedom to the climax, equally lovely and strong, which has been already quoted. And then, when all has been said that matters, Milton abruptly re-enters.

> Have ye beheld the young God o the Seas
> My dispossessor? Have ye seen his face?
> Have ye beheld his Chariot, foam'd along
> By noble winged Creatures he hath made?
> I saw him on the calmed waters scud
> With such a glow [of] b(l)eauty in his eyes
> That it enfo[r]c'd me to bid sad farewell
> To all my Empire—

so far Keats, with a Shakespearean reminiscence to end with, and then, with an abrupt Miltonic 'turn',

> farewel sad I took
> And hither came to see how dolorous fate
> Had wrought upon ye, and how I might best
> Give Consolation in this woe extreme—
> Receive the Truth, and let it be your balm.
> Whether through pos'd conviction or disdain
> They guarded silence when Oceanus
> Left murmuring, what deepest thought can tell? (232–46)

And precisely the same thing happens in the speech of Clymene which follows, though since the climax has risen less high the drop from it is less abrupt.

> Grief ove[r]came
> And I was stopping up my frantic ears
> When past all hindrance of my trembling hands
> A voice came sweeter, sweeter than all tune,
> And still it cried, 'Apollo! young Apollo!
> The morning-bright Apollo! young Apollo!
> I fled, it follow'd me and cried Apollo!
> O father and O Brethren had ye felt
> Those pains of mine—O Saturn hadst thou felt
> Ye would not call this too-indulged tongue
> Presu[m]ptuous in thus venturing to be heard. (289–99)

In this second book, though there are plenty of minor alterations which are of interest, there is only one considerable passage which is in itself great enough, and which shows sufficiently clearly the steps by which it was arrived at, to be worth detailed examination. This is the passage towards the end of the book which prepares for and describes the entry of Hyperion. It stood first thus:

> Till suddenly a full-blown Splendour fill'd
> Those native spaces of oblivion
> And every glulph and every chasm old
> And every height and every sullen depth
> Voiceless or filled with hoarse tormented Streams;
> And all the everlasting Cataracts
> And all the headlong Torrents far and near,
> And all the Caverns soft with moss and weed
> Or dazzling with bright and barren gems;
> And all the giant-Gods. It was Hyperion:
> He stood upon a granite peak aloof
> With golden hair of short numidian curl,
> Rich as the colchian fleece. (357–72)

The first alterations are minor ones; for some reason Keats wants another verb in the earlier part, and *was seen* is introduced in the third line, the *every* of *every chasm* being deleted to make room for it; in the ninth line the trisyllabic pronunciation of *dazzling* (why this should be described as a specifically cockney mispronunciation I do not know) is got rid of by re-writing the line as

> Or blazon'd with clear Spar and barren gems

the hypermetric *giant* is cut out of the tenth line; and the uncompleted last line about the Golden Fleece is deleted. But then Keats deletes the whole passage and starts again. I am not clear that he was much exercised to make the lines, as has been suggested, a description of a 'universal human experience'. He wants to make vivid the arrival of the sun-god among his fellow Titans, and he not unnaturally wants to describe it in terms of the sun rising on the particular scenery in which the Titans find themselves. And to call the alteration in the first line 'a phrase which by a stroke of consummate genius gives us the key to the picture' seems to be the kind of extravagant laudation which belittles the writer whom it is intended to praise. If Keats' genius when consummate produces no more than the kind of competent piece of craftsmanship here to be noticed it is a very pedestrian genius. Keats simply sees that *full-blown splendour* is a vague phrase and does not at all tell us what kind of splendour it is; it might for example be that of the rising moon. So he determines that there shall be no room for doubt and alters the line so that it reads

> Till suddenly a splendour like the Morn

Then it occurs to him that *native* spaces does not mean a great deal, and that the *native spaces of oblivion* draws no sort of concrete picture, effectively suggestive though it may be; and further that *fill'd* is a little too abrupt for the effect of the growing dawn which is what he wants. So he inserts a precise line

> Pervaded all the beetling gloomy steeps

after which the more vaguely suggestive line, with the substitution of a characteristic Miltonic adjective for the unsatisfactory *native* will do well enough

> All the sad Spaces of oblivion,

after which the first draft, with one alteration, much for the better, will serve till he comes to the caverns and the giant Gods. The trouble with the caverns, effective though the description of them is in itself, is that their softness with moss and weed is quite irrelevant to the way in which they catch the light; so they disappear altogether; and the trouble with the giant Gods is that we know already from what has preceded that they are there, and do not, or at least should not, need reminding of their presence. So instead of them we have two lines which stress the contrast between the earlier darkness and the dawning light.

> And every gulph and every chasm old
> And every height and every sullen depth
> Voiceless or hoarse with loud tormented Streams:
> And all the everlasting Cataracts,
> And all the headlong torrents far and near;
> Mantled before in darkness and huge shade
> Now ~~showed~~ saw the light and made it terrible.[1]

This recast now allows Hyperion to come more emphatically at the beginning of a line, and the description of him is amplified. His feet much more effectively *touch* the granite peak, and instead of the allusion to the Golden Fleece there is a thoroughly Miltonic phrase. There is also a line (*To the most hateful seeing of itself*) which I think one may safely say would have been better omitted. All its content is implied in what has gone before and in the word *betray'd*, and unless our imaginations have wholly gone to sleep the implication is much more telling than the explicit expression. At all events the passage, as revised, ends:

> It was Hyperion—a granite peak
> His bright feet touch'd and there he stay'd to view

[1] There are two interesting small points in this passage, which show how much Keats' ear is engaged when he is composing, and how all the sounds of a phrase are in his ears at the same time, so that when he is writing fast they get confused. He manages to exorcise the redundant *l* in *glulph*, but it insinuates itself later, and *chasm* was actually written *chalsm* because of the *l* in *old* that was to follow, and *before* was written as *febore*.

The Misery his Brilliant had betray'd
To the most h(e)ateful seeing of itself.
Golden his hair of short Numidian curl;
Regal his shape majestic. . . .

Before we leave this second book it is perhaps not without interest to stop for a moment and consider how much material for *Hyperion* Keats brought back with him from his Scotch tour, that tour which as he said he hoped would 'give me more experience, rub off more Prejudice, use to more hardship, identify finer scenes load me with grander Mountains, and strengthen more my reach in Poetry, than would stopping at home among Books, even though I should reach Homer'.[1] Here are parts of his descriptions of his first waterfall: 'We . . . found it out by the noise . . . then we went on a jut of rock nearly level with the second fall-head . . . at the same time we saw that the water was divided by a sort of cataract island on whose other side burst out a glorious stream—then the thunder and the freshness. . . . What astonishes me more than anything is the tone, the coloring, the slate, the stone, the moss, the rock-weed.'[2] And some of this he repeats in a letter of the next day: 'it surpassed my expectation, in what I have mentioned in my letter to Tom, in its tone and intellect its light shade slaty Rock, Moss and Rock weed'.[3] Now if we turn to the description, at the beginning of the second book, of the den where the bruised Titans mourn we find the thunder of the waterfalls, their position unknown except by their sound, the jutting crags and the slaty ridge,

the solid roar
Of thundrous Waterfalls and torrents hoarse,
Pouring a constant bulk, uncertain where.
Crag jutting forth to Crag, and Rocks that seem'd
Ever as if just rising from a sleep,
Forehead to forehead held their monstrous horns,
And thus in thousand hugest phantasies

[1] MBF, 75 (210). [2] MBF, 67 (169, 170).
[3] MBF, 68 (171).

> Made a fit roofing to this nest of woe
> Instead of Thrones, hard flint they sat upon,
> Couches of rugged Stone and Slaty ridge,
> Stubborn'd with iron. (7–17)

Are any other items in the description, one wonders, drawn from other reminiscences of the tour; what of the roofing and the flint and the iron? *Roofing* Keats uses in the poem on Fingal's cave;[1] and there is the following line in the poem included in the letter to Bailey of July 18th:

> Upon hot sand, or flinty road, or Sea shore iron scurf.[2]

Further, the moss and rock weed which seem so much to have impressed him, though they do not appear in the poem as printed, did appear, as we have seen, in the first draft, in the line

> And all the Caverns soft with moss and weed.

and in that same passage come the chasms that so much impressed him on Ben Nevis.[3]

The description of the Titans

> like a dismal cirque
> Of druid Stones, upon a fo[r]lorn Moor
> When the chill rain begins at shut of eve
> In dull November and their chancel-vault
> The heaven itself is blinded throughout night
> (ii. 34–8)

is clearly a reminiscence though with elaborating touches of the Druid stones outside Keswick. 'We set forth about a mile and a half on the Penrith road, to see the Druid temple . . . those aged stones on a gentle rise in the midst of the Mountains, which at that time darkened all around, except at the fresh opening of the Vale of St. John.'[4]

Again, the *cathedral cavern* of the first book (line 86) was fairly certainly suggested by Fingal's Cave. Keats' account of this shows that he had already the subject of *Hyperion* in mind. 'Suppose now the Giants who rebelled against Jove had taken a whole Mass of black Columns and

[1] MBF, 76 (219).
[2] MBF, 75 (213).
[3] MBF, 77 (223).
[4] MBF, 69 (176).

bound them together like bunches of matches—and then with immense Axes had made a cavern in the body of these columns—of course the roof and floor must be composed of the broken ends of the Columns—such is fingal's Cave. . . . For solemnity and grandeur it far surpasses the finest Cathedrall.'[1] And the *natural sculpture* of the same line is suggested by the passage in the poem which immediately follows the prose account of the cave:

> As I stood its roofing under
> Lo! I saw one sleeping there
> On the marble cold and bare[2]

while further on in the poem the cave is again likened to a cathedral,

> This Cathedral of the Sea.[3]

And while we are engaged with this description of Fingal's Cave it is worth drawing attention to a curious point, relevant not to the debt of *Hyperion* to the Scotch tour, but to its possible debt to a literary source. Writing to George and Georgiana Keats in September of 1819 Keats says that he has discovered that he never sent to them part of the account of the tour, and will now copy out for them part of one of his Scotch letters.[4] He copies out this description of Fingal's Cave almost word for word as it was in the letter to Tom Keats of July 1818 except for one odd difference. Writing to Tom he says, as we have seen, 'Suppose now the Giants who rebelled against Jove . . .'. In writing the later letter he says 'Suppose now the Giants, who came down to the daughters of Men . . .'.[5] He is of course here confusing the 'Sons of God' and the 'giants' of the sixth chapter of Genesis, but granted this confusion, why the change in the description of the giants? Had he any reason to equate the two sets, those of the Bible and those of Greek mythology? If, as I have suggested, he had read Davies' *Celtic*

[1] MBF, 76 (217, 8). [2] MBF, 76 (219). [3] MBF, 76 (220).
[4] MBF, 147 (446). [5] MBF, 147 (449).

Researches, he had every reason to equate them. Davies says a great deal of 'the giants of Babel', explains that they were the same as the giants of other primitive mythologies, and says specifically, 'Sanchoniathon, speaking of those people who were dispersed from Babel, says, "These are the people who are described as *Exiles* and *Wanderers*, and at the same time are called the *Titans*.—Euseb. P.E.L. i" '.[1] And also, 'The wars . . . between the *Gods* and the *Titans* are themes of the ancient poets. The descriptions of them contain many particulars, borrowed from antecedent events and dates. They belong to the original dispersion of the *Giants* from Babel.' The identification therefore in the two letters of the two sets of giants seems to me to strengthen considerably the probability of Keats' indebtedness to Davies.

In the third book the attempt to maintain the allegiance to Milton is almost abandoned. There is still a certain amount of Miltonic idiom, a few inversions, like *tumults dire*, *olives green*, *bright elixir peerless*, a possible reminiscence of *dim suffusion*[2] in *half-shut suffused eyes* (44), a fairly certain one of *Dorian mood Of Flutes and soft Recorders*[3] in *soft warble from the dorian flute* (12), and one perhaps even clearer of *Samson Agonistes*[4] in '*For me, dark, dark, And painful vile oblivion seals my eyes*' (81). But there is a great deal more in this book than in the other two that is definitely un-Miltonic in diction, and the whole is completely un-Miltonic in spirit. As Keats turns from the Titans, and from Hyperion in particular, to the young God who is to supersede him, he turns to give expression to an idea which was in his mind when he wrote *Sleep and Poetry*, which he has expressed in his letters since then, and which he is going to express yet more clearly in *The Fall of Hyperion*. At the beginning of this third book Apollo is still in the realm of Flora and old Pan, and the white-handed nymphs smiling upon the flowers and the

[1] Davies, pp. 83, 130.
[2] *P.L.* iii. 26.
[3] Ib. i. 550.
[4] *S.A.* 80.

trees, which Keats described in *Sleep and Poetry*; and just as Keats says that he must pass these joys for

> a nobler life
> Where I may find the agonies, the strife
> Of human hearts (*Sleep and Poetry*, 123–5)

so Apollo only reaches his full godhead, leaving behind the ignorance which though fearless was aching, through anguish and through knowledge. And this idea, because he feels it profoundly, Keats cannot express in a borrowed style; the style in which he does express it would doubtless not have been what it is if it had not been for the influence of Milton, but it is now Keats' own, not an imitation. And it is perhaps not insignificant that in the lines

> yet I can read
> A wondrous lesson in thy silent face (111–12)

we catch an echo not of Milton but of Shakespeare;

> Your face, my thane, is as a book where men
> May read strange matters.[1]

And the echo was even clearer before alteration, since the second line started with a deleted *Matte*.

We may perhaps conclude this brief examination of *Hyperion* by glancing at Keats working on the last passage of the poem before he abandoned it.

> Thus the God,
> While ~~his~~ level-glanced beneath his temples soft
> His eyes were stedfast on Mnemosyne;

then he deletes these two lines and writes

> While his enkindled eyes with level glance
> Beneath his white soft temples, stedfast kept
> Upon Mnemosyne: and

then he deletes *and* and writes *Trembling with ligh* in the margin as the beginning of the line. The next line starts

> And while a

[1] *Macbeth*, I. v. 63.

but the *a* is deleted and the line continued

throughout his ~~limbs~~ frame

and then the whole line is deleted and a new start made, but even this is not very prosperous, since

And wild commotion throughout

is cancelled as soon as written, a false start *And his* made and cancelled, and the line at last achieved as

Soon wild commotions shook him, and made flush

and the next line starts

All his white,

but is completed as

All the immortal fairness of his limbs,

and the next line written

Roseate and pained as any ravish'd nymph—

the *any* first altered to *a* and then the line cancelled, and Keats has a disastrous spasm of the old fatal Leigh Hunt influence.

Into a hue more roseate than sweet pain
Gives to a Nymph new-r

but *new-ravish'd* is going to be too much for Keats even in this mood, and he completes the line

Gives to a ravish'd Nymph when her warm tears
Gush luscious with no sob—

After this unfortunate and incongruous interlude the next few lines move smoothly till the climax is reached.

So young Apollo anguishd:
~~Even~~ his very hair, his golden tresses fam'd,
~~Keep~~ Kept undulation round his eager neck

Here *graceful* is inserted between *Kept* and *undulation* as though the rather meaningless *eager* was to be cancelled; but *graceful* is little better, and is deleted. Then

> During the Pain Mnemosyne upheld
> Her arms as one who prohesie'~~d~~s. At lenght
> Phoebus

(the omission of one letter and the transposition of two others is characteristic of Keats in a hurry) then *Phoebus* is deleted and the line written

> Apollo shreikd—and lo he was the God!
> And godlike

But that is felt to be somewhat abrupt, and another attempt is made,

> Apollo shreikd—and lo from all his limbs
> Celestial

and with that word, so far as we know, Keats' *Hyperion* ends, since there is no authority for the pencilled completion in Woodhouse's transcript. Here then is the conclusion of the poem as Keats left it:

> Thus the God,
> While his enkindled eyes with level glance
> Beneath his white soft temples, stedfast kept
> Trembling with ligh[t] upon Mnemosyne:
> Soon wild commotions shook him, and made flush
> All the immortal fairness of his limbs,
> Into a hue more roseate than sweet pain
> Gives to a ravish'd Nymph when her warm tears
> Gush luscious with no sob. Or more severe;—
> More like the struggle at the gate of death;
> Or liker still to one who should take leave
> Of pale immortal death, and with a pang
> As hot, as death's is chill, with fierce convulse
> Die into life. So young Apollo anguishd:
> His very hair, his golden tresses fam'd,
> Kept undulation round his eager neck.
> During the Pain Mnemosyne upheld
> Her arms as one who pro[p]hesies. At lenght
> Apollo shreikd—and lo from all his limbs
> Celestial

And so ends the great experiment. For all its greatness it was no more than an experiment; in a sense it was even a failure; Keats' reach had exceeded his grasp and he knew it. But he learnt more from the failure than any facile success could have taught him; he learnt power and control, and just because so much of *Hyperion* was 'mere' craftsmanship, work that had to be done in 'an artist's humour', and partly against the grain, he learnt more about the use of his tools than in any other way he could have acquired. And with this new-learnt knowledge he turned to a more congenial theme.

IV. *THE EVE OF ST. AGNES*

ABOUT the 18th of January 1819 Keats went down to Chichester, to stay for a few days with 'old Mr. Dilke',[1] and on the 23rd he and Brown walked over to Bedhampton to stay with Mr. John Snook.[2] There he was ill, and 'did not go out of the Garden Gate but twice or thrice during the fortnight I was there'.[3] His comment on the trip, apart from the mention of two dowager card parties in Chichester, is that 'nothing worth speaking of happened at either place'.[4] Well, opinions differ as to what is worth speaking of; but we find it hard to agree with Keats' estimate when we read his next sentence. 'I took down some thin paper and wrote on it a little poem call'd St. Agnes' Eve.' That was at least something which the readers of English poetry have thought worth speaking of ever since. It is true that, rightly or wrongly, Keats never did rate *The Eve of St. Agnes* so high as his friends then, and critics since, have rated it, and when we come to examine *Lamia* we shall I think discover the reason, and possibly agree with him. There is a wide difference, not so much in execution as in temper, between the two poems. And it is true also that Keats, fresh from his labours, which were disappointing him, on the far harder and greater *Hyperion*, must have felt, and was justified in feeling, that *The Eve of St. Agnes* was a slighter thing. But in its kind, even though that kind be slight, it is not far short of perfection. It has not the power of *Hyperion*, nor the 'sort of fire' of *Lamia*; nor has it the superb and serene mastery of the greatest of his Odes. But Keats has at last entered triumphantly into his kingdom. There is none of the fumbling and the sense of insecurity which marred the beauties of *Isabella*. The control of the metre is complete; the narrative moves straight forward with neither halt nor hurry; the pictures have strength and clarity of line; and the outstanding

[1] MBF, 114 (317).
[2] MBF, 104 (302).
[3] MBF, 105 (304).
[4] MBF, 114 (318).

beauties, of which there are many, are not irrelevant adornments but parts of a harmonious whole. Whatever else *The Eve of St. Agnes* may be, it is the deliberate work of a trained craftsman; and as such it richly repays examination.

And for such an examination, to help us in the fascinating business of looking over the craftsman's shoulder while he is actually at work, we have a greater wealth of material than for any other poem of Keats, or for more than a very few other famous English poems. We have, in the first place, all but seven stanzas of what is almost certainly the first draft of the poem, and we can watch the whole of its development. In the second place we can watch, as I hope to show, Keats' imagination working on his material, selecting from here, there, and everywhere in his reading, taking hints from Shakespeare and Mrs. Radcliffe, Boccaccio and Mother Bunch, and fusing them into his design.

There are extant, besides the printed version of the 1820 volume, four written copies of the poem, and the relations between these are of importance for our study.

1. A copy in Keats' own writing (wanting the first seven stanzas), now in the Widener library at Harvard University.
2. A transcript by Woodhouse, in the possession of the Marquess of Crewe.
3. Another transcript by Woodhouse, also in the possession of the Marquess of Crewe.
4. A transcript by George Keats, now in the British Museum.[1]

Of these the first, the holograph, is almost certainly the first draft. It is so heavily corrected that it is hard to believe that there was any earlier state; and furthermore it is quite clear that in many of the stanzas the poet is writing as he composes; there are frequent false starts, half-lines scratched out before the whole new line is written, and other indications that this is not the work of

[1] *See Note H* (*page* 303).

a man who is merely making final corrections in a more or less complete manuscript. Finally, the physical characteristics of this draft correspond with Keats' own description. The paper is so thin that in examining it one feels somewhat dangerously like Keats himself with his line of Shakespeare which he felt might be blown away.

Woodhouse's first transcript was certainly made from this draft. With one exception the discrepancies are mere trivialities of spelling and punctuation, and such things as the reading of *thine* for *thy*; in several cases where Keats has erased a word without substitution, and so left a line incomplete, Woodhouse writes the deleted word, and in one or two cases, where the state of the holograph is desperate, he simply leaves a gap. The one exception, which for the moment makes one wonder whether Woodhouse had the holograph in front of him, turns out on examination to be the exception that proves the rule. In stanza XXIX, line 3, the holograph reads *and with anguish spread thereon*, whereas Woodhouse reads *and with care quick spread thereon.* And observing this in an apparatus criticus one is tempted to say that Woodhouse could not have had *with anguish* in front of him. But the puzzle is resolved by the holograph. Keats wrote *anguish* as an alteration, and because of difficulty with the deleted word below he wrote *an* (and wrote it badly at that) and then left a space and wrote *guish*. Woodhouse read the latter, not unnaturally, as *quick*, and then made the best he could, though not a very good best, of the ill-written *an*.

This first transcript of Woodhouse, therefore, would be of no importance, since we have the holograph from which it was taken, if it were not for one thing, namely that we have not got the holograph of the first seven stanzas, which, one may exasperatedly suppose, were detached by the too generous Severn.[1] The Woodhouse transcript is

[1] It appears that Severn had a habit, which, however well intentioned, was unfortunate for subsequent investigators, of distributing fragments of Keats' manuscripts to interested friends. A scrap for example with an early version of stanza LX of *Isabella* is endorsed 'M.S. of John Keats given to Henry Wreford at Rome May 1st. 1863 by Joseph Severn'.

then our only authority for the first draft of those stanzas (though it gives us of course only the final state of the first draft), since the seven stanzas which are attached in another hand to the holograph were almost certainly not copied from a manuscript at all but from the 1820 edition. And in those opening stanzas Woodhouse includes one which was cancelled between the first and second drafts and of which we should otherwise have no knowledge at all.

Woodhouse's second transcript is, however, of more importance, or perhaps it would be more accurate to say that the corrections in it are of more importance. He says of this second transcript: 'This copy was taken from Keats' original MS. He afterwards altered it for publication, and added some stanzas and omitted others. His alterations are noticed here. The Published copy differs from both in a few particulars. Keats left it to his Publishers to adopt which they pleased, and to revise the whole.' And he adds a note at the end of the transcript 'Copied from J. K.'s rough MS. 20 April 1819'. By that date then the first draft as we have it was 'finished', and it appears that for some months it was laid aside, and picked up again in September, since Keats writes to Taylor in that month, 'Since I finish'd it (Otho) I have finish'd Lamia: and am now occupied in revising St. Agnes' Eve'.[1] And that this revision implied the writing of a wholly fresh copy is made clear from a note in Woodhouse's second transcript opposite stanza 4 (in his numbering), 'This stanza is omitted in the corrected copy'. For the readings of this corrected copy, this second, and, I think, so far as Keats the independent artist was concerned, final, state of the poem we have then the corrected Woodhouse transcript. But we also have further and corroborative evidence in George Keats' transcript. Keats wrote to Georgiana Keats on January 15, 1820, towards the end of George Keats' visit to England, 'George is busy this morning in making copies of my verses'.[2] It is not a rash conjecture

[1] MBF, 140 (414). [2] MBF, 161 (492).

that one of these copies was that of *The Eve of St. Agnes*, now in the bound volume of George Keats' transcripts in the British Museum. And since this coincides almost exactly with Woodhouse's second transcript with its corrections, we may, I think, assume that in these two transcripts we have reproduced for us Keats' final manuscript, though not of course unhappily the steps between the end of the first draft and the end of the second. One could wish that it were possible to determine whether the Woodhouse or the George Keats transcript was the later in date, but the external evidence is not conclusive, and the internal evidence is somewhat conflicting. Woodhouse does indeed note with regard to the revised, and ultimately rejected, conclusion to the poem, 'Altered in 1820', but his other corrections may, or may not, have been noted earlier; and of the very few discrepancies between the two transcripts some appear to point in one direction and some in the other, though with a balance, I think, in favour of George Keats' transcript being the later. The details of these discrepancies will be found in the notes,[1] and the determination of the point is in any case of minor importance, since from the two transcripts, agreeing as closely as they do, we can see, with the exception of one or two doubtful words, the poem exactly as Keats had made it when he left it to his publishers to 'adopt which they pleased, and to revise the whole'.

I have repeated this phrase from Woodhouse's note, since if we pay proper attention to it it warns us to beware of accepting with any confidence as being Keats' own such alterations as were made between the final draft and the printed version. Some of these were probably his own and one may feel reasonably confident about it where a word which seems to be an improvement appears for the first time in print; as for example the substitution of *regardless* for *uneager* in the first line of stanza VIII, and that of *Flushing* for *Heated* in the second line of stanza

[1] *See Note I (page 303).*

XVI. But we can have no certainty even about these, and, of the rest, some we know and some we guess to have been made in deference to the susceptibilities of the publishers and the supposed susceptibilities of readers, while others are reversions from the second draft to the first, whether because Keats rejected his second thoughts very shortly after the careful revision during which he recorded them, or, as seems to me very much more likely, simply because the publishers happened to prefer and adopt the earlier version, and Keats in proof-reading acquiesced in their choice. For this reason I propose to give at the end of our examination of the poem what has not, so far as I am aware, been given *in extenso* before, namely George Keats' transcript, since that I believe gives us the nearest approach we can make to the poem in the final form which Keats intended.

The second aspect of Keats' craftsmanship which a study of this poem illumines is what is commonly called his 'use of his sources'. That is a dangerous phrase, and it is too often interpreted in a way which evokes a ridiculous picture of a creative artist sitting at his table surrounded by half a dozen books and flitting hurriedly from one to another in search of an idea or a phrase, feverishly turning the interminable pages of *The Mysteries of Udolpho* to find an oaken gallery, and then seeking in Shakespeare for an epithet for trumpets; picking a quince from *Romeo and Juliet*, a gourd from *The Arabian Nights*, and a complete dessert from *Paradise Lost*; and unable to draw a picture of a lover in his lady's chamber without going to Boccaccio to find it. No original artist works like that, but only a pedestrian compiler, 'if such one there be', of inharmonious mosaic. But however original a literary artist is, part, and probably a large part, of the material on which his selecting and shaping imagination works is the reminiscences of his reading. And, so long as we do not jump too hurriedly to conclusions, the pleasure of watching the artist at work is greatly enhanced when we can watch him shape and select. But the greater part of this material is in a kind of superior rag-bag of the artist's mind, in which the scraps are not docketed with their provenance, as though they were in a card-catalogue; so that he cannot tell to what kind of garment, owned by whom, this bit of flannel, or that piece of gingham, or that other attractive bit of silk originally belonged. It must be the commonest experience to any one who reads at all and who ever uses a pen, if for no more than writing letters, that he finds himself using phrases of which he does not know whether they are quotations, or half-quotations, or his own. So too, one may reasonably presume, with the artist. Occasionally, of course, one can see the artist at work on a specific and even acknowledged 'source', as was Shakespeare in many of his plays, or Keats himself in *Isabella*. But, for the most part, 'sources' are of the vaguer and less conscious kind, and the exploration of them is as seductive as it is perilous. The trouble is that the search after sources is too much like the collection of stamps or other objects of the collector's passion; and the discovery of a possible rarity, which the other collector has missed, is apt, in the first flush of enthusiasm, to make the collector unduly reluctant to examine the perforation and watermark. It will be as well, then, to consider for a moment what kind of evidence one can look for in estimating the probabilities that a suggested source was in fact a source. In the first place, the author may state in so many words, or indicate by other unmistakable signs, that he has read the author, book, poem, or passage in question. In the second place he may, by records however disjointed, so blaze the trails of his discursive reading and thinking, that the trained woodsman, if skilful enough and patient enough, can with some certainty follow him, as Professor Lowes followed Coleridge in the most brilliant piece of detective criticism that this century has produced. Again, still in the realm of external evidence, we may have the records of the author's friends as to his reading, whether in general, or specifically in regard to a particular piece of work. When we move to internal evidence we are on much more treacherous ground. In the work of any writer we find innumerable parallels to the work of others. In some instances the parallel is so close, or involves such a striking word or collocation of words, that we feel that mere coincidence will not suffice to account for it, and that we are justified in saying, 'This is a reminiscence, conscious or unconscious, of that'. From such instances we move in a descending scale through the parallels which are introduced in notes by 'This is probably a reminiscence of . . .' to those which have to be contented with 'This may remind one of . . .'. This internal evidence never amounts to proof; and isolated pieces of it are of little more than casual interest. Its value is almost entirely cumulative; if we have reason to suspect that a given work is a source, every additional verbal parallel, or parallel in situation, greatly increases the probability that our conjecture is a sound one. And when both external evidence and a sufficient bulk of internal evidence appear to lead us in the same direction we may feel reasonably sure that we are on the author's trail.

I am going to suggest for examination, as the four main sources of *The Eve of St. Agnes*, apart from the folk-lore element, Shakespeare, especially *Romeo and Juliet*; Mrs. Radcliffe; *The Arabian Nights*; and a French translation of Boccaccio's *Il Filocolo*.

Keats' familiarity with Shakespeare needs no proof. He regarded Shakespeare as his 'Presider'; throughout the letters he is perpetually quoting him, and shows too that sure proof of familiarity which consists in quoting without the use of quotation marks; and two of his copies of Shakespeare, the folio now at Hampstead, and the edition in America,[1] bear evidence of his careful reading of certain

[1] Keats' own copy of Johnson and Steevens' edition of Shakespeare, in seven small volumes, is in the possession of Mr. George Armour, of Princeton. Professor Caroline F. E. Spurgeon's *Keats's Shakespeare* (Clarendon Press, 1928) made accessible all that in that edition seemed of interest in the way of Keats' annotations and underlinings, together with a good deal of the similar material from the Folio and the Poems in the Dilke collection at Hampstead.

plays in the shape of frequent underlinings and occasional annotations.

That Keats was at least acquainted with Mrs. Radcliffe's work appears from his own letters. Writing to Reynolds in March 1818 he says: 'I am going among Scenery whence I intend to tip you the Damosel Radcliffe—I'll cavern you, and grotto you, and waterfall you, and wood you, and water you, and immense-rock you, and tremendous-sound you, and solitude you.'[1] And writing to George and Georgiana Keats in February 1819, in allusion to the titles of his last written poems (*The Pot of Basil*, *St. Agnes' Eve*, and *The Eve of St. Mark*), he says: 'You see what fine Mother Radcliffe names I have.'[2] Neither of these passages implies more than a nodding acquaintance. But when in *The Romance of the Forest* we find, as the refrain of one of the pieces of verse with which Mrs. Radcliffe tries, with imperfect success, to enliven the more tedious passages of her narrative, the line

> Love wave his purple pinions o'er my head[3]

and then turn to Keats' early poem *To Hope*, and find as the last line of three verses

> And wave thy silver pinions o'er my head,

then we rub our eyes and begin to wonder. And when we read in the *Sicilian Romance* that 'The sun, involved in clouds of *splendid* and *innumerable* hues, was setting',[4] and remember that Keats wrote '*Innumerable* of stains and *splendid* dyes', and, further, that in the next line he first deletes his *damasked* for no very apparent reason to substitute *sunset*, then we wonder more, and begin to think that some further investigation along these lines might be illuminating.[5] The idea that Keats, in *The Eve of St. Agnes*, was indebted to Mrs. Radcliffe was first

[1] MBF, 51 (123).
[2] MBF, 114 (322).
[3] *RF*, vol. i, c. iii, p. 86 (c. iii, p. 44).
[4] *SR*, vol. i, c. iii, p. 96.
[5] It is a small point, but perhaps worth remarking, that in *A Sicilian Romance* Mrs. Radcliffe several times alludes to 'Baia' (not Baiae); which may account for the odd rhyme in the *Ode to Maia*.

propounded by Professor M. H. Shackford,[1] in a most interesting paper at which Miss Lowell aimed a boomerang which was much more destructive on its inward than its outward journey. But Professor Shackford confined her attention to *The Mysteries of Udolpho*, and, by so limiting her own range, she missed, as I think and hope to show, discovering the range of Keats.

As to *Il Filocolo*, another American scholar, Professor H. Noble MacCracken, advanced the idea[2] that Keats was indebted to this tale of Boccaccio. But he made the mistake of confining his attention to the original version, and the difficulties of supposing that Keats read *Il Filocolo* in the original are almost insuperable. Eight months later than the composition of *The Eve of St. Agnes* he could only manage Ariosto at the rate of 'six or eight stanzas at a time',[3] and that Keats could have ploughed through the infinite tediousness of *Il Filocolo* at a rate of progress so dragging as that to which his unfamiliarity with the language would have condemned him is a supposition which we would only entertain under the compulsion of the strongest evidence. Of such evidence, of evidence strong enough to outweigh the intrinsic improbability of his thesis, Professor MacCracken produced none at all. What he did show, and it was worth showing, was that there is a close parallel between the situation in *The Eve of St. Agnes* and the situation in one section of *Il Filocolo*, and one or two parallels in detail. But he adduced no verbal parallels which could persuade one to reject the probabilities. After all, the situation in *The Eve of St. Agnes* is not so peculiar that an imaginative artist could not invent it for himself, without recourse to a model; and if we were faced with the alternatives that Keats either read the romance in Italian or did not read it at all, there can be no doubt which of the two is the more

[1] *The Eve of St. Agnes and The Mysteries of Udolpho*, by M. H. Shackford, *Publications of the Modern Language Association of America*, vol. xxxvi, No. 1 (March, 1921).

[2] 'The Source of Keats's *Eve of St. Agnes*', by H. N. MacCracken, *Modern Philology*, vol. v, No. 2 (October 1907).

[3] MBF, 147 (465).

credible. On the other hand, the resemblances in situation are so close that, apart from the question of language, Professor MacCracken's thesis does not merit the cavalier dismissal which is all the attention Miss Lowell sees fit to accord it. We should feel happier if there were some way in which Keats could have read the *Filocolo*. And so there was. It is true that there appears to have been at that date no English translation of it.[1] But there was a French translation. And from what Keats says himself, quite apart from the evidence of the Ronsard sonnets, and the probability, pointed out by Sir Sidney Colvin,[2] that he had read Gombauld's *L'Endimion*, it appears that he had at least adequate facility in French. He begins his remarks about Ariosto with the comment, 'In the course of a few months I shall be as good an Italian scholar as I am a french one'. There is then no intrinsic improbability in the conjecture that Keats read Boccaccio's tale in French, and if he had read Mirabeau's translation of the *Decameron* he might well have looked round for other French translations of Boccaccio.

The internal evidence as to the sources will be more readily examined in detail in connexion with the different sections of the poem for which the particular sources seem to have been used.

I propose that we should examine the poem in some detail, trying to watch as it were both the mind and the hand of the craftsman, to see Keats' imagination working on his material, stimulated by some parts of it, modifying others, and rejecting others, and to see also his technical skill labouring to secure the finished result that he wants. In any such survey it is ridiculous to be dogmatic; the only person who can know how an artist's mind works is the artist himself, and even he is probably none too clear about it. On the other hand, perpetual qualification becomes tedious. I hope therefore that any reader

[1] There was a translation of part of *Il Filocolo*; '*Thirteen most pleasant and delectable questions, entituled, Philocopo . . . turned in English by H. G.* London, 1587 (?1567)', but it does not contain the relevant part of the story of Fleury and Blanchefleur.

[2] SC, 175.

who is interested enough to follow this examination will realize that, outside deductions which can be safely made from an examination of the actual script of the holograph, where some degree of certainty is attainable, any blunt statement of what Keats did or did not do should be read with a tacit qualification of 'probably' or 'one may conjecture' which in the interests of brevity and clarity is suppressed.

The germ of the poem was a piece of folk-lore. And for all the wealth of beauty that sprang from it, Keats did not himself lose sight of what the seed had been, since in August of 1819, four months after the poem was structurally complete, he writes to Bailey of a poem 'call'd St. Agnes' Eve on a popular superstition'.[1] What then was this popular superstition, and whence did Keats derive his knowledge of it? The commentators are content to refer us to Brand's *Popular Antiquities*[2] and to Burton's *Anatomy of Melancholy*. Brand quotes Ben Jonson (or misquotes him):

> And on sweet St. Agnes' night
> Please you with the promised sight
> Some of husbands, some of lovers,
> Which an empty dream discovers

Burton is a very little more explicit:

> "Tis their only desire if it may be done by Art, to see their husbands picture in a glass, they'll give anything to know when they shall be married, how many husbands they shall have, by *Crommyomantia*, a kind of divination with Onions laid on the Altar on St. Agnes' Eve or Night, to know who shall be their first husband.' (III. ii. 3. 1.)

I can see no reason to suppose that the subject 'was

[1] MBF, 133 (399).

[2] *Observations on Popular Antiquities*: by John Brand. Newcastle (for J. Johnson, London), 1777. There was another edition, arranged and revised with additions by Henry Ellis, in 1813. F. T. Palgrave says that a chap-book (see p. 108, note 3) is mentioned and quoted from by Brand in a 1795 edition; but in neither of the above editions can I find any mention or quotation that extends the meagre account of the ceremonies of St. Agnes' Eve, and no 1795 edition is discoverable in either the British Museum or the Bodleian Library.

more probably suggested to Keats'[1] by Burton than by Brand, or by Jonson direct: nor very much reason to suppose that it was suggested to him by either, since the two of them put together give us no more of the method of divination than a fasting dream. There seems no very cogent reason for pursuing a printed source at all. On the authority of Woodhouse the 'subject was suggested by Mrs. Jones'. It is perhaps enough title to fame for this mysterious lady that she is responsible for the inception of *The Eve of St. Agnes*, but at any rate that is all the title she has, since we know nothing else of her except that she borrowed a book from Keats.[2] But it is reasonable enough to suppose that she was some one he met at Chichester, and tempting to suppose that it was actually on the 20th of January, when Keats was there, that she suggested the subject. If so, the least she could do was to tell Keats, if he did not know it already, the folk-lore about St. Agnes' Eve. At any rate Keats either invented, or learned from Mrs. Jones or from elsewhere, the details of the prescribed observances which are so signally lacking from Brand and Burton. In Keats we have the following points: the maiden must retire fasting; she must not look behind; she must not speak; she must lie on her back; if she follows the ceremonial she will see her adoring lover. The way in which the 'ceremonies due' are catalogued does not read as though Keats were inventing them; and if we are determined to prefer a printed source to Mrs. Jones we shall find it in the shape of a chap-book entitled *Mother Bunches Closet newly broke open*.[3] The relevant passages in this are as follows:

'Why then I will tell you in the first place, you must observe

[1] de S, 465.

[2] SC, 560; at the end of Woodhouse's list (now in the Pierpont Morgan Library in New York) of Keats' books is a list of persons to whom Keats had given or lent books. The occurrence of Mrs. Jones' name here seems to dispose of Miss Lowell's elaborated and quite unnecessary theory that 'Mrs. Jones' was a pseudonym used by Keats to conceal the identity of Mrs. Brawne (AL, ii. 154–5).

[3] *Mother Bunches Closet newly broke open*; Part the First; Burslem; Printed for the Stationers, n.d.; and various other printings, with a few minor differences, but agreeing in all essentials.

> St. Agnes's day which is the 21st of January, and on that day let no man salute thee; and at night before thou goest to bed put on the best shift thou hast, and when thou liest down, lay thy right hand under thy head, and say these words, now the *God of love send me my desires*; then go to sleep as soon as possible, and you shall be sure to dream of him who will be your husband, and see him stand before you, and you may take notice of him and his complexion, and if he offer to salute thee, do not deny him, but shew him as much favour as thou canst.'

That does not get us very far, but it is worth quoting for some interesting parallels which we shall notice later. Five pages later, however, we get more detail, and even though it is to do this time with St. Thomas, that need not seriously disturb us:

> 'Take a St. Thomas's onion [what, one wonders in passing, is this mysterious vegetable?] pare it, and lay it on a clean handkerchief under your pillow; and put on a clean smock and as you lie down, lay your arms abroad, and say these words
>
> Good St. Thomas do me right;
> And bring my love to me this night,
> That I may view him in the face,
> And in my arms may him embrace
>
> Then *lying on thy back* with thy arms abroad go to sleep as soon as you can, and in your first sleep you shall dream of him who is to be your husband and he will come and offer to kiss you; do not hinder him, but catch him in thy arms, and strive to hold him, for that is he.'

This indeed gives us an unnecessary onion; but it gives us the lying on the back; it also gives us a clean smock, which Keats perhaps used, and the point that in the dream there will be an embrace, which is not indeed mentioned by Keats as part of the ceremonies due, except by implication in a finally rejected stanza of the second draft, but which does become the climax of the narrative.

A few pages later we revert to St. Agnes, with fuller detail:

> 'But for all there be so many bad days in this month I can tell you of one day which is lucky, and many young men and maids

have a deal of heart's ease on that day, or the day after shall let you understand; it is the 21st. called St. Agnes' day. This St. Agnes has a favour for young men and maids and will bring to their bedsides their sweethearts if they follow my rules, on this day you must be sure to *keep fast*, and neither eat nor drink all that day, nor night, neither let man woman or child kiss thee on that day; and thou must be sure when thou goest to bed to put on a *clean shift* and the best thou hast, and clean clothes on thy head; for St. Agnes loves to see all clean when she comes. When thou liest down lie as *straight as thou canst*, lay thy hands under thy head and say

> Now St. Agnes play thy part,
> And send to me my own sweetheart;
> And show me such a *happy bliss*,
> This night of him to have a kiss.

And be sure to fall asleep as soon as you can and before you awake out of your first sleep you shall see him come before you.'

We still have not found directions for silence, but these also come later: 'speak not a word' and 'then go to bed without speaking a word'.

Here then is a detailed statement of the ceremonies and their outcome, with the single exception of the prohibition against looking behind. There were probably other chap-books with much the same record of the details of the popular superstition, from which Keats could derive his knowledge, if he did not get it orally from Mrs. Jones. And we can leave Mrs. Jones and Mother Bunch, and possibly others, to share the distinction of being the old dames of stanza v. If we incline to Mother Bunch there are at least two verbal parallels which may strengthen our inclination.

There then is the bare material of the superstition. It is time to turn to the poem and see what Keats made of it, and how he used the obviously wide latitude which it offers to the artist for expansion and embroidery and the interweaving of other themes.

In this examination of the poem I have made almost no attempt at general criticism, that type of criticism which introduces the critic in the role of showman, with pointing finger indicating the beauties of the work. Such criticism will be found, if it is desired, in Leigh Hunt's *London Journal* for January 1835, where he printed the whole poem with a running commentary between the stanzas; and a revised version of this will be found in *Imagination and Fancy*. It shows Leigh Hunt at his best, and whatever we may think of Hunt as an original poet, his critical best was of a very high order. Other critics in turn have tried their hands at it; and perhaps one of the highest tributes we can pay to the poem is to say that it has emerged from this handling untarnished. But I think that critics would do well to take warning from a footnote in Sir Sidney Colvin's *Life of Keats*.[1] There stands there, as he first wrote it, a long passage on two or three stanzas of *Isabella* which is as perfect a piece of expository criticism, in its restraint and taste and insight, as one can hope to find, a model of what such criticism should be. And yet, looking back on it after thirty years, its author notes that it now seems to him 'somewhat officious and over-explanatory'. If he felt so, I think that the rest of us had better keep our clumsy hands away from the exquisite and fragile beauties of such a poem as *The Eve of St. Agnes*. They are patent enough, not of that elusive kind that we need go looking for them behind a cicerone with a flash-lamp. And indeed *The Eve of St. Agnes* is one of those works which deserve, as I believe, the most patient and exact study that we can give them, and will most richly reward the patient reader by disclosing to him their beauties, as though Keats' shut rosebud should slowly expand before his eyes, but which resent, and punish, any attempt to force them to display those beauties. I have tried therefore in the remainder of this chapter to help the study, and leave the bud to expand as it chooses.

First, before he will introduce his main actors, Keats, with his dramatist's instinct, is going to set his stage, and make the cold bite into the marrow.

[1] SC, 395.

I

St. Agnes' Eve—Ah bitter cold it was;
The owl for all his feathers was a-cold,
The hare limp'd trembling through the frozen grass,
And silent were the flock in sheltered fold—
Numb were the Beadsman's fingers while he told
His rosary, and while his frosted breath,
Like pious incense in a censer old,
Seem'd taking flight for heaven without a death,
Past the sweet virgin's picture while his prayers he saith.

There is the most astonishing cumulative effect of cold about this stanza as we feel in turn with the bird; the wild beast; the domesticated beast, partly sheltered; the man, indoors but still cold and numb; and the effect rises to its climax in the freezing picture of the frosted breath. And before the stanza is finished Keats is, I think, standing not in the chapel of his Radcliffean castle, but in one of the coldest places in all literature, where also it was 'bitter cold', and where also it was silent, with not a mouse stirring, the platform before the castle at Elsinore.

In the second draft Keats altered *cold* to *chill*, primarily no doubt, as he explained in a letter to Taylor[1] when protesting against this particular error in the proofs, to avoid the echo with *cold* on the next line; perhaps partly also to avoid the exact Shakespearean quotation. He corrected the fourth line to read *And silent was the flock in woolly fold*; the incense came more vividly *from* a censer, and there are two minor alterations in the last line.[2]

II, III

The next two stanzas are devoted to elaborating the picture of the Beadsman, and the impression of cold. Had Keats any original for the Beadsman? I suspect him of being a composite picture. There is a ghost in *Henry VI*

[1] MBF, 206 (536).

[2] There is, I think, no doubt that the first draft read *sheltered*. Woodhouse's second transcript reads (before correction) *sheltered*; the first transcript at first had a gap, indicating that Woodhouse had trouble in reading the word and *woolly* is pencilled in, as though later from the second draft.

who is 'of ashy semblance, meagre, pale, and bloodless';[1] there is an apothecary in *Romeo and Juliet* whose looks were 'meagre',[2] and, in the next scene to the apothecary, a friar who was 'barefoot'.[3] There is a stream of minor ecclesiastics in Mrs. Radcliffe of whom two in particular seem worth observing. In *The Romance of the Forest* there is a chapel of the abbey 'where the hymn of devotion had once been raised, and the tear of penitence had once been shed; . . . where austerity anticipated an earthly purgatory';[4] here, as one of the characters comments, 'are probably deposited the ashes of some ancient monk, who, after having spent a life of abstinence and prayer, sought in heaven the reward of his forbearance upon earth'.[5] And in *A Sicilian Romance* 'an old man issued from the vault with a lighted taper in his hand . . . who appeared to be a friar, and who had been doing penance at the monument of a saint'.[6] And there is also a man in *The Mysteries of Udolpho*, though he does not appear *in propria persona*, but in an incidental piece of verse, whose eyes *ache* and whose *spirit fails*.[7] Anyway, here is Keats' Beadsman, 'meagre, barefoot, wan', with his lamp and his penance, and his failing spirit.

His prayers he saith, this patient holy man,
Then takes his lamp and riseth from his knees,
And back returneth meagre, barefoot, wan,
Along the chapel aisle by slow degrees;
The sculptur'd dead on each side seem'd to freeze
Emprison'd in black purgatorial rails:
Knights, ladies, praying in dumb orat'ries
He passeth by, and his weak spirit fails
To think how they may ache in icy hoods and mails.

Northward he turneth through a little door,
And scarce three steps, ere Music's golden tongue
Flatter'd to tears this aged man and poor.
But no—already had his death bell rung,

[1] *2 H VI*, III. ii. 162.
[2] *R & J*, v. i. 40.
[3] *R & J*, v. ii. 5.
[4] *RF*, vol. i, c. ii, p. 38 (c. ii, p. 21).
[5] Ib., vol. i, c. v, p. 183 (c. v, p. 88).
[6] *SR*, vol. ii, c. xii, p. 98.
[7] *MU*, vol. iii, p. 334 (c. xxxiv, p. 63).

The joys of all his life were said and sung—
His was harsh penance on St. Agnes' Eve:
Another way he turn'd ; and soon among
Black ashes sat he for his soul's reprieve,
And all night kept awake, for sinners' souls to grieve.

In the second of these two stanzas our ears may catch an echo of a phrase which Keats underlined in *Troilus and Cressida*. 'Helen's *golden tongue*',[1] and of a line in *Richard II*, 'And some will mourn in *ashes*, some *coal-black*'.[2]

In the second draft Keats made one minor alteration in stanza II, and in stanza III changed *turn'd* (to avoid the repetition from the first line) to the plainer *went*, *Black* to *Rough*, and, again to avoid an echo, *souls* in the last line to *sake*.

Having used his Beadsman to give the atmosphere of cold and silence Keats now wishes to transfer our attention from him to the scene of festivity which is to be the setting for the opening of the main action. In the first draft it takes him two stanzas to do it:

But there are ears may hear sweet melodies,
And there are eyes to brighten festivals,
And there are feet for nimble minstrelsies,
And many a lip that for the red wine calls—
Follow, then follow to the illumin'd halls,
Follow me youth—and leave the Eremite—
Give him a tear—then trophied banneral
And many a brilliant tasseling of light
Shall droop from arched ways this high Baronial night.

For the next stanza, in which he is to give the picture of a great house getting ready for an entertainment, it would have been unnatural if Keats' imagination had not travelled back to the scene at the end of the first Act of *Romeo and Juliet* where the musicians are waiting, the serving men enter and conduct a brisk bustle for fifteen lines, and then 'Enter all the Guests and Gentlewomen to the Maskers'.

That ancient Beadsman heard the prelude soft,
And so it chanc'd, for many a door was wide
From hurry to and fro—and now aloft,
The silver snarling trumpets 'gan to chide;

[1] *T & C*, I. ii. 112. [2] *R II*, V. i. 49.

The level chambers ready with their pride
Seem'd anxious to receive a thousand guests:
The carved angels ever eager-eyed
Stared, where upon their heads the cornice rests,
With hair blown back, and wings put cross-wise on their breasts.[1]

(Woodhouse notes that the figures of the angels were probably suggested by figures in the Temple church.)

In the second draft the weak *and now aloft* is changed to *Soon, up aloft*, *The level* is changed to *High-lamped*, and the over-personification of *Seem'd anxious* is altered to the more pictorially vivid *Were glowing*.

And now we are ready for the full scene of festivity, and the introduction of the first of the main actors, and of the 'popular superstition' *motif*.

At length step in the argent[2] revelers
With plume, tiara, and all rich array;
Ah what are they? the idle pulse scarce stirs,
The muse should never make the spirit gay;
Away, bright dulness, laughing fools away,—
And let me tell of one sweet lady there
Whose heart had brooded all that wintry day
On love, and wing'd St. Agnes' saintly care,
As she had heard old Dames full many times declare.

This is clearly not very satisfactory. The intended contrast between the irrelevant background of the merry-making and the important central figure is clear enough, but it is clumsily handled, and there seems no particular reason why the muse should not upon occasion make the spirit gay. So in the second draft Keats recasts the central

[1] There is a small point in this stanza which seems to me decisive for the view that the seven stanzas attached for completeness to the holograph, but not in Keats' hand, were taken direct from the printed version and not from any manuscript. The reading *level* in line 5 is the one instance (except the unimportant reading of *while* for *as*) in which the printed version goes back to the reading of the first draft against that of the second. And the writer of the seven stanzas here reads *level*, though in all other cases he takes the reading of the second draft.

[2] HBF says that Woodhouse's transcript reads *urgent*; but the word in both transcripts is clearly *argent*.

section of the stanza entirely, with two alterations in the first line, one for vividness and one for rhyme.

> At length burst in the argent revelry,
> With tiara and plume and rich array,
> Numerous as shadows haunting fairyly
> The brain, new stuff'd, in youth with triumphs gay
> Of old romance. These let us wish away,
> And turn sole thoughted, to one Lady there
> Whose heart had brooded, all that wintry day,
> On love and winged St. Agnes' saintly care,
> As she had heard old Dames full many time[s] declare.

And now Keats is ready to use his knowledge of the details of the superstition, whether derived from Mrs. Jones or from Mother Bunch or from elsewhere.

> They told her how upon St. Agnes' eve
> Young virgins might have visions of delight,
> And soft adorings of their loves receive
> Upon the honied middle of the night,
> If ceremonies due they did aright;
> As, supperless to bed they must retire,
> And lay supine their beauties lily white,
> Nor look behind nor sideways, but require
> Of Heaven with upward eyes for all that they desire.

One can hardly doubt that the fourth line is a reminiscence of a line in *Measure for Measure*[1] which Keats underlined,

> Upon the heavy middle of the night

and I think that one can also see an interesting instance of the working of association in the epithet *honey'd*, when we remember a collocation in a line on *Julius Caesar*,[2]

> the *honey-heavy* dew of slumber.

The phrase *lily white*, which in itself is odd, since the beauties in themselves might as well be dark as fair, is perhaps Keats' adaptation of Mother Bunch's 'clean shift' and St. Agnes' love of seeing all clean; as the requiring of heaven for all that they desire recalls the 'now the God of love send me my desires' of the same directions.

In the second draft the adorings are *from* the loves, and

[1] *M for M*, IV. i. 37.

[2] *JC*, II. i. 230.

the virgins are no longer to *lay* their beauties, as Mother Bunch tells them to 'lay' their hands, but to *couch* them. And this suggests that when Keats was recasting the preceding stanza and altering this he had running through his head two lines from *Romeo and Juliet*:[1]

> where unbruised *youth* with *unstuff'd brain*
> Doth *couch* his limbs

At this point the second draft inserts a complete stanza which does not appear in the printed version:

> 'Twas said her future lord would there appear
> Offering as sacrifice—all in the dream—
> Delicious food even to her lips brought near:
> Viands and wine and fruit and sugar'd cream,
> To touch her palate with the fine extreme
> Or relish: then soft music heard; and then
> More pleasures followed in a dizzy stream
> Palpable almost: then to wake again
> Warm in the virgin morn, no weeping Magdalen.

With regard to this there are two problems. First, where does it come from? There is almost no hint of it in Mother Bunch, and though we do in her find mentions of repasts in connexion with similar ceremonies they would hardly touch any palate with the fine extreme of relish, consisting as they do of satisfyingly unromantic bread and cheese and beer. There can be hardly a doubt that this stanza comes direct from a source more distant and more romantic, namely from *The Arabian Nights*.[2] The same sequence there is a matter almost of common form, delicious food, soft music, and more pleasures, with no qualifying *almost* to detract from their extremely frank palpability. Here is a passage typical of many:

'When the first compliments were over, we sat down upon

[1] *R & J*, II. iii. 37.

[2] The two editions in English of *The Arabian Nights* which would have been readily accessible to Keats are *Arabian Nights Entertainments* translated from the French by M. Galland, London, 1785 (and 1789), and *The Arabian Nights Entertainments, carefully revised and occasionally corrected from the Arabic, with introduction and notes by Jonathan Scott*; 6 vols., London, 1811. Of these Scott's is the more readable, and the references here are to his edition

a sofa, and there conversed together with the highest satisfaction. We had the most delicious refreshments served up to us; and after eating, continued our conversation till night. We then had excellent wine brought up, and fruit adapted to promote drinking; and timed our cups to the sound of musical instruments. . . . The lady of the house sung herself, and by her songs raised my passion to the height. In short, I passed the night in full enjoyment.'[1]

Or again:

'She commanded a collation to be brought; and immediately a table was covered with several baskets of fruits and sweetmeats. . . . They rose from the table; ten slaves took musical instruments. . . . The young lady then made him sit down by her, and began to caress him.'[2]

Or again:

'Other ladies covered a table with dry fruits, sweetmeats, and everything proper to relish the liquor. . . . Some of the ladies brought in musical instruments, and when everything was ready, they invited me to sit down to supper. The ladies sat down with me, and we continued a long while at our repast. They that were to play upon the instruments and sing arose, and formed a most charming concert. . . . It was past midnight ere these amusements ended. At length one of the ladies said to me, You are doubtless wearied by the journey you have taken today; it is time for you to retire to rest; your lodging is prepared: but before you depart choose which of us you like best to be your bedfellow.'[3]

And if besides the wine and the fruit and the *relish* we want the *viands* we shall find those too in the description of the 'splendid entertainments, at which the most delicate viands were served up'.[4]

We shall have to observe some further interesting parallels in detail when we come to the 'feast of fruits' and to one or two other points, particularly the carpets and the matting, which have caused trouble. But it is perhaps

[1] Scott, vol. ii, p. 241, *Story by the Christian Merchant.*
[2] Ib., pp. 362–4, *Story of the Barber's Second Brother.*
[3] Id., vol. i, pp. 282, 3, *History of the Third Calender.*
[4] Id., vol. iv, p. 178, *Story of Abou Hassan.*

worth while calling attention here to a page in the story of the Inchanted Horse, which bears a close resemblance to the central situation in *The Eve of St. Agnes*. I am suggesting later that if we want to find a source from which Keats may have drawn this situation we shall find it in Mrs. Radcliffe or in Boccaccio, and there are some striking verbal parallels which make it seem likely that Keats had both these writers in his memory. But the general outline, and some of the details, are here also in *The Arabian Nights*.

> 'In the next room to this the princess lay, as appeared by the light, the door being open, through a silk curtain, which drew before the doorway, whither Prince Firoze Shaw advanced on tip-toe, without waking the eunuchs. He drew aside the curtain, went in, and without staying to observe the magnificence of the chamber, gave his attention to something of greater importance. . . . He crept softly towards the bed, without waking either the princess or her women, and beheld a beauty so extraordinary, that he was charmed, and inflamed with love at the first sight. . . . After these reflections on his situation, and on the princess's beauty, he fell on his knees, and twitching gently the princess's sleeve, pulled it towards him. The princess opened her eyes, and seeing a handsome man on his knees, was in great surprise; yet seemed to show no sign of fear.'[1]

That Keats had read some at least of *The Arabian Nights* is clear from his letters;[2] and indeed it would be strange if he had not. And it is entirely characteristic of his 'combining' imagination that he should insert pictures from them in the very un-Oriental setting of his romantic Gothic castle.

The second problem is why this stanza was omitted from the printed version. Why it was inserted is clear enough. Something of the kind is badly wanted to prepare us for what follows. Every reader who has read the poem with any degree of attention must have wondered why Angela's first thought when she has consented to Porphyro's 'stratagem' is the provision of 'cates and dainties'.

[1] Id., vol. v, pp. 215, 6.

[2] *MBF*, 76 (218); 114 (324).

Porphyro has said nothing about them. Nor has he said anything about music. Food, one might think, is reasonable enough, Porphyro or no Porphyro, since the fasting Madeline will be hungry when she wakes. But why does Angela suddenly interject the information that Porphyro will find an apparently irrelevant and highly unnecessary lute? The answer to these vexing difficulties is in the rejected stanza. Why then, having been once wisely inserted, was it rejected? The answer to that is, I suppose, Woodhouse and Taylor. Keats, as we shall see, had trouble with them about a later stanza or stanzas, and acquiesced against his own judgement. And if they objected there they would certainly object here, and find this stanza, in spite of the last line, and the comically precautionary 'all in the dream' and 'almost', which might have allayed the apprehensions of the most censorious, too 'sensual' or whatever other epithet they used to register their disapprobation. Hence an essential stanza is omitted and the structure of the poem gravely weakened.

The next stanza is straightforward, and indeed in view of the stanza which follows almost unnecessary:

> Full of this whim was thoughtful Madeline;
> The music yearning like a god in pain
> Touch'd not her heart, her maiden eyes divine,
> Fix'd on the floor saw many a sweeping train
> Pass by—she heeded not at all—in vain
> Came many a tiptoe amorous cavalier,
> And back retir'd; not cool'd by high disdain,
> But she saw not—her heart was otherwhere,
> She sigh'd for Agnes' dreams, the sweetest of the year.

In the second draft the third line opens *She scarcely heard*. One point of possible interest is the provenance of the heroine's name. I do not know that we need look further than its sound, which we know was grateful to Keats' ear; 'beautiful name, that Magdalen',[1] he says in a letter. And, for what it is worth, he found Adeline in *The Romance of the Forest*,[2] and Maddelina in *The Mysteries of Udolpho*.[3]

[1] MBF, 51 (124). [2] *RF*, passim. [3] *MU*, vol. iii, c. vii (c. xxxii).

From this point to the end of the poem we have before us Keats' own first draft, and the business of following his methods becomes correspondingly more complicated and more fascinating.[1]

VIII

The next stanza is to be devoted, somewhat repetitively, to increasing the impression of Madeline's abstraction, and Keats starts

She danc'd along with vague uneager look—
  Her anxious ~~lips~~ mouth full pulpd with rosy thought~~s~~—
The hour was near at hand—and

But *look* is vague, and there seems no rhyme for it in prospect; so make it more definite by writing *eyes*, and then *sighs* will do for the rhyme; the second line is all very well in itself, but it perhaps demands a pictorial attention on the part of the reader which may distract him, so simplify it, and at the same time add an additional touch; and lengthen the third line so that *sighs* comes easily at the end of it:

She danc'd along with vague uneager eyes—
  Anxious her lips, her breathing quick and short
The hallowed hour was near at hand—she sighs

and then three lines write themselves:

  Amid the Timbrels, and the throng'd ressort
  Of Whispersers in anger or in sport—
'Mid Looks of Love, defiance, hate and scorn;
She was hoodwink'd with fancy—all a mort
Save to St. Angnes and her Lambs unshorn
And all the Bliss to be before tomorrow morn

[1] I have endeavoured to make the stages of development clear by a method which indicates what words Keats at any given moment of composition had before him, but does not represent the appearance of the draft as we now have it, nor indeed as Keats saw it. For example, in the stanza which we are about to examine Keats did not write the first three lines and then delete them and re-write them as shown in the second version; but by corrections and interlinear insertions he got them into a condition which a compositor would have set as the second version. This method, though it occupies a good deal of space, seems to be the only way in which the stages of development can be made easy to follow, and the distracting labour of interpreting the brevity of an apparatus criticus avoided.

She was seems a trifle dull, and a waste of space, so cut it out, and let the line start with the emphatic word

Hoodwink'd with faery fancy

Here there are some fairly clear Shakespearean echoes. The picture of the whisperers is that of the ball in *Romeo and Juliet*,[1] and the actual word may be a reminiscence of Capulet's 'whispering tale in a fair lady's ear'.[2] In the preceding scene Cupid is 'hoodwinked',[3] and 'all amort' is a common enough Elizabethan phrase, as in *The Taming of the Shrew*, 'what, sweeting, all amort'.[4]

The alterations in the second draft are unimportant, and the first draft is reverted to for the printed text, except that there is one important alteration which appears in the printed text for the first time, *regardless* being preferred to *uneager*.

IX

The action has been held up since the end of stanza VI by Madeline's abstraction, and it is now time, and perhaps more than time, for the entrance of the second main actor.

So purposing each moment to retire
  She lingered fearful who might. . . .

But there has been enough of this suspense, so delete any more about the hesitation and get on with the action:

She lingered still—meantime across the Moors
  Had come young Porphyro with heart afire
For Madeline. Most piteous he implores
  All Saints

But that is not altogether satisfactory; *piteous* suggests a feebleness which is certainly out of place at the first introduction of the hero, and in any case he needs, as it were, a *locus standi* for his implorings; so go on after *Madeline* thus:

Within the Portal Doors

Sh . . .

[1] *R & J*, I. v.
[2] Ib. I. v. 27.
[3] Ib. II. iv. 4.
[4] *T of S*, IV. iii. 36.

(presumably going to be *shelter'd*, but on second thoughts let us have a more vivid picture, and also keep him as yet a little more outside, so)

> Beside the Portal Doors
> Buttress'd from Moonlight stands he and implores
> All saints to give him sight of Madeline
> But for one moment in the tedious hours
> That he might gaze—or speak, or knell. . . .

But somehow or other we have to get to the end of this stanza, and also find a rhyme; and both can be done by giving a kind of crescendo of approach:

> That he might gaze, and worship all unseen—
> Perchance speak,—kneel—touch—kiss—in sooth such things have been.

(weak though the ending is).

Keats wavered a good deal as to his hero's name. He is first Porphyro. In some places, but not in all, in the first draft this is altered to Lionel, but in the second draft he is uniformly Porphyro. Where this name came from I do not know. In his work on *Hyperion* Keats had come upon and used Porphyrion, and may well have done no more than adapt a sound which he liked. By the end of this stanza we have added a significant touch to the lighting of the stage, moonlight, now for the first time mentioned, which is to be of importance later, and we have got the hero, if not on to the stage, at least into the wings ready for his entrance.

X

And now for his entrance:

> He ventures in wrapped in a dark disguise
> Let no Man see him, or a hundred Swords
> Will storm his heart for all his amorous sighs

First a verbal alteration, *cloak'd up in* taking the place of *wrapped in a*. But then other points occur. Does the dark disguise seem a trifle cowardly? And surely the amorous sighs are both feeble and irrelevant. So Keats scratches it all out and starts again in an impatient hurry to which the misspellings testify:

> He ventures in—let no damn'd whisper tell
> All eyes be muffeld or a hundered sords [altered to *sowrds*]
> Will storm his heart—Love's fevrous Citidel;[1]

Then three lines move easily:

> For him those Chambers held barbarian hords
> Hyena foemen, and ~~bloo~~ hot blooded Lords
> Whose very dogs would execrations bark
> Against his ~~Ho~~ Name and Lineage

The first alteration in the last half-line is a curious one, the *A* of *Against* being deleted, the *g* capitalized, and an apostrophe put in front of it; what was coming we cannot tell since Keats then deletes the whole half-line, re-writes it, and goes on, introducing the third actor,

> Against his Lineage—not a soul affords
> Him any Mercy in that Mansion dark
> Save one old Beldame nigh to loose the . . .

One can hardly resist the sinister conjecture that the demands of rhyme are conducting the line to the inevitable conclusion *vital spark*; but happily Keats cannot bring himself to write it down, let alone allow it to stand, and so has to go back, change *bark* to *howl* (for the better), *dark* to *foul* (probably for the worse) and complete the stanza otherwise, so that it runs:

> Whose very dogs would execrations howl
> Against his Lineage—not a soul affords
> Him any Mercy in that Mansion foul
> Save one old Beldame weak in body and in Soul—

In the second draft *damn'd* is changed to *buzz'd* and the slightly too colloquial *not a soul* to *not one breast.*

The general picture of the entry of the lover into the festivities of his foemen is clearly that of *Romeo and Juliet*, and the dogs perhaps come through a reminiscence of

[1] *storm* is an amusing word; Keats is so full of the *sw* with which he has been having so unsuccessful a struggle at the end of the last line that it carries over into the new line, and he starts his *storm* with *sw* and then corrects).

Sampson's remarks in the first scene of that play about 'a dog of the house of Montaguc',[1] while part at least of the composite picture of the old Beldame is surely Juliet's nurse, Romeo's one friend in the house of the Capulets. It is worth while stopping for a moment, before Keats goes on to draw her in more detail, to consider what other elements there may be in his picture. There is a selection of old attendants in Mrs. Radcliffe of whom the most significant for our purposes is Dorothée in *The Mysteries of Udolpho*. She says of herself 'I am old, and—a little matter *startles* me'[2] and 'I wonder what it is makes my old limbs *shake* so, to night'.[3] Emily 'drew one of the massy *armchairs* . . . and begged Dorothée would *sit down*, and try to compose her spirits',[4] and later 'Dorothée, at first, carried the lamp, but her hand trembled so much with infirmity and alarm, that Emily took it from her, and offered her arm, to support her feeble steps'.[5] There is also Gloritie in the Philocope, but her similarity is rather in her position in the plot than in physical characteristics, and consideration of her can be for the moment deferred. There are also perpetual confidential attendants in *The Arabian Nights*.

Apart from resemblances to two of these passages there is little to comment on in the next stanza, which seems to have written itself, the three changes being made *currente calamo*.

XI

Ah happy chance! the aged Beldam came
~~Tottering~~ shuffling along with ivory headed ~~staff~~ wand
To where he stood hid from the Torches flame
Behind a ~~huge~~ broad hall pillar, far beyond
The sound of Merriment and chous bland.
He startled her—but soon she knew his face
And grasp'd his fingers in her palsied hand
Saying "Mercy Jesu! Hie thee from this place
They are all here tonight, the whole bloodthirsty race.

[1] *R & J*, I. i. 9.
[2] *MU*, vol. iii, p. 359 (c. xxxv, p. 68).
[3] Ib., vol. iv, p. 32 (c. xli, p. 90).
[4] Ib., vol. iv, p. 55 (c. xlii, p. 94).
[5] Ib., vol. iv, p. 52 (ib.).

It is perhaps worth remarking how the earlier picture of *Buttress'd from moonlight* is repeated with differences but the same motif, and worth recalling that in *The Mysteries of Udolpho* Emily 'as she passed these *pillars* feared to turn her eyes towards them almost expecting to see a figure start out from behind their *broad* shafts'.[1] In the second draft, to avoid the repetition of the last line of the preceding stanza, the *Beldam* becomes a *creature*; and in the printed version some one, presumably the Woodhouse-Taylor combination, sacrificed scansion to propriety by reading *Mercy Porphyro* for *Mercy Jesu*.

XII

This stanza is devoted to emphasizing Porphyro's peril:

> "Get hence! Get hence! there 's dwarfish Ferdinand
> He had a fever late and in his fit
> He cursed thee and thine both house and land:
> There 's old Francisco Mendez not a wit
> Tamer for all his Palsy

But an apparently endemic Palsy is not thought well of, and the names for some reason do not give satisfaction. *Ferdinand* becomes *Hildebrand*, and *Francisco Mendez* is first metamorphosed into *Lord Maurice Lacey*; but this change of nationality is felt to be inconvenient and he ends his career as a cosmopolitan *Lord Maurice*, and we have

> "Get hence! Get hence! there 's dwarfish Hildebrand
> He had a fever late and in the fit
> He cursed thee and thine both house and land:
> Then
> ~~And~~ There 's old Lord Maurice ~~Lacey~~ not a wit
> More tame for his gray hairs—Alas me! flit!
> Flit like a Ghost away"—"Ah Gossip dear
> We're safe enough—here in this arm chair sit
> And tell me how"—Good Gods, not here not here
> Follow me Child,—hush hush. . . .

It looks as though a *for . . . fear* or *lest . . . hear* rhyme were

[1] *MU*, vol. iii, p. 7 (c. xxvi, p. 8).

coming, but first *Good Gods* is toned down to *Good Saints*, and then *hush hush* is deleted and the line concluded:

> Follow me Child,—or else these stones will be thy bier."

The second draft has only one minor correction, reading *Then there's that old Lord Maurice.*

XIII

The next stanza goes very smoothly, with only three corrections:

> He followed her along a passage dark
> Brushing the Cobwebs with his lofty Plume
> And as she muttered 'Well a—welladay'
> He found him in a little moonlight room
> Pale casemented and silent as the tomb.
> Now tell me where is Madeline' said he,
> O tell me Goody by the holy loom
> Which none but holy Sisterhood may see
> When they St. Agnes wool do weave full piously"

The first line is altered, presumably for the sake of rhyme before the third line was completed, into

> He followed through a lowly arched way.

The room becomes *Pale latticed high and silent*... and the expletive *do* and the feeble *full* are got rid of in the last line which reads:

> When they St. Agnes' wool are weaving piously"

In the second draft Keats is determined that we shall have no excuse for forgetting that it is cold, and the room becomes *Pale*, *latticed*, *chill*.

The mention of the lowly arched way in the first correction offers as good a stopping-point as any other for a consideration of the whole setting of the poem. The scene is some kind of vaguely mediaeval castle, of which the main features seem to be a chapel with aisles, which is only used in the introduction, galleries dusky or oaken, wide stairs, Gothic windows with stained glass, hanging lamps, an iron gate, arras on the walls, some anachronistic carpets on the floor, and draughts. The inhabitants use tapers to light their way along the passages. In a tale of this kind Keats was not likely to trouble his head about historical accuracy; what he wants is a congruous setting for his story; and this is not a period castle at all, but one of those from the 'Novel of Mystery and Terror' whether it be the *Castle of Otranto* or one of those which beetle so frequently in the pages of Mrs. Radcliffe. For the general characteristics of these uncomfortable but 'romantic' residences it matters little whether we turn to Mrs. Radcliffe or to others of her school; but there are in her descriptions certain points of detail which seem to indicate that Keats built such portions of his castle as he required according to her specifications rather than those of others. Let us therefore put together a number of representative passages from Mrs. Radcliffe. 'She took a lamp in her hand, and with cautious, fearful steps descended through the long winding passages to a private door, which opened into the church of the monastery. The church was gloomy and desolate; and the feeble rays of the lamp she bore, gave only light enough to discover its chilling grandeur. As she passed silently along the *aisles* . . .'[1] 'the *cold* air of the *aisles* chilled her . . . the *moonlight, that streamed through a distant gothic window*. . .'.[2] '*Ferdinand* descended into a large vaulted hall; he crossed it towards a *low arched* door';[3] 'After waiting a few minutes, he forced back the *gate*, which was heavy with *iron work*, and *creaked harshly on its hinges*';[4] 'the dim glass of the *high-arched* windows, *stained* with the colouring of monkish fictions'[5]; 'a window of the same order (Gothic), whose pointed arches still exhibited fragments of *stained glass*';[6] 'evening threw its melancholy twilight through the *painted casements*, and deepened the gloom of the *oak* wainscoting';[7] 'this gallery

[1] *SR*, vol. ii, c. xii, p. 97; cf. st. II. [2] *MU*, vol. i, p. 242 (c. ix, p. 47).
[3] *SR*, vol. i, c. iii, p. 91; cf. st. XIII, 'He followed through a lowly arched way'.
[4] *RF*, vol. i, c. ii, p. 37 (c. ii, p. 21); cf. st. XLI, 'the iron porch' and 'the door upon its hinges groans'.
[5] *SR*, vol. ii, c. ix, p. 29. [6] *RF*, vol. i, c. ii, p. 37 (c. ii, p. 20).
[7] *MU*, vol. iii, p. 119 (c. xxx, p. 27).

opened into another, long and winding, which led to the *grand staircase*';[1] 'The gallery terminated in a *large old stair-case, which led to a hall below*';[2] 'Having passed up the great staircase, and through the *oak gallery*';[3] 'the faded tapestry with which the chamber was hung';[4] 'the great hall of his castle, where the costly tapestry that adorned the walls with pictured exploits of his ancestors, the *casements of painted glass enriched with armorial bearings, the gorgeous banners* that waved along the roof';[5] 'the wind was high . . . she perceived the *arras*, with which the room was hung, *wave* backwards and forwards';[6] 'sumptuous tapestry, which it was now too dark to distinguish, hung upon the walls, and depictured scenes from some of the antient Provencal romances';[7] 'from the centre of the ceiling descended a silver lamp';[8] 'the hall was sufficiently lighted by the large tripod *lamp*, which *hung* in the vaulted roof; and, while she should wait till Annette should bring a taper . . .'.[9] We have there all the features of Keats' castle, except the carpets, and there are, as we shall see later, a number of passages of more detailed resemblance. It is time to return to the narrative, which we interrupted in the middle of Angela's speech.

XIV

St. Agnes! Ah! it is St. Agnes eve—
 Yet Men will murder upon holidays:
Thou must hold water in a Witches sieve
 And be liege Lord of all the elves and fays
  To venture so—in truth it doth amaze—
  Young Signor Porphyro—St. Agnes Eve!
  Gods help! my Lady fair the Conjuror plays
  This very night—good agels her deceive—
But let me laugh awhile I've mickle time to grieve."

[1] *SR*, vol. i, c. i, p. 11. [2] *SR*, vol. i, c. iii, p. 91.
[3] *MU*, vol. iii, p. 375 (c. xxxvi, p. 70).
[4] Ib., vol. iii, p. 364 (c. xxxv, p. 68).
[5] Ib., vol. iv, p. 107 (c. xliv, p. 103), cf. st. xxiv.
[6] *RF*, vol. ii, c. viii, p. 9 (c. viii, p. 136).
[7] *MU*, vol. iii, p. 350 (c. xxxv, p. 66).
[8] *RF*, vol. ii, c. x, p. 117 (c. xi, p. 185).
[9] *MU*, vol. iii, p. 241 (c. xxxiii, p. 48).

First *in truth it doth* was cancelled in favour of *it fills me with*, but then the whole parenthesis was deleted and nothing substituted. Woodhouse fills in the gap in his first transcript with *To see thee Lionel*. The passage evidently exercised Keats, since in the second draft he tries an entirely different reading:

> To venture so about these thorny ways
> A tempting Be'lzebub.

The idea of holding water in a sieve is common enough and I do not know that we need look for a specific source for its introduction here, even though the witch in *Macbeth* proposes to sail in a sieve;[1] and it is possible that the idea of power over the fairies in connexion with venturing into peril was a reminiscence either of Huon of Bordeaux, read in the French or in Berners' translation,[2] or more probably on Sotheby's translation of Wieland's *Oberon*,[3] which was a popular book at the time.

XV

The next stanza was first written straight through and Keats then went back and polished it. Here it is in the unfinished form:

> Feebly she laughd in the bright languid Moon
> While Porphyro upon her face doth look
> As doth an Urchin on an aged Crone
> Who keepeth closed a wondrous riddle book
> As spectacle'd she sits in chimney nook—
> But soon his eyes grew brilliant when she told
> His Lady's purpoise, and he scare could brook
> Tears at the though of those Enchantments cold—
> Sweet Madeline asleep among those legends old.

The first line for some reason caused the most trouble. First he tries

> Feebly she laugheth in the languid moon

[1] *Macbeth*, I. iii. 8.

[2] '*The ancient, honorable, famous and delightfull historie of Huon of Bordeaux*'; London, 1601. (But it is more than doubtful whether Keats could readily have secured access to this.)

[3] *Oberon, a poem, from the German of Wieland*; by W. Sotheby. London, 1798.

Then puts in *bright* again and writes an *s* in over the *eth* but without deleting the latter, and then deletes *bright* again, so that we have

> Feebly she laugh$\overset{s}{e}$th in the languid moon

Then the Urchin is made more vivid by becoming a *puzzled* Urchin, and Madeline's situation is changed from the vague *among* to *in lap of*. Finally *and he scare could brook Tears* is deleted, as though Keats was conscious of the misuse of *brook*, but nothing is substituted. In the second draft *But soon* becomes *Sudden*, and the tears become *Sighs*.

I feel sure that there is some source for the Urchin and the riddle-book; it may of course be a recollection of Keats' boyhood or of a scene that he has remembered, but I suspect a literary source without any success in confirming the suspicion.

There is one very odd textual point about this stanza, over which I am as much puzzled as the Urchin. In two places, the reading of *Like* at the beginning of line 3, and the reading of *And* at the beginning of line 9, the printed text differs from the first draft, and from Woodhouse's second transcript, but agrees with Woodhouse's first transcript. The alterations themselves might no doubt have been inserted in the second draft after the second transcript had been made; but how in the world did they find their way into the first transcript?

XVI

As the excitement of the action rises, so does that of the composition. Keats starts off in full career for three lines and into the fourth.

> Sudden a thought more rosy than the rose
> Flush'd his young Cheek and in his painfle heart[1]
> ? riot fierce—and then doth he propose
> This Stratagem

Then *more rosy than the rose Flush'd his young Cheek* is

[1] Buxton Forman reads this word as *head*, I think unnecessarily; the word is cramped at the end of the line and the apparent *d* may well be *r* followed by an uncrossed *t*.

deleted, *rosy* inserted between *a* and *thought*, and *Heated his Brow* substituted in the second line, but the first line is left incomplete, though with the insertion of *rosy* before *thought*. Then the beginning of line 3 comes in for treatment. First the opening word, whatever it was, is changed to *Made* and then both this and *riot fierce* are deleted and *Made purple riot* written above, and finally *This* is changed to *A*, so that we are left with this:

> Sudden a rosy thought
>   Heated his Brow and in his painfle heart
> Made purple riot:—then doth he propose
>   A Stratagem. . . .

and are ready to go on

> that Makes the Beldam start—
> 'A cruel Man and impious thou art—
> Sweet Lady, let her pray and sleep and dream
> Alone with her good angels far apart
> From wicked Men like thee: by Christ I deem
> ~~Thou art not~~
> ~~Thou canst not be the Youth~~
> Thou canst not surely be the same ~~as~~ that thou didst seem'

Finally *by Christ* is altered to *O Christ*.

In the second draft the first line is completed:

> Sudden a thought came full blown like a rose

(which one can hardly believe that Keats would ever have altered to the more obvious and weaker reading of the printed version), and the heart became *pained* rather than *painful*. *O Christ* had from the outset not a chance of passing the duumvirate of censors. *Away* is significantly pencilled in in Woodhouse's first transcript, and between that and the *Go! go!* which was finally sanctioned there is little to choose in the matter of anility. We can if we like amuse ourselves by catching an echo in this stanza of two Shakespearean phrases:

> Make a riot on the gentle brow[1]

and

> riot and dishonour stain the brow.[2]

[1] *KJ*, III. i. 247. [2] *1 H IV*, I. i. 85.

XVII

'I will not harm her, by the great St. Paul;
Says Porphyro,—O may I ne'er find grace
When my weak voice shall uto heaven call
If one of her soft ringlets I misplace
Or look with ruffian passion in her face—
Good Angela, thou hearest how I swear

So far so good, but *swear* is going to cause trouble with rhymes, particularly if the end of the stanza is already in mind, since the foemen will have more than one ear between them, and there had better be several bears. So the end of the line is at once re-written:

believe me by these tears—
Or I will even in a moments space
Awake with horrid shout my foemen's ears,
And beard them though they be more fang'd tham wolves and bears'.

But Keats is determined that Porphyro is going to swear somewhere in the stanza, so he goes back to the second line and changes *says* to the mouth-twisting *swearth*. On the opposite page to the text, in Woodhouse's first transcript, some one (as we shall meet him again, let us call him *X*[1]) has made various entries in pencil. Whether swearing by the saints in general was less reprehensible than swearing by an individual saint, or for some other reason, he ends the first line with *By the Saints I swear* and makes the two consequential alterations of *Quoth Porphyro* in the second line and *send to Heaven its prayer* in the third. What authority, if any, *X* had for his alterations one cannot tell; but they appear in the printed version, though with modifications, one of which greatly improves the end of the third line.

The last line is something of an oddity. Why should wolves and bears be *fanged*? The characteristic weapon

[1] Unless Woodhouse wrote a very different hand in pencil from what he wrote in pen, *X* is not Woodhouse, but he is some one who for some of his entries, particularly where he is filling in gaps, had the draft before him, though in other places he coincides with the printed version against the draft and the transcripts.

of the bear is its hug, not its teeth; and why should the teeth even of wolves be described in terms more appropriate to snakes? The answer, I think, lies in an interesting piece of association. Wolves and bears are mentioned together three times in Shakespeare,[1] but in one of the passages in which they are so linked there is a mention a few lines earlier of an 'adder blue';[2] and in *Hamlet*[3] we find:

my two schoolfellows,
Whom I will trust as I will adders fang'd,
They bear the mandate.

XVIII

The next stanza goes smoothly enough:

'Ah! why will you affright a feeble Soul?
A poor weak palsy stricken churchyard thing
Whose passing bell may ere the morning toll;—
Whose prayers for thee each mornd and evening
Were neer missed—' Thus planing doth she bring
A gentler speech from burning Porphyro,
So gentle and of such deep sorrowing
That the old Beldam promises to do
Whatever he shall say, betide her weal or woe.

wilt thou is substituted for *will you* in line 1; the possible tolling of the passing bell is advanced to *midnight*; and *Dame* is written in above a cancelled Beldam, while *promises to do* is deleted and nothing substituted. In the second draft the last three lines become:

So woeful and of such deep sorrowing
That Angela gives promise she will do
Whatever he shall wish, betide her weal or woe

XIX

The next stanza has a false start,

Which was, as all who ever lov'd will guess

which is at once deleted and a fresh start made:

Which was to guide him in close secrecy
To Madeline's Bedchamber, and there hide
Him in a Closet if such one there be—

[1] *WT*, II. iii. 186; *Timon*, III. vi. 106; ib., IV. iii. 190.
[2] *Timon*, IV. iii. 182.
[3] *Hamlet*, III. iv. 203.

But this does not satisfy him, and with deletions and insertions the following is arrived at:

> Which was to lead him in close secrecy
> Even to Madeline's Chamber, and there hide
> Him in a Closet if such one there be—
> That he might see her beauty unespied
> Or win perhaps that night a peerless bride
> While legion'd faries cl

the opening of this word, whatever it was to be, is deleted and the line completed

> round her pillow flew

but *flew* does not promise well for rhyme, and this phrase is deleted in favour of

> pace'd the Coverlet
> And pale enchantment held her sleepy-eyed.
> O when on such a night have lovers met
> Since Merlin pay'd the demons all the monstrous debt.

O when is then altered to *Never*, and *the demons* to *his Demon*, so that the last two lines run

> Never on such a night have lovers met
> Since Merlin paid his Demon all the monstrous debt.

So, after a good deal of toil, the stanza has been completed. Of the two outstanding features of it, the legioned fairies and Merlin, the sources of the one are fairly clear and of the other very obscure. The fairies seem to be suggested by the famous passage on Queen Mab in *Romeo and Juliet*,[1] of which passage Keats underlined a considerable portion, together with a passage in Milton's *At a Vacation Exercise* (which any one who is convinced that Keats drew his folk-lore from Brand will be pleased to find quoted in *Popular Antiquities*):

> Good luck befriend thee Son; for at thy birth
> The Faiery Ladies daunc't upon the hearth;
> Thy drowsie Nurse hath sworn she did them spie
> Come tripping to the Room where thou didst lie;
> And sweetly singing round about thy Bed
> Strew all their blessings on thy sleeping Head.[2]

[1] *R & J*, I. iv. 55–96.

[2] *At a Vacation Exercise*, 59–64.

But I have an uneasy feeling that there is something else behind, something which suggests a more orderly and slower progress of a ranged body of fairies than the gallop of Mab in her chariot or the dance in the *Vacation Exercise*.

That, however, is a trivial difficulty compared with the trouble about Merlin. If ever there was a passage which bears all over it the marks of derivation from a literary source, this is it. The wording of '*the* monstrous debt' has just the implications of many phrases in Milton, e.g. '*that* small infantry';[1] it is something that we are presumed to know about without more elaboration. But what is it that we ought to know about? Leigh Hunt was puzzled by it and honestly makes no bones about saying so, remarking that though Merlin was the son of a demon and conversant with the race he is aware of no debt that he owed them. Buxton Forman[2] attempts to make very short work of Leigh Hunt's difficulties by denying that there are any. He thinks that the monstrous debt was Merlin's own monstrous existence, which was paid when he disappeared by the working of one of his own spells upon him by Viviane; and that the 'never on such a night' refers to the tempest which was supposed to have swept over the woods of Broceliande the night after the magician was spell-bound. He supports the first part of his contention by a quotation from Dunlop's *History of Fiction*:

> 'The demons, alarmed at the number of victims which daily escaped their fangs since the birth of our Saviour, held a council of war. It was there resolved that one of their number should be sent to the world with instructions to engender on some virgin a child who might act as their vice-gerent on earth, and thus counteract the great plan that had been laid for the salvation of mankind.'

Professor de Sélincourt[3] thinks that Buxton Forman is right about the debt but wrong about the source, since 'the simile was obviously suggested to his mind by the storm which he conceives as bursting out upon the

[1] *Paradise Lost*, i. 575
[2] HBF, ii. 74 n.
[3] de S, 468.

meeting of Porphyro and Madeline, as before on the meeting of Merlin and Viviane, and no mention of the storm is made in Dunlop'. This is all very well until we come to examine the passage in front of us. Leigh Hunt had every right to be puzzled; the natural implication of 'the monstrous debt' is some kind of compact between Merlin and 'the demons' or 'his Demon', of the Faust-Mephistopheles type, in which there is as it were a contractual obligation which has ultimately to be satisfied. Merlin's existence, for which he had no responsibility, can hardly be so thought of. And 'his Demon' is surely the oddest possible way of alluding to Merlin's demon father. Further, no doubt there was a storm over Broceliande, but this hinders rather than helps us, since up to this point there has been no mention of a storm in *The Eve of St. Agnes*. 'On such a night'; what kind of night? So far the impression has been one of icy moonlight and if anything of stillness, to which has been added in stanza xv an impression of enchantments and faerie. If the storm is relevant Keats is most inartistically anticipating in his own imagination something of which he is to give his readers no hint for seventeen more stanzas. For an artist as keenly aware of significance as was Keats surely some much more exact parallelism than this is needed. What is wanted is a meeting of lovers by night, which is connected in some way with the payment of a recognized debt by Merlin to some one who can be naturally described as 'his Demon'. If the lovers are, as one naturally supposes, Merlin and Vivian, they must be meeting, even though Vivian's love is assumed, *as* lovers, and not when Vivian is on the point of treachery. Keats possessed a book vaguely described by Woodhouse as a 'History of King Arthur' which might throw some light if we could identify it. Mr. E. Vinaver has kindly called my attention to a passage in the old French romance of Merlin,[1] which has perhaps some significance; Merlin tells 'Nivienne' of 'la plus biele petite

[1] *Merlin*, edited by G. Paris for the Société des Anciens Textes Français. Paris, 1886.

chambre que je sache', in which two lovers lived, died, and were buried together. Merlin and Nivienne visit the room in which the tomb is built, and Nivienne insists on spending the night there. From there on the story proceeds as usual with Nivienne enchanting Merlin and imprisoning him in the tomb. This has a touch more of the required atmosphere, but is not I think adequate. Also we can find a few touches of what is wanted in the Elizabethan play of *The Birth of Merlin*, but nothing that is really satisfactory. That Keats is here alluding to some episode in a history of Merlin which he has read I have as little doubt as that the particular episode is still waiting for discovery.

XX

The next stanza represents almost the last moment of easy composition in the poem; there are one or two of the common hurried misspellings and one moment of hesitation.

> 'It shall be as thou wishest' said the Dame
> All cates and danties shall be stored there
> Quickly on this feast night;—by the tambour frame
> Her own Lute thou wilt see—no time to spare
> ~~And~~ For I am slow and feeble, and scare dare
> On such a Catering tust my dizzy head:
> But wait an hour's time ~~as thy~~
> and kneel in prayer

This is then at once altered to

> But wait an hour passing—kneel in prayer
> The while—Ah thou must needs the Lady wed
> Or may I never leave my grave among the dead.'

In the second draft the opening of the seventh line is altered to

> Wait here my child with patience

and *Ah* is altered to *Sooth*.

For twenty stanzas, though there have been plenty of alterations and improvements, Keats has been writing with fair ease and fluency. But now, as the crisis of the action approaches, the fever of composition increases, and one can study with an excitement almost painful the workings of the creative spirit in the throes of creation. And at this point, to avoid too much interruption and delay when we come to the actual study, it will be as well to set out in general the sources on which Keats appears to have drawn. Let us take first *Il Filocolo* in the French translation[1] in which we are supposing Keats to have read it, if he read it at all. Blanchefleur is imprisoned in a tower, with Gloritie. Fleury (otherwise Philocope), her lover, has designed to secure entrance by being sent up in a large basket of flowers, and the basket is raised carefully 'jusques à l'une des fenestres de la chambre de Blanchefleur, ou Gloritie la receut'. Philocope then nearly ruins the plan by over anxiety. 'A cause du grand desir de la veoir, il se haulsa le visaige si que Gloritie jecta soubdainement ung tresgrand cry: Mais incontinant qu'elle le cogneut' (cf. *startled her, but soon she knew his face*), Gloritie locks the chamber door and becomes 'joyeuse oultre mesure, de sorte qu'elle ne pouoit croyre ce qu'elle veoyoit', as much *filled with amaze to see* him as Angela was to see Porphyro. As Porphyro asks *Now tell me where is Madeline*, Philocope 'demanda à Gloritie que faisoit Blanchefleur', and continues, 'Gloritie ma chere soeur je te prie la me faire veoir diligemment d'autant qu'a peine l'ardeur et desir me promettront de tant viure'. And just as after Porphyro's speech of such deep sorrowing Angela consents to take him to Madeline's chamber and there hide him in a closet that he might see her beauty unespied, and he swears not to harm her, so in the *Philocope* Gloritie says 'Mais pour ne tumber en pareille peine et contenter ton desir, je te mettray en ceste prochaine chambre, dont tu pourras veoir à ton ayse ta chere amye Blanchefleur festoyer avecq les aultres, jusques à la nuyct que le te musseray derriere les courtines de son lict'; this

[1] *Le Philocope de Messire Jehan Boccace Florentin. . . . traduictz d'Italien en Francoys par Adrian Sevin.* Paris, 1542.

contents Philocope, though he expects to find the time as long as Porphyro found the endless minutes; 'Ce conseil pleut moult à Philocope, jacoit qu'il luy fust grief d'attendre tant, Parquoy Gloritie le mena en la chambre, et le feit jurer et promettre de ne faire oultre leur deliberation'. Gloritie then goes to find Blanchefleur whom she discovers 'fort melancoliée et pensive' (like the *thoughtful* and *pensive* Madeline *sighing for Agnes' dreams* of stanzas VII and XXI), whom she comforts by relating a vision she has had of Fleury who came into the room 'revestu de couleur quasi de *vermeilles roses*' and 'te regardoit *dormir en ton lict doulcement*'. And in the dream Fleury tells Gloritie that the gods 'm'ont promis qu'elle (Blanchefleur) me sera presentement et toujours ma loyalle espouse' (as Porphyro hopes *to win perhaps that night a peerless bride*). Blanchefleur is comforted and begins the festivities, while Porphyro watches from the next room. He '*deuint par pitié semblable au mort*' but later '*ayant repris vigueur* il regarda plaisamment son seul bien'. (Porphyro first 'grew faint', but later 'his heart revives'.) He 'demoura en ceste sorte ce jour entier *qu'il pensoit durer à jamais*'. Then when night comes Gloritie 'prepara le riche lict, et abaissées les courtines, elle mist Philocope à l'endroit qu'ilz auoient ensembles deliberé, et le pria bien fort d'attendre en la maniere qui auoit esté dicte'. There follows a long conversation between Gloritie and Blanchefleur in which there is one phrase which perhaps recalls to us, though its context is different, Porphyro's situation of peril with not one breast to afford him mercy; 'si l'Admiral s'en apperceuoit il vous feroit mourir cruellement sans aulcune misericorde'. At length, when we have become as weary of it as Fleury, the conversation ends, and Gloritie withdraws; Blanchefleur 'se coucha au riche lict: et en estendant ses braz pour y trouuer son loyal amy, elle commença à pleurer amerement et dist. O Fleury ma seulle esperance. . . . Helas si tu y fusses, tu me feroys tres gracieuse compaignie: Et neantmoins il fault qu'vne *craintiue* iouuencelle dorme seulle en si grand et riche lict. O saincte Venus quand me tiendrez vous promesse? . . . je cognoys impossible que mon desir sorte à effect pour la loigntaine demeure de mon tresriche et seul amy, au lieu de qui (O Citharée) te plaise enuoyer en mon estomach le *doulx sommeil* et les amyables atouchemens. . . . Et autant de foys qu'elle nommoit Fleury elle jectoit ung tresgrande souspir, et les braz estanduz vers le lieu ou Philocope estoit, elle s'endormit en souspirant. . . . Quand elle fut endormie il se despouilla tout nud, et se mist entre les bras d'icelle et la baisa doulcement neantmoins elle ne s'esueilla, ains Philocope la print devant entre ses braz. . . . La chambre luysoit aumoyen des *deux escharboncles* comme s'il fust iour clair, parquoy en la regardant il disoit. . . . O pourquoy dors tu tant sans me sentir? . . . O excellente damoyselle *reveille toy*, à ce que tu cognoisses ta joye en tes braz. . . . Reveille toy O ma seulle esperance. . . . Ce pendant il la baisoit sans cesse, la regardant evidemment. . . . et appelloit souuent *l'ame alienée du dormir*'. There follows a passage which is only worth recording as showing Keats' instinct for selection and omission at work, since, wishing to translate the whole episode to the higher romantic plane, he omits all but one of the merely physical details, and selects the one emotional touch. 'Il la descouuroit, et regardoit avecq amoureux oeil son delicat estomach, et *sa desirante main* en toucheoit les ronds et blancs tetins, lesquelz il baisoit souuent. . . . Et le tenant print si grand plaisir qu'il luy sembla oultre *passer en joye les regions des dieux*.' One seems to catch an echo of this in sound as well as in sense when Porphyro is 'beyond a mortal man impassion'd far'. He longs to wake her, but dares not do it suddenly, and so speaks to her in a low voice; 'mais l'ame qui pensoit en sommeil l'auoir faincetement entre les braz, ne luy concedoit le reueil, pource qu'elle auoit en dormant non moindre plaisir que celluy de Philocope: Toutesfois à la fin elle contraincte, se reueilla estraignant les braz, et dist. Helas mon ame qui te ravist? A l'heure Philocope respondit. Doulce damoyselle confortes toy, car les dieux m'ont donné à toy ainsi nulle personne ne t'en pourra priuer.

Elle oyant la voix humaine toute estourdie du sommeil et *de la paoeur* voulut fuyr le lict, crier, et appeller Gloritie, mais Philocope la retint fort, et soubdainement luy dist. O gratieuse damoyselle ne te vueilles escrier, et ne vueilles fuyr celluy qui t'ayme plus que luy. Je suis le tien Fleury, *conforte toy et chasse toute craincte*. . . . Neantmoins Blanchefleur ne le pouoit croyre, et regardant en doubte trembloit comme le fueille, mais à la fin Philocope la reconforta et asseura peu à peu, tant qu'elle l'embrassa et baisa tant amoureusement en souspirant qu'a peine sa vie peut souffrir son incomprehensible plaisir.'

So much for Boccaccio in his French dress. Are we justified in thinking that Keats had read the narrative? Opinions will no doubt differ. I feel myself that the obvious resemblance in the general situation, and the cumulative effect of a considerable number of resemblances in detail, do not indeed constitute proof, but are enough to create a strong presumption that Keats was drawing upon his memories of Boccaccio. And now for Mrs. Radcliffe. We have already seen the resemblances between her castle and Keats', and some other points of contact, particularly in the figure of Angela. But there are resemblances much closer than these, resemblances which seem to be beyond the range of chance coincidence. First there is the detailed description of a room: 'In a large oriel *window of painted glass*, stood a table, with a *silver crucifix*, and a *prayer-book* open . . . the *lute*[1] itself, lying on a corner of the table.'[2] Then there are two passages from *The Italian*, in which Vivaldi is watching Ellena: 'She was rising from a small altar where she had *concluded the service*; the glow of devotion was still upon her countenance as she raised her eyes, and with a rapt earnestness fixed them on the heavens. . . . But, while he thus hesitated, he heard her sigh, and then with a sweetness peculiar

[1] It should perhaps be observed that there are several lutes in *The Arabian Nights*.

[2] *MU*, vol. iv, p. 61 (c. xlii, p. 95); cf. st. xxv, 'her *silver cross*', and xx, 'her own *lute*'.

to her accent, *pronounce his name*. During the trembling anxiety with which he listened to what might follow this mention of his name. . . .'[1] 'To ask himself, whether it was honourable thus to *steal* upon her *retirement*, and become an unsuspected observer of her secret thoughts. . . . Ellena was alone, sitting in a *thoughtful attitude and holding her lute she appeared lost to a consciousness of surrounding objects*, and a tenderness was on her countenance, which seemed to tell him that her thoughts were engaged by some interesting subject. . . . Vivaldi, while he listened to this, was immovable; he seemed as if *entranced*. . . . From this moment Vivaldi seemed to have *arisen* into a new existence; the whole world to him was *Paradise*'.[2] And another in the *Sicilian Romance*: 'At these words Hippolitus started from his seat, and clasping his hands in fervent joy "Enchanting sounds!" cried he, in a voice tenderly *impassioned*; "*could* I but believe ye,—could I *but* believe ye—this world were *paradise*".'[3] Another from the *Romance of the Forest*: 'When he approached the bed he heard her *gently breathe*, and soon after sigh . . . and then heard her sing in her sleep . . . some notes of a melancholy little air. . . . He *undrew the curtain, and saw her lying in a profound sleep*.'[4] Then there are several awakenings: 'She unclosed her eyes, and joy once more illumined his soul';[5] 'The lady *breathing a deep sigh, unclosed her eyes*';[6] and, perhaps the most significant, 'She gazed at him for a moment in speechless *affright*, while he, *throwing himself on* his knee at the bedside, *besought her to fear nothing*. . . . I have bribed a servant of the castle to open the gates, and, before tomorrow's dawn, you shall be far on the way to Venice.'[7] In the *Sicilian Romance* the hero thus addresses the heroine: ' "Come, my love, the keys are ours, and we have not a moment to lose";

[1] *It*, vol. i, pp. 19, 20; cf. st. XXVI, 'her vespers done', and st. XXXV.
[2] Ib., vol. i, pp. 58–61; cf. st. XXVIII, '*Stol'n* to this *Paradise*, and so *entranced*'.
[3] *SR*, vol. i, c. iii, p. 113; cf. st. XXXVI. 'Beyond a mortal man *impassion'd* far'.
[4] *RF*, vol. iii, c. xiv, p. 17 (c. xv, p. 272).
[5] *AD*, p. 70.
[6] *SR*, vol. ii, c. xiv, p. 159.
[7] *MU*, vol. ii, pp. 264, 267 (c. xx, pp. 125, 126).

. . . they descended to the hall. . . . This they crossed.'[1] There are again perpetual ditties, usually mournful, for example 'the mournful songs of past times';[2] 'a melancholy little air, one of the popular songs of her native province',[3] and one of these is connected with a lute and another with Provence.[4] Then in *The Mysteries of Udolpho* there is the constant background of carousal, which Mrs. Radcliffe characteristically describes as 'the wild uproar of riot, not the cheering gaiety of tempered mirth';[5] and one of the allusions to this is noticeable for the way in which the noise ceases; 'the distant carousals of Montoni and his companions—the loud contest, the dissolute laugh and the choral song, that made the halls re-echo. At length, she heard the heavy gates of the castle shut for the night, and those sounds instantly sunk into a silence'.[6]

Some of these parallels are obviously trivial, and in isolation would be evidentially valueless; others are more striking; and some almost beyond the range of coincidence. Taking them *en masse* it appears to me hard to resist the conclusion that Keats had read Mrs. Radcliffe with a retentive memory. One last parallel, which is as it were the prize exhibit of this collection, and I feel clinching, shall be kept for display in its proper place.

One would expect to find some traces of indebtedness to *The Rape of Lucrece*, seeing that the situations have at least the connexion of strong contrast. But though Keats had read the poem, as his underlinings testify, I can find, with two very doubtful exceptions, no trace whatever of 'influence', let alone any specific parallels. And in general treatment, there could hardly be a divergence wider than that between the elaborate, ornate, and 'conceited' long-windedness of Shakespeare, and the rich simplicity of Keats. There are points of indebtedness to other passages in Shakespeare, and to certain other authors, but these

[1] *SR*, vol. i, c. iii, p. 152.
[2] *MU*, vol. iv, p. 411 (c. lvi, p. 155).
[3] Ib., vol. ii, p. 60 (c. xvii, p. 90).
[4] *AD*, p. 39; *RF*, vol. iii, c. xviii, p. 184 (c. xix, p. 353).
[5] *MU*, vol. iii, p. 118 (c. xxx, p. 27).
[6] Ib., vol. ii, p. 475 (c. xxv, p. 7).

will be more conveniently treated in their respective contexts. And so let us return to what, after all, is greatly more important than *Il Filocolo* and Mrs. Radcliffe's endless romances, to Keats, shaping into the exquisite beauties of the *Eve of St. Agnes* his various material whencesoever drawn.

XXI

Here, at the beginning of a much more difficult and more tumultuous period of composition, the start is no better than a recording in prose of the necessary idea;

> So saying she hobble'd out busily

This becomes

> So saying she hobble'd off with busy fear.

and the next two lines get written:

> And we will pass the Lover's endless hour;
> The Dame return'd, and whisper'd in his ear

But the second line is thoroughly unsatisfactory, since it does no more than record the passage of time without giving the imagination any help to realize its passage. There is also trouble looming ahead about the rhyme at the end of line 4. So next we have:

> So saying she hobble'd off with busy fear.
> The Lover's endless minutes quckly pass'd;
> The Dame return'd, and whisper'd in his ear
> To follow her, with aged eyes agast
> From fright of any noise[1]

But *any noise* has a kind of comic triviality, and it is changed very much for the better:

> From fright of dim espial—Safe at last,
> Through loneliest passages and . . .

And what? Why 'and' anything? Why not define more particularly? So

> Through lonely arras Galleries

[1] HBF reads these two words as *airy vision*, one of his rare misreadings.

But *arras* is awkward as an adjective, so let us borrow some woodwork from Mrs. Radcliffe's castles and try again:

> Through lonely oaken Galleries they ~~gaind~~ came
> To the Maiden Chamber

The *came* is deleted in favour of *reach* and *To* cut out, so that we have

> they reach
> The Maiden's Chamber silken hush'd and chaste
> Whre closeted he

The last three words at once deleted for

> There in a panting covert to remain,

and this for

> Where he in panting covert ~~must~~ will remain,

And then there are all kinds of trouble about the Alexandrine. First Keats writes

> Love (or possibly 'Lone') purgatory sweet

Then he tries

> In purgatory sweet

And then

> A purgatory sweet

Then he gets rid of purgatory altogether and tries

> Upon the frontier

Then he writes down

> In purgatory sweet

and has another look at it, and then alters *In* to *From* to see if that will do any better, and then exasperatedly cross-hatches the whole thing out and goes over to the next page and struggles to the end of the line with

> From purgatory sweet to view love's own domain

But that will not do either, and after a half-hearted attempt to change *From* to *In* he tries another ending, *or what may he attain* which will not fit on to the beginning, and then deletes the whole line and gives it up as a bad job.

In Woodhouse's first transcript *X* suggests, as emendations for *endless* and *quickly*, *anxious* and *slowly*, but there is no sign of these in Woodhouse's second transcript as corrected.

In the second draft the galleries become *dusky* and the last two lines are completely recast.

XXII

This stanza started

> There secreted,

when it occurred to Keats that, Porphyro being now immobilized, something had better be done with Angela. So he starts again:

> Scare had old Angela the Stair case found
> Ere Madeline, like an affrighted Bird
> Flew past her

But even in the heat of composition Keats' sense of humour does not desert him, and this is too much for it; not even the capital B nor the attempt to improve matters by turning the *Bird* into a *Swan* can remedy this unhappy picture (which nevertheless stays in his mind for a more appropriate context); so he starts again with *Scarce had*, writes *Old An* over it and then deletes both; then

> With fautling hand upon the Ballustrad
>   Old Angela was feeling for the Stair
> When Madeline St. Agnes charmed Maid
>   Rose like a spirit to her unaware,

And the feeble *to her* is deleted and with the aid of Sotheby and perhaps Shakespeare the line becomes

> Rose like a mission'd spirit unaware,[1]

and we go on

> And with her taper's light and gentle care
> Guided her

[1] Translation of Wieland's *Oberon*, Canto v. lxiii, 'Like a commissioned angel of the skies'.

But the taper shall be made more pictorial and the whole picture clearer:

> With silver taper's light and gentle care
> She turn'd and led the aged gossip down
> To ~~the~~ a save level matting—now prepare
> Young Porphyro a-gazing on that Bed

at which point it is necessary to go back and put the rhyme right by transposition two lines above; and now the picture of the bird, but a better bird, much improved, will serve;

> She comes she comes again like ring dove fray'd and fled.

The second draft reverts for some unexplained reason, perhaps the desire for complete simplicity, to the weak *a spirit to her*; reads *taper light* for *taper's light*; and alters *gentle* to *pious*.

XXIII

The next stanza goes its lovely way untroubled till near the end:

> Out went the taper as she hurried in,
> Its little smoke in pallid moonshine died
> She closed the door, she panted; all akin
> To Spirits of the Air and visions wide—
> No uttered syllable or woe betide;
> But to her heart her heart was voluble
> ~~And~~ Paining with eloquence her balmy side
> As though a tongueless nightingale should sweel
> Her barren throat in vain and die heart stifled in her dell.

As this last line is a foot too long *in vain* is first deleted, and then *barren* deleted and *in vain* replaced. The second draft reads *floated* for *hurried*.

Here again, as Sir Sidney Colvin noted, there seems to be a reminiscence of Sotheby:

> Oft in this speechless language, glance on glance,
> When mute the tongue, how voluble the heart.
> (*Oberon*, vi. 17)

XXIV

For showing Keats the pure craftsman delighting in his mastery of his craft these next two stanzas are unequalled in the poem. There is no emotional stress to distract, no excitement of action to hurry him. He is quietly setting his stage for the climax, and he can take his time over making it as richly perfect as it can be made. He remembers the arched windows and the stained glass from Mrs. Radcliffe and possibly the *deux escharboncles*[1] from Blanchefleur's chamber; and he starts with a kind of fluent rough sketch.

A Casement ach'd

But let us make it bigger (? for more light and a better display of glass) and also more defined in outline; so

A Casement tripple archd and diamonded

(we notice that instinct for line, always strong in Keats, which gives first the outline of the window and then fills it with the intersecting tracery of the leading)

With many coloured glass fronted the Moon
In midst ~~of which~~ wereof a shilded scutcheon shed
High blushing gules, upon

But, before the gules is shed on her, Madeline, who was left at the door, must be brought forward; so *upon* is deleted and a colon goes in after *gules*; and pictures from Mrs. Radcliffe come back to him; in one of which he remembers somewhere a silver cross which will catch the light:

High blushing gules: she kneeled saintly down
And inly prayed for grace and heavenly boon;
The blood red gules fell on her silver cross
And her white hands devout

(with, I think, an experimental change of *her white* into *whitest*).

[1] Professor MacCracken makes great play with these—more, I think, than is justified.

Well, there at least is some of the material in the rough; but it will not do as it stands, if only for the purely technical reason that *down* will only rhyme with *moon* and *boon* if one is Burns. And apart from that there is a fumbling of touch in the repetition of *gules*. But most of the material is much too good to let go. So Keats takes it all to pieces, like a man making the stained-glass window of which he is talking, and begins to put the fragments together in a different design. And first he decides that Madeline had better be postponed till the next stanza. He will indulge himself with the luxury of a piece of pure description and give himself ample room for the development of the window and the moonlight. He starts by elaborating the window:

A Casement tipple archd and high

presumably going to end *there was* but he concludes that this had better come at the beginning, and we get

There was
A Casement tipple archd and high
All garlanded with carven imageries
Of fruits & trailing flowers and sunny corn

which is excellent except that it does not rhyme; so *trailing* goes out and the line is completed with *ears parchd* ready to rhyme with the first line when the latter was transposed. But the transposition is not made, because there suddenly recurs to him a word ('knot-grass') from a passage which he had marked in *A Midsummer Night's Dream*[1] that will rhyme with the first line as he first had it in mind. So he starts all over again.

A Casement high and tripple archd there was
  All gardneded [*he is in a hurry now*] with carven imageries
Of fruits and flowers and bunches of knot grass;
  And diamonded with panes of quaint device
  Innumerable of stains and splendid dies
  As is the wing of evening tiger moths;
  And in the midst 'mong ~~man~~ thousand heraldries
  And dim twilight

[1] *MND*, III. ii. 329.

At this point he sees how to give emphasis to both *dim* and *twilight* by separating them, and so cancels them to write

And twilight saints and dim emblasonings
A shielded scutcheon blushd with Blood of Queens and Kings

But now the sixth line is left hanging unrhymed. He makes a minor alteration in the seventh line, so that it starts *In midst whereoft*; then he feels that the line about the stains and dies, even though he is half-conscious that it is a reminiscence, is a fine line in itself, and that the line which follows, even apart from the easily secured rhyme, will not at present take the weight of its predecessor. So for the final touch for his stanza he begins the operation which makes of the tiger moths and their wings one of the richest of even his opulent lines. He first deletes it altogether and starts

As is the tiger moths rich[1]

no, let us have both a more significant word and an alliteration

deep damasked wings

and then the force of association is too much for him; the splendid and innumerable dies when he first met them were the hues of sunset, and he acknowledges his debt by writing *sunset* for *damasked*, and so for the moment left the stanza, for once, we may hope, well satisfied. In the second draft he diminished the over-emphatic *s*'s of the third line by writing *fruit*, went back to the simpler *And in the midst*, and, surely rightly, reinstated *damasked*.

XXV

Keats is now ready to work into his design the other pieces that are left over, and, as he is no longer trying to compress into one stanza the material of two, he has space to develop the second part of his picture, the moonlight and Madeline. The impression of cold can be maintained

[1] *rich* is the accepted reading, but I am not happy about it: the initial letter is not like Keats' initial *r*, and the two that follow are more like *ci* than *ic* (though that is not unlike Keats in a hurry).

by the moon being *wintry*, and the picture of Madeline complete instead of a sketch.

> Full on this Casement shone the wintry moon
> And threw red gules on Madelines fair face

Red is redundant and becomes first *warm* and then *rich* (carried over from the deletion in the last stanza); *face* suffers from all possible disabilities; it suggests no feasible rhyme except *grace* which cannot be deferred till the fourth line; it is feebly Leigh Huntian; and in any case we do not want the heroine red in the face, even though by the operation of lunar cosmetics; so alter it to *breast*, and we have:

> Full on this Casement shone the wintry moon
>   And threw rich gules on Madelines fair breast
> As down she kneel'd for heavens grace and boon
>   Tinging her pious hands together prest
> And silver cross

But the fourth line is not satisfactory, and also it occurs to him that the window of innumerable stains seems incapable of transmitting anything but gules, which is both illogical and dull; so he gets to work on the fourth line, and after a deal of experimentation, of which the stages are obscure, we arrive, with a dubious rhyme, at the end of the fifth line

> Rose bloom fell on her hands together prest[1]
> And on her silver cross soft Amethyst
> And on her hair a glory like a Saint's—
> She seem'd ~~like an immortal agel drest~~
>   silvery angel newly drest,
> Save wings for heaven—Porphyro grew faint
> She knelt too pure a thing, too free from motal taint—

[1] What exactly happened with this line is hard to determine. What we find in the draft, as nearly as print can represent it, is the following:

> ~~And~~ rose ~~with red~~ bloom fell on her hands together
> ~~Tinging her pious~~ hands ~~together~~ prest

The results of the first alteration were meant I think to be

> Tinging with red her hands together prest

the second

> And rose bloom on her hands together prest

the third

> Rose bloom fell on her hands together prest

but this does not at all account for the firm deletion of the first *together* and I

And the stanza is tidied up by the deletion of the final *s* of *Saint's*. In the second draft Keats reverted to the much happier first thought of *warm*, and changed the rather inhuman and metallic silver angel to *a splendid angel*.

XXVI

> But soon his heart revives—

(Porphyro, like Fleury, 'reprit vigueur')

> her prayers said

And now Keats addresses himself to the delicate business of getting Madeline undressed. He probably, as Mr. W. T. Arnold pointed out, called to his aid a passage in Browne's *Britannia's Pastorals*:

> And as a lovely maiden, pure and chaste,
> With naked ivory neck, a gown unlaced,
> Within her chamber, when the day is fled,
> Makes poor her garments to enrich her bed:
> First she puts off her lily-silken gown,
> That shrinks for sorrow as she lays it down;
> Her breasts all bare, her kirtle slipping down,
>
> . . . .
>
> Prepares for sweetest rest.[1]

though I am not clear that there is anything very specific there by way of parallel except the *unlaced* and the *slipping down* and the latter could at least as well have been derived from a visual as from a literary memory. However, with whatever memories, Keats begins:

> She lays aside her veil

cannot make any combination of the words before us that will make a line with *together* omitted. And one cannot help wondering, though it would upset the idea that Keats was wanting more varied colour, whether *rose* did not start life as a verb, in contrast to *down she kneeld*.

There is one interesting small point, which indicates the rapidity with which Keats wrote when composing. In line 7 as altered there is clearly an *a* wanted before *silvery*. And Keats omitted it because he thought it was there. The *d* of *seem'd* is not only badly made, but widely spaced from the rest of the word, and Keats' eye was caught by it as he re-wrote the line and took it for the *a* that was needed.

[1] *Britannia's Pastorals*, I. v. 807 et seqq.

But this is the first that we have heard of a veil, and anyway it is not important, so cut it out and try

> She strips her hair of all its wreathed pearl

and then try this the other way round,

> its pearled wreath

and go on

> Unclasps her bosom jewels

but this (apart from the awkwardness of *bosom* as an adjective) is going too fast and leaves the hair unfinished, so delete it and write

> And twists it one knot upon her head

But Keats now knows that he is getting well out of his depth, so the whole thing disappears and he starts again, having made up his mind we may suppose that in this unfamiliar region the only thing for it is rigorous compression:

> But soon his heart revives—her prayers done

(changed first, to avoid the awkward dissyllable, into *her prayers soon done* and then into *her praying done*)

> ~~Sh~~Of all ~~her~~its wreathed pearl she strips her hair
> Unclasps her warmed jewels one by one

So far so good; but now comes a desperate moment which can only be indicated by an attempt to represent the agitations of the draft:

> ~~her bursting~~
> Loosens ~~her‸boddice~~ ~~from her~~
> ~~her Boddice lace~~ string
> ~~her Boddice and her bosom bare~~
> her

One can almost see Keats arriving, at the fourth attempt and with clenched teeth, at the end of the line and a rhyme for *hair*, even though grammar has been sacrificed to get there; and hear the sigh with which he writes the final and undeleted *her* but refuses to write *Boddice* for the fourth time. At this point he turns the page and tries the line again, this time with happier success:

> Loosens her fragrant boddice and doth bare
> Her

But by now it is time for a new attempt, and after an idle moment of recuperation, in which he goes back and counts the stanzas he has written, he numbers[1] this one (the first he has numbered since he started) and advances to the attack once more.

> Anon
> But soon his heart revives—her praying done
> Of all its wreathed pearl her hair she strips
> Unclasps her warmed jewels one by one
> Loosens her fragrant boddice: and down slips
> Her sweet attire

At any rate we are once for all done with the boddice; but Keats finds himself stuck in the middle of a line when he wants to be at the end of it; so he alters *and down slips* to *to her knees*, which allows him to hold the verb up as long as he wishes, makes the consequential alteration of *frees* for *strips* in the second line, and takes up line 5 again. First he tries

> Her sweet attire falls light

and then

> creeps down by

which was presumably to continue

> slow degrees

when it occurs to him to put the degrees earlier and the knees here, and he arrives at

> Loosens her fragrant boddice: by degrees
> Her sweet attire creeps rusteling to her knees
> Half hidden like a Syren of the Sea
> And more melodious

[1] The numbering of this stanza (26) and of the only other which he numbered (33), coinciding as it does with that of the printed text, indicates that Keats had cut out the 'additional' stanza between III and IV more or less as soon as it was written.

But he finds that associations have run away with him, since there is no point in Madeline being either more or less melodious than a Syren (unless he had for the moment intentions of making her rather than Porphyro sing like Mrs. Radcliffe's damsels); so

> Half hidden like a Mermaid in sea weed
> She stands awhile in thought; and sees

the line being then completed by the insertion of *dreaming* before *thought*,

> In fancy fair Saint Agnes in her bed
> But dares not look behind or all the charm is ~~fled~~ dead

In the second draft the *praying* is specified as *vespers*, the attire becomes *rich* instead of *sweet*, the seventh line opens

> Pensive awhile she dreams awake

and *fled* comes in again for *dead*.

There at last, after all the difficulties, is Madeline rather summarily undressed, and she is left shivering in the midst of her discarded raiment with no hint of Mother Bunch's clean shift or any other shift. But all the King's horses and men will not drag Keats back over this stricken field again, and, nightdress or no nightdress, Madeline must be got safely into bed as rapidly as may be.

XXVII

> Then stepping forth she slips

deleted at once;

> The charm fled not—she did not look behind;
> Soon trembling in her soft and chilly nest

('chilly'; no wonder).

At this point it seems better to give up the first line altogether, so it is cancelled and we start with the second, and go on

> She lay and had not seen her

also cancelled;

> She lay ~~and as~~ and till the poppied warmth of sleep

also cancelled; but it has contained an idea which is retained:

> She lay, in sort of wakeful swoon perplext

and this only requires transposition to serve

> In sort of wakeful swoon perplext she lay
> Util the poppied warmth of sleep opprest
> Her soothed Limbs, and Soul fatigued away;
> Flown like a thought until the morrow day;
> Blissfully havend both from joy and pain
> Shut like a Missal where swart paynims pray—

Several alternatives are tried, *Like a shut Missal*, *Like a clasp'd Missal*, and finally

> Clasp'd like a Missal where swart paynims pray—
> ~~Dead to~~ Blinded alike from Sunshine and from rain
> As though a rose should ~~shut close~~ shut and be a bud again.

The source of the missal has not been satisfactorily explained, but an interesting suggestion about it, which may be the solution and is certainly worth recording, was made by Professor F. N. Scott, of the University of Michigan:[1]

'If a certain missal was much written and talked about in literary circles at this time, and if further it was a missal that had been used by Christians dwelling among the swart paynims (all of whom, as good Mohammedans, are pretty regular in their praying), there is a chance that this was the book that touched the poet's imagination and supplied the simile.

'As it happens, a copy of a missal which meets these conditions is now in the British Museum. It appears in the catalogue as *Missale mixtum secundum regulam beati Isidori dictum Mozarabes. . . . In regali civitate Toleti* 1500. The character of this missal, and its repute among book fanciers of Keats's time, are indicated by notes upon Lord Spencer's copy at Althorp, in T. F. Dibdin's *Bibliotheca Spenceriana*.'

The account of the missal is in vol. i, pp. 135–144 of Dibdin's work; it is a printing of the 'Gothic' ritual, as

[1] In a letter to the *New York Evening Post*, May 3, 1911, quoted by AL, vol. ii, pp. 173, 4.

emended by St. Isidore, in the seventh century; and the significant sentence in Dibdin is:

> 'The overthrow of the Goths, by the Moors and Arabs, succeeded in the four following centuries: but although many of the former preferred exile to the Moorish government, yet, a great many of them, having a few churches granted them for the free exercise of their worship, continued to be mingled and domesticated with the conqueror; still using, but in a form probably somewhat corrupted, their Gothic ritual of worship.'

XXVIII

This stanza was as it were written backwards. The idea with which it opens is ultimately deferred till the fourth line, and the idea which occurs to Keats' mind last is ultimately chosen to open with. Keats starts *in medias res* with

> Her slumbrous breathing

and deletes it; then

> The listning Porphyro her breathing heard
> And when

and deletes that, and remembering the hero of the *Romance of the Forest* who heard the breathing, and Vivaldi in *The Italian* who as he listened was entranced and felt himself in Paradise, he writes

> The entranced Porphyro stol'n to Paradise

and deletes that; but by this experimental method, and by allowing association to work, the material has been assembled and it can now be arranged.

> Stoln to this Paradize and so entrance'd
> Porphyro gazed upon her empty dress
> And listen to her breathing, if it chanc'd
> To wake into a slumbrous tenderness
> Which when he heard ~~he breath'd himself~~
> that minute did he bless
> And breath'd himself: then from the closet crept
> Silent as Fear, and ? not with

But he decides to elaborate the simile of Fear, so that whatever he did not do disappears (the word is illegible from heavy deleting), and we have first

Silent as Fear amid a wilderness

then he experiments with *Noiseless* for *Silent* and goes back to *Silent* again but leaves both standing; then deletes *amid* and writes *in a wild* and then alters *wild* to *wide*, so that the line stands

Silent
Noiseless as Fear in a wide wilderness
And o'er the silent carpet hushing

changed to

And over the hush'd carpet silent stept
And tween the Curtains peep'd, and lo! how fast she slept

The second draft reads *where lo!* for *and lo!*

XXIX

Then by the bed side where the fading Moon
Made an illumed twilight soft he set
A Table light, and stilly threw theron
A Cloth of woven crimson gold and jet—

The third line is re-written as

A Table, and with anguish spread theron

and he continues:

O for some drowy morphean amulet
The boisterous midnight Clarions of the feast
~~Sounded though faint and far away~~
~~Came Sound in his ears~~
And kettle drums and far heard clarinet
Reach'd his scar'd ears.

But something now has to be done about the rhymes for the end of the stanza; so he goes back to the line about the Clarions, and first tries

Clarions of the Ball

and then

The boisterous midnight festive Clarions

and then returns to the line that he was engaged with and writes it as

> in
> Affray'd his ears though but ~~with~~ faintest tones:
> The Hall door shuts again and all the noise is gone

which means going back, making both the Clarions and the tones singular and then playing about with tenses, first making the last line past to suit *affray'd* and then making it present again and altering *affray'd* to suit it.

This stanza continued to exercise him more than most in his final revision. The moon becomes *faded*, and the illumed twilight becomes *a dim silver twilight*; *with anguish* becomes *half anguished*, and *faintest* becomes *dying*; and there is an extremely interesting alteration of *midnight* as an epithet of Clarion to *braying*. I suggested that as early as the first stanza Keats had *Hamlet* in his mind; and here again surely he is at Elsinore, hearing

> The *Kettle-drum* and trumpet thus *bray* out
> The triumph of his pledge.[1]

That this passage was running in his head will become clear beyond any reasonable doubt when we come to stanza XXXIX, but this reading of *braying*, which only George Keats records, seems to me decisive, since, though trumpets no doubt bray in other places in Shakespeare, they do not elsewhere bray in connexion with both Kettledrums, and wassailers, and a bloated King, and Rhenish.

XXX

This stanza starts with deceptive facility, but when we get to the feast of fruits there is as vexatious a time as with either the window or the undressing.

> ~~But~~
> ~~And still she slept:~~
> And still she slept an azure-lidded sleep
> In blanched linen, smooth and lavender'd;
> While he from forth the closet brough a heap
> Of candied ~~sweets~~ sweets with

[1] *Hamlet*, I. iv. 11.

then the sweets become first *fruits* and then specified fruits. For some of them he goes to *Romeo and Juliet*,

> *Lady Cap.* Hold, take these keys and fetch more spices, Nurse.
> *Nurse.* They call for *dates* and *quinces* in the pastry[1]

for some to *The Arabian Nights* passim, and for Samarcand and Fez pretty certainly to the great gazetteer in the eleventh book of *Paradise Lost*[2] (it is worth noticing that he keeps Milton's spelling of Samarc*h*and), and for the creamed curd perhaps to *The Winter's Tale*, 'The queen of curds and cream'[3] though the collocation is common enough.

> Of candied apple Quince and plumb and gourd
> With jellies soother than the dairy[4] curd
> And lucent syrups smooth with ?

dairy gets altered to *creamed* and *smooth* (if it is *smooth*) to *tinct*, but what the syrups were originally smooth with is a matter of conjecture. The word was clearly not at first *cinnamon*, even if there were any reason to suppose that cinnamon would make a syrup smooth. The word as it stands is *ciannamon* or, more probably, *crannamon* and one cannot help wondering whether Keats started with his cream here and then transferred it more appropriately to the curd in the line above.

But the complications increase when we get on to the more recondite confectionery. Keats starts

> And sugar'd dates ~~from~~ that o'er Euphrates fard

but after this there is such a welter of writing and re-writing and deletion in the draft that it is difficult to give any ordered notion of it. Keats is determined that he is going to have manna and dates; the dates are sometimes sugared and sometimes not; they are going to be (for rhyme) *transferred* from somewhere in something, but whether in Brigantine or Bragantine or Argosy is for long uncertain (the faring across Euphrates is given up almost as

[1] *R & J*, IV. iv. 1, 2.
[2] *Paradise Lost*, XI. 389, 403.
[3] *WT*, IV. iii. 161.
[4] HBF reads this word as *daisy*, I think wrongly.

soon as thought of). I fancy too that in the obscurity of the heaped fruit and the interlinear deletions there lurk some hitherto unsuspected peaches, though they had only a short life. There is no question that the provenance of the dates is to be Fez from the outset, and of the spiced dainties Samarchand; but there is a deal of hesitation as to what kind of Samarchand it is to be. First it was *wealthy*, and finally it was *silken*, but in the intermediate or cocoon stage heaven knows what it was. Buxton Forman thinks that the word is either *quilted* (with the surprising explanation that if silk is rich quilted silk is richer) or *guilded* (for *gilded*); I should read the word as *glutted*, which seems to me just possible for Keats, though not satisfactory. At any rate, after all the trouble, a feast of fruits is prepared to make the mouth water, and much more luscious than that repast about whose cooling there was no fear, which has been supposed, rightly or not, to be the model for it.[1]

And still she slept an azure-lidded sleep
  In blanched linen smooth and lavender'd;
While he from frorth the closet brough a heap
  Of candied apple Quince and plumb and gourd
  With jellies soother than the creamed curd
  And lucent syrups tinct with cinnamon
  Manna and daites in Argosy transferrd
  From fez—and spiced danties every one
From silken Samarchand to cedard lebanon

The second draft reads *brought from the cabinet* and *creamy*. And also, it will be remembered, adds the stanza which makes this one, which otherwise is no better than an ill-attached adornment, an integral part of the story.

XXXI

These Delicates with glowing hand he

but *heap'd* is going to be troublesome, so delete *he* and insert *he heap'd* before *with*; that at least is what Keats intended; but being in a hurry he inserts the words first

[1] *Paradise Lost*, v. 331 et seqq.

And kettle drum and far heard clarinet

~~Reaches his scared ear~~

Affray & his ears though but ~~with~~ in faintest t

The Hall door shuts again and all the noise i

~~And~~ But ~~still she slept~~:

And still she slept an azure-lidded sleep

In blanched linen, smooth and lavender'd

While he from forth the closet ~~brought~~ a hea

Of candied ~~sweet~~ ~~fruit~~ apple ~~with~~ quince and plumb and go

With jellies soother than the ~~sauce~~ creamed curd

And lucent syrups tinct with cinnamon

~~And sugared date~~

ar[go]sy Manna and daites in ~~Brigantine~~ ~~Manna and~~

sugared dates transfe

~~In Brigantine from Fez~~

From Fez - and spiced dainties every on

From ~~wealthy~~ silken Samarchand to cedared Leban

he heaped

These Delicates with glowing hand ~~he~~

On golden salvers and in baskets brigh

Of ~~twisted~~ wreathed silver: sumptuous they stan

Amid the quiet of St Agnes' night,

Filling the chilly room ~~with~~ with perfume li

And now - my love ~~~~ my seraph fair

Thou art my heaven and I thine Eremite

Open thine eyes for meek St. Agnes' sake

A PAGE OF THE HOLOGRAPH OF *THE EVE OF S*

Or I shall drowse beside thee, so my soul doth ache.

~~Thus clasping his warm unnerved arm~~
~~Sunk in her pillow. Shaded was her sleep~~
~~By the dusk curtains; & dreamless of alarm~~

~~And was~~
Then whispering his warm unnerved arm
Sunk in her pillow. Shaded ~~were~~ was her dreams
By the dusk Curtains! 'Twas a midnight charm
Impossible to melt as iced stream!
The lustrous salvers ~~in~~ the moonlight gleam
Broad golden fringe upon the carpet lies
~~Broad golden fringe lies wealthy on the~~

It ~~seem'd~~ he never never ~~could~~ redeem
From such a stedfast spell his lady's eyes
And ~~stood~~ mus'd awhile entoil'd in woofed
Phantasies

33

Awakening up, he took her hollow lute,
Tumultuous, and in chords that tenderest be
He play'd an ancient ditty long since mute
In Provence call'd La belle dame sans mercy
Close to her ear ~~he held~~ touching the Melody;
Wherewith disturb'd she utter'd a soft moan
He ceas'd -- ~~her breathing ceas'd~~ she panted quick -- and suddenly
Her blue half frayed eyes wide open shone --
Upon his knees he sunk pale ~~as~~ as smooth sculptured stone

N THE HARVARD UNIVERSITY LIBRARY

between *glowing* and *hand*, sees that it is wrong, and deletes the caret, but even so is too impatient to go back far enough, and inserts the new caret after *with*.

he heap'd
These Delicates with ‸ glowing hand
On golden salvers and in baskets bright
Of ~~twisted~~ wreathed silver—sumptuous they stand
Amid the quiet of St. Agnes' night,
And now saith he my seraph

But this is getting on too fast and besides is not going to provide a rhyme for *night*, so delete and elaborate on the fruit and the cold:

Filling the chilly room with perfume light
~~Teeming~~
And now saith he my Seraph may awake,

which is weak, and at once emended to

And now my Love, my Seraph fair awake!
Thou art my heaven and I thine Eremite
Open thine eyes for meek St. Agnes' sake
Or I shall drowse beside thee, so my Soul doth ache.

XXXII

We have had enough of Porphyro standing by his dessert; it is time he acted;

~~Thus~~ So whispering, his warm unnerved arms
Sunk in her pillow. Shaded was her sleep
By the dusk curtains; dreamless of alarms
And[1]

Then all this is deleted and a fresh start made:

Thus whispering his warm unnerved arm
Sunk in her pillow. Shaded ~~were~~was her dream~~s~~
By the dusk Curtains. 'Twas a midnight charm
Impossible to melt as iced stream!
The lustrous salvers ~~on~~ in the moonlight gleam
Broad golden fringe lies wealthy on the f
It seems he never neve can redeem
From such a stedfast spell his Lady's eyes

[1] The corner of this page is badly stained and the words hard to decipher. There is I think no doubt of the plural of both *arms* and *alarms*, and there was certainly a word written in above *sleep*, though I cannot decipher it.

So back two lines and secure the rhyme, and make a change of tense in the next line:

Broad golden fringe upon the carpet lies
It seemd he never neve could redeem
From such a stedfast spell his Lady's eyes
And ~~stood~~ mus'd awhile entoild in woofed Phantasies.

In the second draft the salvers become dishes, and the reading of the printed text *in the retired quiet of the night* is given by *X* in pencil in Woodhouse's second transcript.

The reminiscences of *The Arabian Nights* in these last four stanzas are I think quite unmistakable. In the introduction to Scott's edition Keats would find syrups, creams, and confections;[1] he would also find very exactly the broad gold fringe; 'cotton mattresses . . . over these a covering of *broadcloth* trimmed with *gold* lace and *fringes hanging over to the ground*'.[2] And he would find not only the supposedly anachronistic carpet on which the fringe lies, but also perhaps the matting of an earlier stanza; 'the terrace floor below the platform being first matted is covered with the finest carpets'.[3] In the tales themselves he would find apples, peaches, quinces, and gourds (though not plums), and spices.[4] He would find, in a passage quoted earlier, the 'baskets' of fruits,[5] and the setting of the table in others, e.g. 'the slave in a little time brought a collation of fruits upon a small silver table, which she set down'.[6] He would find innumerable carpets, and more fringes, here connected with the cloth for the table, 'He had an eating cloth bordered with rich fringe, and whenever any person was present about meal-time he used to call out to his black servant, 'Lay the fringed cloth!'[7] He would also find here, as well as in Milton, Euphrates[8] and Samarcand.[9]

[1] Scott, Intro., p. viii. [2] Ib., p. lxi. [3] Ib., p. lxii.

[4] Ib., vol. i, pp. 147, 148, 244; *Story of The Three Calenders* (and *passim*).

[5] Id., ii. 264. And compare also, for the *golden dishes*, 'a table in the middle covered with dried sweetmeats, the choicest and most exquisite fruits of the season, raised in pyramids, in seven gold basons'; iv. 208–9, *Story of Abou Hassan.*

[6] Id., ii. 445, *History of Aboul hassen and Schemselnihar.*

[7] Id., vi. 112, *Story of the Avaricious Cauzee.*

[8] Id., iv. 78, *History of Ganem.* [9] Id., i. 2.

XXXIII

Now, pursuing the ordinary sequence of *The Arabian Nights*, music is needed.

> Awakening up, he took her hollow Lute,
> Tumultuous, and in chords that tenderest be
> He play'd an ancient ditty long since mute
> In Provence call'd 'La belle dame sans mercy'[1]
> Close to her ear he held the Melody;

altered first to *he touch'd the Melody* and then to *touching the Melody*:

> Wherewith disturb'd she uttered a soft moan
> He ceas'd—her breathing ceas'd—and suddenly
> Her blue half-frayed eyes wide open shone:—
> Upon his knees he sunk pale as smooth sculpturd stone.

Her breathing ceas'd is changed to *she panted quick*; and in the second draft *half-frayed* is changed to the straightforward *affrayed* and *smooth* to *fair*. There is an interesting small point in the last line. The line actually stands

> Upon his knees he sunk pale, ~~as~~ as smooth sculpturd stone

with the comma deleted. I think that there can be no doubt that Keats first wrote *he sunk pale, as* . . . where *as* was not the preposition but the beginning of another word, probably *ashen*, and then deleted both this and the comma and completed the line as we have it.

Of the probable sources of this stanza so far as it is concerned with Madeline's frightened awakening enough has already been said, and in one of the passages from Mrs. Radcliffe we have the sinking to the knees. But for the rest of the last line there is another passage in Mrs. Radcliffe, which seems to me much the most

[1] Keats took the title from the title of a poem by the old French court poet Alain Chartier, which he knew, as Leigh Hunt tells us, in the translation ascribed to Chaucer. But neither here nor in his own poem of the same name did he take anything but the title.

significant of all as evidence of Keats' memories of her works:

> 'his countenance became fixed, and touched as it now was by the silver whiteness of the moonlight, he resembled one of those marble statues of a monument which seem to bend, in hopeless sorrow, over the ashes of the dead, shewn
>
> by the blunted light
> That the dim moon through painted casements lends[1]
>
> *The Emigrants*.'

XXXIV

The next stanza moves easily:

Her eyes were open but she still beheld
Now wide awake, the vision of her sleep :
There was ~~some~~ a painful change,—that nigh expell'd
The Blisses of her dream so pure and deep:
At which ~~she~~ ? [a deleted word, probably a jumble of a repeated *she* and *sighd*]
fair Madeline began to weep
And moan forth little words with many a sigh
While still her gaze on Porphro would keep
Who with an aching brow and piteous eye
Feared to move or speak she look'd so dreamingly—

In the second draft *witless*, which was written in the margin of the first draft, is substituted for *little*, and the last two lines read

Who knelt with joined hands and piteous eye
Fearing to move. . . .

XXXV

~~At length~~ she speaks, 'Ah Porpyro but
~~"Ah Porphyro, saith she but~~ even now
Thy voice was at sweet tremble ~~by~~ in mine ear
Made tuneable by every sweetest vow
And thy kind eyes were spiritual and clear
How change'd at thou how pallid, chill and drear

[1] *MU*, vol. i, p. 190 (c. vi, p. 38). Mrs. Radcliffe's acknowledgement of the source of the line and a half of verse led Miss Lowell, in her anxiety to convict Professor Shackford of inaccuracy, to attribute to Mrs. Radcliffe 'another book', otherwise unknown to literary history. The lines are from *The Emigrants, a Poem in Two Books*, by Charlotte Smith, London, 1793.

Give me that voice again my Porphiro!
Those looks immortal ~~and that~~
—— those complainings dear
O leave me not in this etenal woe
Ah! if thou diest my love I know not where to go!

Here I think he had in mind for the fourth line a line and a half which he had underlined in his Shakespeare

your tongue's sweet air
More tuneable than lark to shepherd's ear[1]

but this is altered in the second draft to

And tun'd devout with every softest vow.

And from this as well as one or two other instances one may guess that Keats was more keenly aware of his direct borrowings from Shakespeare than of those from others and took deliberate steps to modify them. The second draft opens the stanza with *Ah Porphyro said she*, makes Porphyro *cold* instead of *chill*, and his eyes *sad* instead of *kind*. In Woodhouse's first transcript a gap is left after *again* in the sixth line, and *X* has filled the gap with the remarkable reading *sweet Prospero*, and Buxton Forman notes, with even less explicability, that the insertion was probably made by Keats himself. On the opposite page *X* 'indulges the Muse' (one feels that that would have been his own phrase) on his own account, with

Give me again that voice's warbling flow

but this effort mercifully got no further than a pencilled note.

XXXVI

And now after the breathing-space of one or two stanzas which have more or less written themselves Keats comes to the climax of the action, which he knows must be handled with a rare combination of perfect delicacy and perfect firmness. And it is not going to be too easy. For the opening of the stanza he has recollections of Hippolitus who was tenderly *impassioned* by his lady's voice; and

[1] *MND*, I. i. 183.

Fleury who seemed 'passer en joye les regions des dieux'; and perhaps a passage in which 'in the *deep serene* of the heavens . . . the *stars* now seemed to *tremble*, and now to emerge with purer splendour'.[1] But for the conclusion of the stanza he has to rely on his own imagination and his own taste.

Impassion'd far beyond a mortal man
  At these voluptuous ~~words~~ accents he arose
Ethereal, ~~fulshd~~ flush'd and

At this point, *ethereal* having suggested a star, he goes back and transposes the two halves of line 1, and goes on

like a throbbing star

~~Was either~~

(a most mysterious opening, but I cannot make anything else of the second word)

Seen 'mid the sapphire heaven's deep repose
With her bright dream he m

Followed by

In her bright dream he m

and then

Into her dream he melted as the rose
Blendeth ~~her p~~ its perfume with the violet.

and then *perfume* deleted and *odour* substituted.

~~A ? as one~~
Solution sweet.

and this too deleted and nothing put in to fill the gap, and the line completed

Meantime the frost wind blows

~~Darkness~~
Like ? alarum pattering the sharp ?
Against the Casement gloom—St. Agnes moon had set.

Then he tries *Window's gloom* and then tries making first the casement and then *windows* dark, so that the line finally stands

Against the windows dark—St. Agnes moon had set.

[1] *MU*, vol. iii, p. 365 (c. xxxv, p. 69).

The second word in the eighth line was certainly not *Loves* at first and it would be interesting to find what it was. It appears to have begun *Lot*, but then *Loves* was so heavily written over it that conjecture is precarious. And the word at the end of the line is not in the least degree like *sleet*, though I see nothing else that it can have been meant to be.

Almost miraculously successful as this may seem to us, in giving the picture which Keats wanted to give, and yet not breaking the tone of the poem, it did not satisfy him, and in the second draft he changes the last two lines of the preceding stanza and recasts most of this, as follows:

> (Give me that voice again my Porphyro
> Those looks immortal those complainings dear)
> See while she speaks his arms encroaching slow
> Have zon'd her, heart to heart—loud, loud the dark winds blow.
> For on the midnight came a tempest fell.
> More sooth for that his close rejoinder flows
> Into her burning ear:—and still the spell
> Unbroken guards her in serene repose.
> With her wild dream he mingled as a rose
> Marryeth its odour to a violet.
> Still, still she dreams.—louder the frost wind blows,

(Woodhouse II reads *quick* for *close*.)

This alteration Keats showed to Woodhouse, as well as probably some more drastic ones of which we have no record; and the board of censors got to work. Some of the correspondence is worth giving, showing as it does the kind of temper in which Keats was working at the time of the revisions.

Woodhouse writes to Taylor on the 20th of September 1819, and says that a week earlier Keats had come to see him in town.[1]

> 'He wanted I believe to publish The Eve of St. Agnes & Lamia *immediately*: but Hessey told him it could not answer to do so

[1] The original letter is in the Pierpont Morgan Library in New York. I have quoted from it at some length since it seems to be of sufficient interest to deserve correct quotation. Sir Sidney Colvin quoted two sentences (SC, p. 366) with minor inaccuracies which do not affect the sense. Miss Lowell (AL, vol. ii, pp. 317–20) quoted it more or less *in extenso*, but with many errors.

now. I wondered why he said nothing of Isabella: & assured him it would please more than the Eve of St. Agnes—He said he could not bear the former now. It appeared to him mawkish. This certainly cannot be so. The feeling is very likely to come across an author on review of a former work of his own, particularly where the objects of his present meditations are of a more sobered & unpassionate character. The feeling of mawkishness seems to me to be that which comes upon us where anything of great tenderness & excessive simplicity is met with when we are not in a sufficiently tender & simple frame of mind to bear it: when we experience a sort of revulsion, or resiliency (if there be such a word) from the sentiment or expression. Now I believe there is nothing in the most passionate parts of Isabella to excite this feeling. It may, as may Lear, leave the sentiment far behind: but there is none of that sugar & butter sentiment, that cloys & disgusts.'

To us there is an odd irony in Woodhouse's innocent supposition that Keats' dissatisfaction with *Isabella* was in part due to the objects of his present meditations being of a more sobered and unpassionate character. When Keats wrote *Isabella* he did not know what passionate love was; when he came to revise *The Eve of St. Agnes* he knew all too bitterly well. No wonder that he felt as he did about *Isabella*. And how cynically amused he would have been at the mention in one breath of *Isabella* and *Lear*.

Woodhouse continues:

'He had the Eve of St. A. copied fair. He has made trifling alterations, inserted an additional stanza early in the poem to make the *legend* more intelligible, and correspondent with what afterwards takes place, particularly with respect to the supper and the playing on the Lute—he retains the name of Porphyro—has altered the last 3 lines to leave on the reader a sense of pettish disgust by bringing old Angela in (only) dead stiff & ugly. He says he likes that the poem should leave off with this change of sentiment—it was what he aimed at, & was glad to find from my objections to it that he had succeeded.—I apprehend he had a fancy for trying his hand at an attempt to play with his reader, and fling him off at last—I sho'd have thought he affected the 'Don Juan' style of mingling up sentiment and sneering: but that he had before asked Hessey if he co'd procure him a sight of that work, as he had not met with it, and if the E. of St. A. had not in all probability been altered before his Lordship had thus flown in the face of the public. There was another alteration, which I abused for 'a full hour by the *Temple* clock'. You know if a thing has a decent side I generally look no further—As the Poem was orig'y written, *we* innocent ones (ladies & myself) might very well have supposed that Porphyro, when acquainted with Madeline's love for him, & when 'he arose, Etherial flush'd &c. &c. (turn to it) set himself at once to persuade her to go off with him, & succeeded & went over the 'Dartmoor black' (now changed for some other place) to be married in right honest chaste & sober wise. But, as it is now altered, as soon as M. has confessed her love, P. winds by degrees his arm round her, presses breast to breast, & acts all the acts of a bonafide husband, while she fancies she is only playing the part of a Wife in a dream. This alteration is of about 3 stanzas; and tho' there are no improper expressions but all is left to inference, and tho' profanely speaking, the Interest on the reader's imagination is greatly heightened, yet I do apprehend it will render the poem unfit for ladies, & indeed scarcely to be mentioned to them among the 'things that are'. He says he does not want ladies to read his poetry: that he writes for men —& that if in the former poem there was an opening for a doubt what took place, it was his fault for not writing clearly & comprehensibly—that he sho'd despise a man who would be such an eunuch in sentiment as to leave a maid, with that character about her, in such a situation: & sho'd despise himself to write about it &c. &c. &c.—and all this sort of Keats-like rhodomontade.'[1]

Now Woodhouse's account of the alterations where it refers to what we have in front of us is precisely correspondent with it, both in the comment on the last three lines, and the alteration of Dartmoor, and the insertion of an additional stanza (which it will be noticed he differentiates from 'alterations'), and in the 'winds by degrees his arm round her, presses breast to breast'. And this makes us the more surprised when we read, 'This alteration is of

[1] There is one small point of interest in this letter, apart from the main point about the alterations; it shows that Taylor had either Keats' first draft or one of Woodhouse's transcripts to refer to; and this makes one wonder whether one can write an equation $X =$ Taylor; but I cannot see enough resemblance between X's hand and Taylor's to justify it.

about three stanzas'. The 'alterations' as we have them cover no more than the last two lines of one stanza and the first half of the next, and the second stanza as altered, moving as it does even farther in the direction of 'inference' and away from plain statement than the original, would surely have caused Woodhouse less rather than more distress. The conclusion is then that either Woodhouse meant three lines when he wrote three stanzas, and was quarrelling with the last two lines of stanza XXXV as altered, both of which seem improbable, or that there were at least two completely new (not altered) stanzas of which we have no trace. But this supposition when we come to look at it is not much more satisfactory, since to write two stanzas which shall describe the hero 'acting all the acts of a bonafide husband', and yet write them so that there 'are no improper [in Woodhouse's sense] expressions but all is left to inference' seems to be a task whose difficulty amounts to impossibility. It looks at first sight as though the connexion between the corrected stanzas as we have them told against the supposition that there were at one stage two completely new stanzas inserted at that point; but further consideration at least leaves room for doubt. It is true that the mention of the loud winds at the end of stanza XXXV is immediately followed by the explanatory 'For on the midnight rose a tempest fell' at the beginning of XXXVI. But there is an extremely abrupt transition from the slowly encroaching arms to the loud winds, there seems no very good reason why the tempest should make his *close rejoinder* more sooth, as *for that* implies, and the close rejoinder itself is more puzzling still, since none has yet been made, and before one is made, in the next stanza, there is a further reference to the winds. So that the transition which seemed at first so natural appears at least possibly to have been the result of a neat short-circuit operation, with the excision of the offending portion. In view of the fact that Woodhouse's account of the alterations corresponds so exactly to the alterations that we have down to the description of the encroaching arms, but then contains a phrase which corresponds if anything more accurately to the unoffending first draft than to the second as we have it, one would have little doubt that Keats in his anti-mawkish, anti-Isabella mood, being determined that this poem at least was not going to be 'weak-sided' and that a touch of realism would stiffen it, a touch let us say more in the vein of Boccaccio than he had permitted himself in the first draft, wrote two explicit stanzas that would put his meaning beyond doubt, and that he then in deference to Woodhouse destroyed them and patched things up as best he could, flinging, I cannot help feeling, a half-contemptuous sop to the rather mild Cerberus, who was insisting on the position being regularized without delay, in the shape of the odd alteration of the *blendeth* of the first draft to the *marryeth* of the second. Woodhouse could at least have the word if he could not have the fact. But Woodhouse's description of the stanzas as leaving all to inference still presents a difficulty which I suggested earlier; and in the upshot one must leave the matter open to conjecture.[1]

XXXVII

'Tis dark—still pattereth the flaw-blown sleet[2]
'This is no dream my Bride! my Madeline
'Tis dark the iced gusts still rave and beat
'No dream Alas! Alas! and woe is mine
Porphyro will leave me here to fade and pine
~~Ah~~ cruel! What traitor could thee higther bring?
I curse not for my heart is lost in thine
Though thou forsakest a deceived thing
A silent mateless dove with sick unpuned wind'

[1] It will be observed that Woodhouse's phrase, 'acts all the acts of a bonafide husband, while she fancies she is only playing the part of a wife in a dream', corresponds much more exactly to the passage in the *Philocope* than to the second draft as we have it.

[2] This is the accepted interpretation of the holograph, but it is far from satisfactory. The last word but two is no doubt finally *flaw*, but it started life as *fa* . . . or *fo* . . . (possibly, indeed, *foam*) with a hyphen after it which has been overwritten by the *b* of *blown*, and the word which is read as *sleet* is, if that is what it is meant to be, unbelievably badly written, even for Keats; it is also quite unlike the word read as *sleet* in the last stanza. If either of them is *sleet* the other has no right to be. But having no better suggestion to offer I leave it as it is.

But the last two lines do not satisfy him and he tries first

> Though thou shoudst leave forsaken a deceived thing

perhaps with some notion that that may do for the Alexandrine, and then cuts out *shoudst leave* but without altering *forsaken* back to *forsakest*. Then he puts in a mysterious *To* before the opening of the last line, deletes the word, and re-writes as

> A Dove folorn and lost with sick unpuned wind.

XXXVIII

> My Madeline! ~~the~~ Dark is this wintry night

Yes, no doubt. But the readers know all about that already, unless Keats has wholly failed in his description; and so, one may suppose, does Madeline. So continue the apostrophe

> My Madeline! Sweet Dreamer! Lovely bride!
> Say, may I be for aye thy vassal blest?
> Thy Beauty's shield, heart-shapd and vermil ~~died~~dyed?
> Ah silver shrine by thee will I take rest

which deletions and insertions turn into

> Ah silver shrine here will my take rest

but I think we may reasonably guess that what Keats meant to leave was

> here will I take my rest

(perhaps with an echo in his mind of

> here
> Will I set up my everlasting rest[1])

> After so many hours of toil and quest
> With tearful(?) features pale and mournful Pilgrim's weeds

But that unhappily has a foot too much, so it is reduced first to

> Pale feautred and in mournful Pilgrim's weeds

[1] *R & J*, v. iii. 110.

and then to

> Pale feautred and in weeds of Pilgrimage
>
> I have found but will not rob thy downy nest!
> Soft Nightingale, but keep thee in a cage

followed by

> Though I have found I can not rob thy nest!
> Soft Nightingale, I'll keep thee in a cage

and then

> I have found but can not rob thy downy nest!
> Soft Nightingale, I'll keep thee in a cage
> To sing to me—but hark! the blended tempest's rage!

(with perhaps a reminiscence of Lear's 'we two alone will sing like birds i' the cage')[1]

The second draft has a recast of this:

> (After so many hours of toil and quest)
> A famish'd pilgrim, save'd by miracle.
> Though I have found, I will not rob thy nest
> Saving of thy sweet self, if thou thinkst well
> To trust, fair Madeline, to no rude infidel.

XXXIX

> Hark! ~~the~~ 'tis an elfin Storm from fairy land
> Of haggard-seeming, ~~but, my love, to us~~
> but a boon in ~~truth~~
> deed
> Arise my Love—the morning is at hand—
> The bloated Wassailers will never heed:
> Let us away my Love with happy speed—
> ~~Over the moors~~ [he is not ready for the moors yet]
> There are no ears to hear, or eyes to see
> Drown'd all in Rhenish and the drench of mead

changed successively to

> the drenching mead
> the sleepy mead.

[1] *King Lear*, v. iii. 9.

partly because *drenching* echoes the sound of *Rhenish* too closely;

> Put on warm cloathing sweet, and fearless be
> Over the bleak Dartmoor I have a home for thee

Then he goes back to line 3 and in view of the *my love* in line 5, substitutes a second *Arise*, and in the last line writes *the dartmoor blak.* But he leaves the prosaic comicality of the warm clothing.

In the second draft he gets rid of this, and also of the too specific localization of the scene, and the last two lines appear as

> Awake, arise, my Love and fearless be
> For o'er the Southern moors I have a home for thee.

In this stanza there are reminiscences of Mrs. Radcliffe, and the *chasse toute crainte* of Fleury, and very clearly of the same passage from *Hamlet*[1] that has already been noticed in connexion with the kettle-drums. Claudius in another passage is the *bloat* king,[2] and when we read

> The King doth wake tonight and takes his rouse,
> Keeps *wassail*, and the swaggering upspring reels;
> And as he drains his draughts of *Rhenish* down
> The *kettle drum* and trumpet thus *bray* out
> The triumph of his pledge

and add from *Macbeth*

> in swinish sleep
> Their *drenched* natures lie as in a death[3]

we cannot feel much doubt that Keats' memory is stored with Shakespearean material to be drawn upon at need.

XL

Keats has been sailing in fairly calm waters for two or three stanzas, but troubles now begin again:

> She hurried at his words, beset with fears
> around
> For there were sleeping dragons all ~~about~~ ;
> Or perhaps at glaring watch with ready spears

[1] *Hamlet*, I. iv. 11. [2] Ib. III. iv. 182.
[3] *Macbeth*, I. vii. 67.

and then to avoid the *p'raps* he deletes *Or* and transposes,

> At glaring watch perhaps with ready spears
> ~~Well~~ Down the wide Stairs a darkling way they found
> heard no
> In all the house was ~~not a~~ human sound,
> ~~But~~
> ~~Though every~~
> ~~But noise of winds besieging the high towers~~(?)
> ~~But the b~~
> ~~But the besieging Storm~~

But he is getting almost as tired of this as of the Boddice, and he gives up the *besieging* motif altogether for the moment, and tries what can be done with lamps.

> ~~The Lamps were flickering death shades on the walls~~
> ~~Without, the Tempest kept a hollow roar~~
> ~~The Lamps were flickring~~
> ~~The Lamps were dying in~~
> ~~But here and there a Lamp was flicking out~~

but at least he has defined for himself the two main ideas of tempest and lamps, so one more attempt, making, with the assistance of Mrs. Radcliffe, or Coleridge,[1] the lamp a hanging one, and remembering the agitations of the arras in *The Romance of the Forest*.[2]

> A drooping Lamp was flicking here and there

but still not right, so

> A chain-droop'd Lamp was flicking by each door
> The Arras ~~flutterd~~ rich with horsemen hawk and hound
> Flutter'd, with cold

but the cold is irrelevant to the fluttering, so why not now go back to *besieging*?

> Flutter'd, in the besieging wind's uproar
> And the long Carpets rose along the gusty floor

XLI

> Like Spirits into the wide-paven hall
> They glide, and to the iron porch in haste

This has the two relevant features of the Radcliffean

[1] *Christabel*, 182.

[2] *RF*, vol. i, c. ii, p. 37 (c. ii, p. 20).

castle, but Keats sees how to make the lines more emphatic by repetition, and emends to

They glide like Phantoms into the wide hall,
  Like Phantoms to the iron porch they glide
Where lay the Porter in uneasy sprawl
  Whith a large empty beaker by his side.

Then he tries *slept* for *lay* but rejects it in favour of *lay* again, and goes on

The wakeful Bloodhound rose and shook his hide
And paced round Madeline all angerless

which will do for the moment till the demands of rhyme have to be satisfied

~~The Chains are loos'd the~~
~~The Chains are~~
By one and one the easy bolts back slide

He wavers backwards and forwards between this and

By one and one the bolts full easy slide

with several deletions and restitutions, and then continues

~~Silent~~
~~Across the pavement lie the heavvy chains~~
The Chins lay silent on the footworn stones
The key tuns, and the Door upon its hinges groans

This has been a bad stanza, and he is weary of it, as the hurried misspellings in the last two lines testify; but it has to be finished somehow, and he goes back to the sixth line to make it rhyme, and finds more trouble waiting.

But with a calmed eye his Mistress owns

followed by

But his unangerd[1] eye his Mistress owns

but this will not do, since there is no reason at all to suppose that Madeline was the mistress of the castle watch-dog, and plenty of reason to suppose the contrary, so

But his unangerd eye an inmate owns

And so for the moment this trying stanza rested. In the second draft the beaker becomes *huge*, and the eye *sagacious*.[2]

[1] *unangerd* is uncertain; *angerless* gives it a certain probability, but *calmed* has intervened; and I have a suspicion that the word is *assured* or *assuaged*.

[2] Woodhouse was in trouble with this stanza. He could not read either

XLII

And now, in sight of the end, Keats finds less trouble.

And they are gone—Aye, ages long ago
These Lovers fled into a night of Storms
That night the Baron dreamt of many a woe
And all his warrior ~~saw~~ Guests with shades and forms
Of Witches Deamons and large ~~charnal~~coffin worms
Were long benighmare'd. Angela ~~ne'er told~~
the old
Died palsy twitch'd with meagre face deform
The Beadsman after thousand aves told
For aye unsought for slept among his ashes cold—

The only difficulties are in the second and third lines, with *night* occurring twice. First I think he tried *into a Morn of Storm* and then changed the second *night* to *Morn* and reverted to *night* in the second line, to give the picture of the lovers escaping in the darkness and the Baron sleeping on benightmared long after they have gone. Finally the plurals are all turned into singulars, and *long* with too little consideration altered to *all* and the stanza for the moment left. It is perhaps worth while giving it in full again, since here we have the atmosphere, the temper, in which Keats wished to leave his poem when he first wrote it in January of 1819. It is a conclusion perfectly in key with the tone of all that has gone before.

And they are gone—Aye, ages long ago
These Lovers fled into the night of Storm
That Morn the Baron dreamt of many a woe
And all his warrior Guests with shade and form
Of Witch and Deamon and large coffin worm
Were all benighmare'd. Angela the old
Died palsy twitch'd with meagre face deform
The Beadsman after thousand aves told
For aye unsought for slept among his ashes cold—

In the second draft, in a mood, one may guess, more in key with *The Cap and Bells* than with *The Eve of St.*

unangerd, or whatever the word is, nor *inmate*, so takes the last readings that he can make out, *calmed* and *Mistress*. But he very oddly reads *quick his calmed* and the *footway* stones.

Agnes, Keats altered the end of this stanza, so that the poem concludes

Angela went off
Twitch'd by the palsy—and with face deform
The Beadsman stiffen'd—'twixt a sigh and laugh
Ta'en sudden from his beads by one weak little cough

The following is *The Eve of St. Agnes* as I believe Keats himself left it after his revision of September 1819, and before his publishers began to 'adopt which (reading) they liked and to revise the whole'; it is the British Museum transcript, with no other alterations than those of three obvious errors, 'tiard' for 'tiara', 'tim'd' for 'tun'd', and 'found' for 'heard'.

St. Agnes' Eve—Ah bitter chill it was!
The Owl for all his Feathers was acold;
The hare limped trembling thro' the frozen grass,
And silent was the flock in woolly fold:
Numb were the beadsman's fingers while he told
His rosary, and while his frosted breath
Like [pious] incense from a censer old,
Seem'd taking flight for heaven without a death
Past the sweet Virgin's Picture, as his prayer he saith.

His prayer he saith, this patient, holy Man,
Then takes his lamp and riseth from his knees
And back returneth, meagre, barefoot, wan,
Along the chapel aisle by slow degrees:
The sculptur'd dead on each side seem to freeze,
Emprison'd in black purgatorial rails:
Knights, Ladies, praying in dumb Orat'ries
He passeth by and his weak spirit fails
To think how they may ache in icy hoods and mails.

Northward he turneth through a little door,
And scarce three steps, ere Music's golden tongue
Flatter'd to tears this aged Man and Poor:
But no—already had his death bell rung;
The joys of all his life were said and sung:
His was harsh penance on St. Agnes' Eve:
Another way he went and soon among
Rough ashes sat he for his Soul's reprieve,
And all night kept awake for sinners' sake to grieve.

That ancient Beadsman heard the prelude soft;
And so it chanc'd, for many a door was wide
From hurry to and fro. Soon, up aloft,
The silver snarling trumpets 'gan to chide:
High-lamped chambers, ready with their pride
Were glowing to receive a thousand guests:
The carved angels, ever eager-eyed
Star'd where upon their heads the cornice rests,
With hair blown back, and wings put crosswise on their breasts.

At length burst in the argent revelry,
With tiara and plume and rich array,
Numerous as shadows haunting fairyly
The brain, new stuff'd, in youth with triumphs gay
Of old romance. These let us wish away,
And turn sole thoughted, to one Lady there
Whose heart had brooded, all that wintry day,
On love and winged St. Agnes' saintly care,
As she had heard old Dames full many time[s] declare.

They told her how upon St. Agnes' Eve
Young virgins might have visions of delight,
And soft adorings from their love receive
Upon the honied middle of the night,
If ceremonies due they did aright:
As, supperless to bed they must retire,
And couch supine their beauties lily white;
Nor look behind nor sideways, but enquire
Of heaven with upward eyes for all that they desire.

'Twas said her future lord would there appear
Offering as sacrifice—all in the dream—
Delicious food even to her lips brought near:
Viands and wine and fruit and sugar'd cream,
To touch her palate with the fine extreme
Of relish: then soft music heard; and then
More pleasures followed in a dizzy stream
Palpable almost: then to wake again
Warm in the virgin morn, no weeping Magdalen.

Full of this whim was thoughtful Madeline:
The music yearning like a god in pain
She scarcely heard; her maiden eyes divine,
Fixed on the floor, saw many a sweeping train
Pass by—She heeded not at all—in vain
Came many a tiptoe, amourous Cavalier,
And back retired; not cool'd by high disdain,
But she saw not: her heart was otherwhere:
She sigh'd for Agnes' dreams the sweetest of the year.

She danc'd along with vague uneager eyes,
Anxious her lips, her breathing quick and short.
The hallowed hour was near at hand: she sighs
Amid the timbrels, and the throng'd resort
Of whisperers in anger and in sport;
Mid looks of love, defiance, hate and scorn,
Hood wink'd with faery fancy; a la mort,
Save to St. Agnes and her lambs unshorn,
And all the bliss to be before to-morrow morn.

So purposing each moment to retire,
She lingere'd still. Meantime, across the moors,
Had come young Porphyro, with heart afire
For Madeline. Beside the portal doors,
Buttress'd from moonlight, stands he, and implores
All saints to give him sight of Madeline,
But for one moment in the tedious hours,
That he might gaze and worship all unseen;
Perchance speak, kneel, touch, kiss—in sooth such things have been.

He ventures in: let no buzz'd whisper tell:
All eyes be muffled, or a hundred swords
Will storm his heart love's fev'rous citadel:
For him those chambers held barbarian hordes
Hyena foemen, and hot blooded Lords,
Whose very dogs would execrations howl
Against his lineage: not one breast affords
Him any mercy, in that mansion foul,
Save one old Beldame, weak in body and in Soul.

Ah! happy chance! the aged creature came,
Shuffling along with ivory headed wand,
To where he stood hid from the torches flame,
Behind a broad hall pillar, far beyond
The sound of Merriment and chorus bland:
He startled her; but soon she knew his face,
And grasped his fingers in her palsied hand,
Saying, "Mercy Jesu! hie thee from this place;"
"They are all here to-night, the whole bloodthirsty race."

Get hence! Get hence! there 's dwarfish Hildebrand:
He had a fever late, and in the fit
He cursed thee and thine both house and land:
Then there 's that old Lord Maurice, not a whit
More tame for his grey hairs—Alas me! flit!
Flit like a Ghost away"—"Ah Gossip dear,
We're safe enough; here in this arm chair sit,
And tell me how"—"Good Saints! not here, not here;
Follow me child or else these stones will be thy bier."

He follow'd through a lowly arched way
Brushing the cobwebs with his lofty plume,
And as she utter'd "Wella—well-a-day!"
He found him in a little moonlight room,
Pale, lattice'd, chill, and silent as a tomb.
"Now tell me where is Madeline" said he,
"O tell me Goody by the holy loom
Which none but secret sisterhood may see
When they St. Agnes wool are weaving piously."

"St. Agnes! Ah! it is St. Agnes' Eve—
Yet Men will murder upon holy days:
Thou must hold water in a witch's seive,
And be liege lord of all the Elves and Fays,
To venture so about these thorny ways
A tempting Be'lzebub:—St. Agnes' Eve!
God's help! my Lady fair the conjuror plays
This very night: good Angels her deceive,
But let me laugh awhile, I've mickle time to grieve."

Feebly she laugheth in the languid Moon,
While Porphyro upon her face doth look,
Like puzzled Urchin on an aged Crone,
Who keepeth clos'd a wondrous riddle book
As spectacled she sits in chimney nook.
Sudden his eyes grew brilliant, when she told
His Lady's purpose; and he scarce could brook
Sighs, at the thought of those enchantments cold:
Sweet Madeline asleep in lap of Legends old.

Sudden a thought came fullblown like a rose,
Heated his brow, and in his pained heart
Made purple riot: then doth he propose
A stratagem, that makes the beldame start:
A cruel Man and impious thou art:
Sweet Lady, let her pray and sleep and dream
Alone with her good angels, far apart
From wicked Men like thee: O christ, I deem
Thou canst not surely be the same that thou didst seem.

"I will not harm her; by the great St. Paul,
Sweareth Porphyro; "O may I ne'er find grace,
When my weak voice shall unto heaven call,
If one of her soft ringlets I displace,
Or look with ruffian passion in her face:
Good Angela beleive me by these tears:
Or I will, even in a Moments space,
Awake with horrid shout my foemen's ears
And beard them, though they be more fange'd than wolves and bears.

"How canst thou terrify a feeble Soul?
A poor, weak, palsy-stricken, churchyard thing,
Whose passing bell may ere the midnight toll;
Whose prayers for thee, each morn and evening,
Were never miss'd"—Thus plaining doth she bring
A gentler speech from burning Porphyro;
So woeful, and of such deep sorrowing,
That Angela gives promise she will do
Whatever he shall wish, betide her weal or woe.

Which was, to lead him, in close secrecy,
Even to Madeline's chamber, and there hide
Him in a closet, if such one there be;
That he might see her beauty unespied,
Or win perhaps that night a peerless bride,
While legione'd fairies pac'd the Coverlet,
And pale enchantment held her sleepy eyed.
Never on such a night have lovers met
Since Merlin pay'd his demon all the monstrous debt.

"It shall be as thou wishest:" said the Dame:
All cates and dainties shall be stored there
Quickly on this feastnight: by the tambour frame,
Her own lute thou wilt see:—no time to spare,
For I am slow and feeble and scarce dare
On such a catering trust my dizzy head:
Wait here my child with patience: kneel in prayer
The while: sooth thou must needs the Lady wed,
Or may I never leave my grave among the dead."

So saying, she hobbled off with busy fear.
The lovers endless minutes quickly passed;
The dame return'd, and whisper'd in his ear
To follow her, with aged eyes agast
From fright of dim espial. Safe at last,
Through many a dusky gallery, they gain
The Maiden's chamber silken, hush'd, and chaste;
Where Porphyro took covert, pleas'd amain:
His poor guide hurried back with agues in her brain.

Her fault'ring hand upon the Ballustrade,
Old Angela was feeling for the stair,
When Madeline, St. Agnes' charmed Maid,
Rose, like a spirit to her, unaware:
With silver taper['s] light, and pious care
She turn'd, and down the aged gossip led
To a safe level matting. Now prepare,
Young Porphyro; a gazing on that Bed;
She comes, she comes again, like ring dove fray'd and Fled.

Out went the taper as she floated in;
Its little smoke in pallid moonshine, died:
She clos'd the door, she panted, all a kin
To spirits of the air, and visions wide:
No uttered syllable, or woe betide:
But to her heart, her heart was voluble,
Paining with eloquence her balmy side;
As though a tongueless nightingale should swell
Her throat in vain, and die, heart-stifled in her dell.

A casement high and triple arch'd, there was,
All garlanded with carven imag'ries
Of fruits, and flowers, and bunches of knot-grass,
And diamonded with panes of quaint device;
Innumerable of staines and splendid dyes
As are the tiger moths deep damask'd wings;
And in the midst, 'mong thousand heraldries,
And twilight saints, and dim emblazonings
A shielded scutcheon blush'd with blood of Queens and Kings.

Full on this casement shone the wintry moon,
And threw warm gules on Madeline's fair breast,
As down she knelt for heaven's grace and boon:
Rose bloom fell on her hands together prest,
And on her silver cross, soft amethyst,
And on her hair a glory, like a Saint;
She seem'd a splendid angel, newly drest
Save wings, for heaven:—Porphyro grew faint:
She pray'd, too pure a thing, too free from mortal taint.

Anon his heart revives: her vespers done,
Of all its wreathed pearls her hair she frees;
Unclasps her warmed jewels, one by one;
Loosens her fragrant boddice; by degrees
Her rich attire creeps rustling to her knees:
Half hidden, like a Mermaid in sea weed,
Pensive awhile she dreams awake, and sees
In fancy fair St. Agnes in her bed,
But dares not look behind or all the charm is fled.

Soon trembling in her soft and chilly nest,
In sort of wakeful swoon, perplexed she lay,
Untill the poppied warmth of sleep oppress'd
Her soothed limbs and soul fatigued away:
Flown, like a thought, until the morrow day;
Blissfully haven'd both from joy and pain;
Clasp'd like a Missal, where swart Paynims pray,
Blinded alike from sunshine and from rain,
As though a rose should shut and be a bud again.

Stol'n to this Paradise and so entranc'd,
Porphyro gaz'd upon her empty dress,
And listene'd to her breathing if it chance'd
To wake into a slumbrous tenderness;
Which when he heard that minute did he bless,
And breathed himself: then from the closet crept,
Noiseless as fear in a wide wilderness,
And over the hush'd carpet, silent, stept,
And 'tween the curtains peep'd, where lo!—how fast she slept.

Then by the bed side, where the faded Moon
Made a dim silver twilight, soft he set
A table, and, half anguished, threw thereon
A cloth of woven crimson, gold, and jet:—
O for some drowsy morphean amulet!
The boisterous, braying, festive clarion,
The kettle drum and far heard clarinet,
Affray his ears though but in dying tone:—
The Hall door shuts again, and all the noise is gone.

And still she slept an azure-lidded sleep,
In blanched linen, smooth, and lavender'd,
While he brought from the cabinet a heap
Of candied apple, quince, and plum, and gourd;
With jellies soother than the creamy curd,
And lucent syrup[s], tinct with cinnamon:
Manna and dates, in Argosy transferr'd,
From Fez: and spiced da[i]nties, every one,
From silken Samarcand to cedar'd Lebanon.

These delicates he heape'd with glowing hand
On golden dishes, and in baskets bright
Of wreathed silver: sumptuous they stand
In the retired quiet of the night,
Filling the chilly room with perfume light.—
And now my love my seraph fair awake!
Thou art my heaven, and I thine Eremite:
Open thine eyes for meek St. Agnes' sake,
Or I shall drowse beside thee, so my soul doth ache."

Thus whispering, his warm, unnerved arm
Sunk in her pillow. Shaded was her dream
By the dusk curtains: 'twas a midnight charm
Impossible to melt as iced stream:
The lustrous salvers in the moonlight gleam;
Broad golden fringe upon the carpet lies:
It seem'd he never, never could redeem
From such a stedfast spell his Lady's eyes;
So mus'd awhile, entoil'd in woofed Phantasies.

Awakening up, he took her hollow lute,—
Tumultuous,—and in chords that tenderest be,
He play'd an ancient ditty long since mute,
In provence call'd "La belle dame sans merci:"
Close to her ear touching the melody;—
Wherewith disturbe'd, she uttere'd a soft moan:
He cease'd—she panted quick,—and suddenly
Her blue affrayed eyes wide open shone:
Upon his knees he sunk pale as fair sculptur'd stone.

Her eyes were open, but she still beheld,
Now wide awake, the vision of her sleep:
There was a painful change, that nigh expell'd
The blisses of her dream so pure and deep:
At which fair Madeline began to weep,
And mourn forth witless words with many a sigh
While still her gaze on Porphyro would keep;
Who knelt, with joined hands and piteous eye(s),
Fearing to move or speak, she look'd so dreamingly.

"Ah, Porphyro!" said she "but even now
Thy voice was at sweet tremble in mine ear,
And tun'd, devout, with every softest vow;
And those sad eyes were spiritual and clear:
How chang'd thou art! how pallid, cold and drear!
Give me that voice again, my Porphyro;
Those looks immortal, those complainings dear!"
See while she speaks his arms encroaching slow
Have zon'd her, heart to heart—loud, loud the dark winds blow.

For on the midnight came a tempest fell.
More sooth for that his close rejoinder flows
Into her burning ear:—and still the spell
Unbroken guards her in serene repose.
With her wild dream he mingled as a rose
Marryeth its odour to a violet.
Still, still she dreams.—louder the frost wind blows,
Like love's alarum pattering the sharp sleet
Against the window panes: St. Agnes' moon hath set.

'Tis dark: still pattereth the flaw blown sleet:
"This is no dream my Bride, my Madeline!"
'Tis dark: the iced gusts still rave and beat:
"No dream alas! alas! and woe is mine!
Porphyro will leave me here to fade and pine.—
Cruel what traitor could thee hither bring?
I curse not for my heart is lost in thine
Though thou forsakest a deceived thing;—
A Dove forlorn and lost with sick unpruned wing."

"My Madeline! Sweet dreamer! lovely Bride!
Say may I be, for aye, thy vassal blest?
Thy beauty's shield heart shaped and vermeil dyed?
Ah silver shrine, here will I take my rest
After so many hours of toil and quest,
A famished Pilgrim,—sav'd by miracle
Though I have found, I will not rob thy nest
Saving of thy sweet self; if thou thinkst well
To trust, fair Madeline, to no rude Infidel."

"Hark! 'tis an elfin storm from faery land
Of haggard seeming, but a boon indeed:
Arise arise! the morning is at hand:—
The bloated wassaillers will never heed:—
Let us away my love with happy speed;
There are no ears to hear, or eyes to see,—
Drown'd all in Rhenish and the sleepy mead:
Awake! Arise! my love and fearless be
For o'er the southern Moors I have a home for thee."

She hurried at his words, beset with fears,
For there were sleeping dragons all around,
At glaring watch, perhaps, with ready spears—
Down the wide stairs a darkling way they found.
In all the house was heard no human sound.
A chain droop'd lamp was flickering by each door;
The Arras rich with horseman hawk(e) and hound,
Fluttered in the beseiging winds uproar;
And the long carpets rose along the gusty floor

They glide, like Phantoms, into the wide Hall;
Like Phantoms, to the iron porch, they glide;
Where lay the Porter, in uneasy sprawl,
With a huge empty beaker by his side:
The wakeful Bloodhound rose, and shook his hide
But his sagacious eye an inmate owns:
By one and one the bolts full easy slide:—
The chains lie silent on the footworn stones;—
The key turns, and the door upon its hinges groans—

And they are gone: aye ages long ago
These lovers fled away into the storm.
That night the Baron dreamt of many a woe,
And all his warrior guests, with shade and form
Of witch, and demon, and large coffin worm,
Were all benightmar'd. Angela went off
Twitch'd with the Palsy; and with face deform
The beadsman stiffen'd, twixt a sigh and laugh
Ta'en sudden from his beads by one weak little cough.

V. *THE ODES TO PSYCHE, TO A NIGHTINGALE, TO MELANCHOLY* [1]

KEATS' own account of the *Ode to Psyche* is as follows: 'The following Poem—the last I have written is the first and the only one with which I have taken even moderate pains. I have for the most part dash'd off my lines in a hurry. This I have done leisurely—I think it reads the more richly for it and will I hope encourage me to write other things in even a more peaceable and healthy spirit.'[2] This suggests some rather curious reflections, seeing that the Ode was copied out on the 30th of April 1819.[3] Either Keats had forgotten all about *The Eve of St. Agnes* and the way he wrote it, or he had strange notions of what constituted 'moderate pains'. But I incline to think that the contrast which Keats felt between his methods here and those of earlier poems, the contrast which made him feel as though he was turning over a new technical leaf, was one not so much between careless and careful as between slow and fast composition. It is as though he were measuring 'pains' not by amount of energy but by amount of time expended. And *The Eve of St. Agnes*, for all the care that went into it, does yet bear throughout the marks of rapid composition. Whereas

[1] Of the five Odes written in the spring of 1819 I have selected only three for examination, as illustrating three different aspects of Keats' craftsmanship. The study of the other two, particularly that *On a Grecian Urn*, is of the utmost importance in examining the development of Keats' thought, but does not, I think, throw much additional light on his methods of presenting that thought.

[2] MBF, 114 (367).

[3] Not the 15th, as H. Buxton Forman says. The exact chronology of the Odes is difficult to determine, and not, I think, by external evidence determinable, except as regards *To Autumn*. There is plenty of evidence to assign the other five to the spring of 1819, but nothing to fix their relative order. It is usually assumed that the *Ode to Psyche* is the earliest (even though the first hint of the *Ode on Indolence* is in the same journal letter under the date March 19th (MBF, 114 (339)) and for this assumption the internal evidence seems to me overwhelming. The form of the *Ode to Psyche* appears to be a stage in the development of the stanzaic form of the other Odes, and that Keats should have reverted from that finished form to the irregularities of the *Ode to Psyche* is an almost untenable supposition. I am adopting therefore the usual assumption.

this Ode, though we have not the material which would enable us to watch its growth, has about it just the richness which Keats thought he found in it and which he attributed to 'leisurely' composition. And if Keats' own account is correct, and we have seen reason to trust his accounts of his own processes, this Ode is a most significant milestone in his poetic progress. In writing it he had passed beyond the stage in which the writer is dominated by the imperative, and sometimes almost feverish, instinct to get something down on paper and then hurry to correct and shape it. The trouble with this method is that from the moment when a phrase or a line or two are committed to paper the idea seems to have taken on an embodiment from which it can never after wholly escape. There may be alterations and modifications, but they are alterations and modifications within limits which may be found cramping. It is as though a sculptor with the main lines of a group conceived in his imagination should too hurriedly commit himself to executing it in marble, and then find that without doubt it should have been a bronze. He can modify his composition as he goes along, no doubt, and secure a measure of consonance between design and material, but he knows that it will never be what it should have been; and yet it requires a kind of heroism almost superhuman to discard all the result of his labours and start again. But more leisurely composition tends to keep the pen for longer from the paper, and therefore the ideas and the words in which they are trying to find expression more floating or fluid in the mind, till the idea finds, almost as it were of itself, its inevitable expression. How far Keats had learned his lesson it is impossible to tell. We should need to have before us an undoubted first draft written in the more leisurely mood; and, as I hope to show, there is every reason to suppose that the holograph of the *Ode to a Nightingale* is not the first draft which it has been supposed to be, and no reason to suppose that the holograph of *To Autumn* is the first draft except possibly of the second stanza. But even in that stanza, though there is no question that Keats is composing as he writes, there is yet not the air of hurry that marks the more 'hit-or-miss' stanzas of *The Eve of St. Agnes.* And about all the poems from this time on there is, I think, observable something of that 'richness' which Keats thought he had secured in the *Ode to Psyche* by composing it slowly.

As we have studied *The Eve of St. Agnes* in considerable detail, and shall be watching again Keats' methods of verbal 'carpentry' in the *Ode to a Nightingale* and in *To Autumn*, and as such study easily becomes wearisome, I propose for examination in this Ode no more than some examples of that process of 'distillation' by which Keats manages to concentrate in one line or phrase the full rich essence of images which have hitherto found only partial expression in scattered passages in his earlier work.

At the very beginning of his career there is a picture of May flowers:

> And let long grass grow round the *roots* to keep them
> Moist, *cool* and green (*I stood* . . . 32)

Then there is a passage in *Endymion* in which he thinks of white flowers scattered on a dark-blue background as being like eyes:

> 'Tis *blue*, and over-spangled with a million
> Of little *eyes*, as though thou wert to shed,
> Over the darkest, lushest blue-bell bed,
> Handfuls of daisies. (i. 629)

Then there are two lines in *Hyperion*, which connect fragrance, the one with coolness, and the other with quietness:

> And like a rose in vermeil tint and shape,
> In *fragrance* soft, and *coolness* to the eye (i. 209)

> Where a sweet clime was breathed from a land
> Of *fragrance*, *quietness*, and trees, and flowers
> (ii. 263)

Let us just add to these one line from the *Epistle to George Keats*:

> Crowned with flowers purple, white, and red (88)

And then ask whether there is anything essential in those pictures which is not given in the two perfect lines of the *Ode to Psyche*:

> Mid hush'd, cool-rooted flowers, fragrant eyed,
> Blue, silver-white, and budded Tyrian[1]

And we may notice in passing how the first of these lines together with the next line of the Ode

> They lay calm breathing on the bedded grass

are in turn compressed into

> My head cool-bedded in the flowery grass

of the *Ode to Indolence*, and how various earlier phrases, '*soft* dimpled *hands*',[2] 'fingers *soft* and round',[3] '*soft slumber*'[4] and '*soft closer* of our eyes'[5] are all summed up in the two words *soft-handed slumber*.

And so we arrive at the incense. Keats' imagination has always been full of pictures of incense and of vessels swinging. The room in which Adonis sleeps is

> Full of light, *incense*, tender minstrelsy (*End.* ii. 390)

in *The Eve of St. Agnes* is the

> pious *incense* from a *censer* old (11)

and in *Hyperion*

> *incense teeming* up
> From man to the sun's God (i. 167)

then there is the passage in '*I stood tiptoe . . .*' in which the incense is connected with a temple

> A hymn from Dian's *temple*; while upswelling,
> The *incense* went to her own starry dwelling (197)

Then there is the venerable priest in *Endymion*, and

> From his right hand there *swung* a vase, milk-white
> (i. 153)

and the '*chain*-drooped lamp' in *The Eve of St. Agnes*.

[1] In the letter, *Blue, freckle-pink, and budded Syrian.*
[2] '*Woman! when I behold thee . . .*', i. 16.
[3] *Sleep and Poetry*, 333.
[4] *End.* ii. 329.
[5] *Sleep and Poetry*, 11.

And the essence of all those is compressed into a line and a half

> no incense sweet
> From chain-swung censer teeming.

No wonder that with this power of 'distillation' at work the poem has about it a richness new in Keats' work, and wholly different from that lusciousness, the product of an unchecked exuberance, which marked, and often marred, his earlier work. He has learned how to make the true attar, and though he may not always succeed in making it, he is never again going to be content with anything more dilute.

The *Ode to Psyche* is a milestone also (if a milestone can emulate Sir Boyle Roche's bird) in regard to quite another side of Keats' poetic development, and that the more purely technical. Up to this time, for all of his work which he thought fit to publish, with the sole exception of the three Hymns and the Song to Sorrow in *Endymion* (and in two even of those the irregularities amount to no more than the occasional shortening of a line), he has used as the vehicle for his poetry metres at once regular and recognized. With the exception of one or two trivialities such as *To Hope* he has confined himself to the couplet, decasyllabic and other, using the decasyllabic variety always in its looser form with varying success; *ottava rima*, making a deliberate, though only partly successful, attempt to modify its natural characteristics into suitability for his purpose; blank verse after the Miltonic manner, with all the success that could be expected to attend an effort that was against the grain; the Spenserian stanza, at first in a weakly imitative way, and then quite lately with a superb mastery of a type far more closely knit than the original; and both forms of sonnet, first the Petrarchan exclusively, and then mainly the Shakespearean. But now, in the letter in which he copied the *Ode to Psyche*, he shows himself for the first time attempting a considered metrical experiment. The experiment begins in a dissatisfaction with both the accepted sonnet forms; it leads to the form of the

Ode to Psyche; and it ends by equipping him with one of the most perfect verse forms in English. For a detailed exposition of this experiment I cannot do better than refer the reader to pp. 73–97 of Mr. Garrod's *Keats*,[1] where he will find a model of what such technical analysis can be, should be, and so lamentably seldom is. But I will give a summary of the experiment here, partly because I want to venture a doubt as to whether Mr. Garrod is correct in his interpretation of Keats in one point which is I think of some interest, though it does not at all affect the main issue. In the journal letter to George and Georgiana Keats of February–May, 1819,[2] there occur under the date April 30 three sonnets. Of these the second only is in regular form (Shakespearean). The first, *On Fame* ('How fever'd is that man . . .'), starts out regularly enough with two Shakespearean quatrains and then surprises us with a Petrarchan (strictly speaking pseudo-Petrarchan) sestet, with the rhyme-scheme *e f e g g f*, though it was apparently originally intended to have the scheme *e f e f f e*, that is to be a sestet curiously composed of a third quatrain with two lines rather awkwardly appended and linked by a kind of upside-down rhyme.

On Fame

How fever'd is that Man who cannot look
  Upon his mortal days with temperate blood
Who vexes all the leaves of his Life's book
  And robs his fair name of its maidenhood
It is as if the rose should pluck herself
  Or the ripe plum finger its misty bloom
As if a clear Lake meddling with itself
  Should cloud its pureness with a muddy gloom.
But the rose leaves herself upon the Briar
For winds to kiss and grateful Bees to feed
And the ripe plumb still wears its dim attire
The undisturbed Lake has crystal space—
Why then should man teasing the world for grace
Spoil his salvation by a fierce miscreed

[1] *Keats*, by H. W. Garrod; Clarendon Press, 1926.
[2] MBF, 114 (365–7).

The third sonnet also starts with an illusive appearance and forecast of normality, *a b a b c d c d* in the ordinary Shakespearean form; and then the sestet very literally 'surprises by himself', since at first sight, and taken in isolation, it seems to have the rhyme-scheme *e f g h g h*, i.e. to consist of two lines rhyming neither with each other nor with anything else, followed by a third quatrain. But when instead of listening forward, as at the opening of either third Shakespearean quatrain or Petrarchan sestet we naturally do, we listen back, we find that the first of the apparently unattached lines ends with the *b* rhyme of the first quatrain, and the second with the *c* rhyme of the second quatrain, so that the complete rhyme-scheme of this odd fourteen-line poem is *a b a b c d c d b c e f e f*.

To Sleep

O soft embalmer of the still midnight
  Shutting with careful fingers and benign
Our gloom-pleas'd eyes embowered from the light,
  Enshaded in forgetfulness divine—
O soothest sleep, if so it please thee close
  In midst of this thine hymn my willing eyes,
Or wait the amen, ere thy poppy throws
  Around my bed its dewy Charities—
Then save me or the passed day will shine
Upon my pillow breeding many woes:
  Save me from curious conscience that still lords
Its strength for darkness, borrowing like a Mole—
  Turn the key deftly in the oiled wards
And seal the hushed Casket of my soul

Then in the letter comes the *Ode to Psyche*, and after it Keats writes:

'Incipit altera Sonneta.

I have been endeavouring to discover a better Sonnet Stanza than we have. The legitimate does not suit the language over-well from the pouncing rhymes—the other kind appears too elegiac—and the couplet at the end of it has seldom a pleasing effect—I do not pretend to have succeeded—it will explain itself.'

And then follow fourteen lines of verse, which may or may not be effective, but which, unless any fourteen decasyllabic lines, loosely linked together by any haphazard rhyme-scheme, are to be called a sonnet, have no right to pass under that appellation. Here is their rhyme-scheme, *a b c a b d c a b c d e d e*; and here are they:

> If by dull rhymes our English must be chaind
> And, like Andromeda, the Sonnet sweet,
> Fetterd, in spite of pained Loveliness;
> Let us find out, if we must be constrain'd,
> Sandals more interwoven and complete
> To fit the naked foot of poesy;
> Let us inspect the Lyre, and weigh the stress
> Of every chord, and see what may be gain'd
> By ear industrious, and attention meet;
> Misers of sound and syllable, no less
> Than Midas of his coinage, let us be
> Jealous of dead leaves in the bay wreath crown,
> So, if we may not let the muse be free,
> She will be bound with Garlands of her own.

What Keats is doing here is to carry a Miltonic experiment unwisely beyond the point at which Milton himself, with his practised instinct, knew that the development of the sonnet had reached its limit. Milton, for all that he wrote at least one, and perhaps two, of the greatest of English sonnets, was never happy in the form; and it is characteristic of that impatience of restraint which led him in his work first to discard rhyme, and then, in the choruses of *Samson Agonistes*, even regular metre, that he should prefer to the Shakespearean the greater freedom of the Petrarchan form, and that, finding a restriction even there in the break between the octave and the sestet, he should take with alacrity a hint from della Scala, and run on at the end of the octave. But even so, though the octave and sestet are linked, they are still octave and sestet, and the Miltonic sonnet has a recognizable and vertebrate structure. Of the three sonnets of Keats which we have been examining the first has a structure which is clear, though novel; the second a structure which is clear (when we discover it), though odd; and the third no structure at all.

Now if we compare the first two of these three sonnets with the *Ode to Psyche* we find some unexpected points of resemblance, which put it beyond doubt that Keats is basing his Ode form upon his modification of the sonnet form. The Ode as written out in the letter consists of three sections, lines 1–23, 24–35, 36–67. The first fourteen lines of the poem correspond almost exactly in rhyme-scheme with the first of the sonnets as first written. We have two Shakespearean quatrains followed by a pseudo-Petrarchan sestet on two rhymes; but the sestet is better knit than that of the sonnet, the scheme being not *efeffe* but *effeef* so that there is no danger of its looking like a quatrain.[1] The next nine lines of the first section are metrically in the nature of an appendage, consisting as they do of one inorganic line, two couplets, and a quatrain. But one can hardly help suspecting a stage of composition in which the brooklet did not run but *was*, and so the fifteenth line was organic, not in a sestet but in a septet. If that is so we can see Keats making already a tentative advance towards that insertion of an additional line which is his crowning technical achievement in *To Autumn*.

> O Goddess hear these tuneless numbers, wrung
>   By sweet enforcement and remembrance dear,
> And pardon that thy secrets should be sung
>   Even into thine own soft-chonched ear!
> Surely I dreamt to day; or did I see
>   The winged Psyche, with awaked eyes?
> I wander'd in a forest thoughtlessly,
>   And on a sudden, fainting with surprise,
> Saw two fair Creatures couched side by side
> In deepest grass beneath the whisp'ring fan
> Of leaves and trembled blossoms, where there ran
>   A Brooklet scarce espied
> 'Mid hush'd, cool-rooted flowers, fragrant eyed,

[1] I am taking the reading of the letter, *fan*, in line 10, since otherwise we are left with an 'inorganic' line.

Blue, freckle-pink, and budded Syrian [? for *Tyrian*]
They lay, calm-breathing on the bedded grass;
Their arms embraced and their pinions too;
Their lips touch'd not, but had not bid adieu,
As if disjoined of soft-handed slumber,
And ready still past kisses to outnumber
At tender eye dawn of aurorian love.
The winged boy I knew:
But who wast thou O happy happy dove?
His Psyche true?

The next twelve lines are three straightforward quatrains; that is, if one cares to put it so, they are a Shakespearean sonnet without its final couplet.

O lastest born, and loveliest vision far
  Of all Olympus faded Hierarchy!
Fairer than Phoebe's sapphire-region'd star,
  Or Vesper amorous glow worm of the sky;
Fairer than these though Temple thou hadst none,
  Nor Altar heap'd with flowers;
Nor virgin choir to make delicious moan
  Upon the midnight hours;
No voice, no lute, no pipe no incense sweet
  From chain-swung Censer teeming—
No shrine, no grove, no Oracle, no heat
  Of pale-mouth'd Prophet dreaming!

The next fourteen lines are an oddly exact parallel to the second of the two sonnets. They consist, as that sonnet at first sight appeared to consist, of two quatrains, followed by two inorganic lines, followed by another quatrain. But the two lines, though not so closely linked as the two lines in the sonnet were found to be, are not wholly unattached, since they throw back, though by correspondence, not by rhyme, and outside the confines of the 'sonnet', to lines in the last section.

O Bloomiest! though too late for antique vows;
  Too, too late for the fond believing Lyre,
When holy were the haunted forest boughs,
  Holy the Air, the water and the fire:

Yet even in these days so far retir'd
From happy Pieties, thy lucent fans,
Fluttering among the faint Olympians,
I see, and sing by my own eyes inspired.
O let me be thy Choir and make a moan
Upon the midnight hours;
Thy voice, thy lute, thy pipe, thy incense sweet
From swinged Censer teeming;
Thy Shrine, thy Grove, thy Oracle, thy heat
Of pale-mouth'd Prophet dreaming!

The next fourteen lines (50–63) are described by Mr. Garrod as 'a normal Shakespearean sonnet save that the end-couplet follows the octave instead of following the sestet', but I think that this, though of course technically accurate, somewhat obscures what Keats was doing, particularly since the couplet coming at that point, and being moreover run-on to the following line, does not at all give the effect of the final couplet. Keats here is surely trying yet another form of the modification which he has already tried twice. He wants a break after the octave. He has tried the break (in the sonnet) of two lines rhyming back to the octave; he has tried the break with two lines not rhyming with anything, though recalling earlier lines; and now he will try the effect of a couplet at that point. The poem ends with the appendage of a final quatrain differentiated from its predecessor, and given the air of finality, by the shortening of the second and fourth lines.

Yes I will be thy Priest and build a fane
In some untrodden region of my Mind,
Where branched thoughts new grown with pleasant pain,
Instead of pines shall murmur in the wind.
Far, far around shall those dark cluster'd trees
Fledge the wild-ridged mountains steep by steep,
And there by Zephyrs streams and birds and bees
The moss-lain Dryads shall be lull'd to sleep.
And in the midst of this wide-quietness
A rosy Sanctuary will I dress
With the wreath'd trellis of a working brain;
With buds and bells and stars without a mane; (for '*name*')

With all the gardener, fancy e'er could feign
Who breeding flowers will never breed the same—
And there shall be for thee all soft delight
That shadowy thought can win;
A bright torch, and a casement ope at night
To let the warm Love in.

But now, before we go on to examine the third stage of Keats' experiment let us go back to the letter and see why he was experimenting at all, and what in his opinion were the defects of the two recognized sonnet forms which he wished to modify. Mr. Garrod, following, as I judge from a footnote, Sir Sidney Colvin's edition of the letters, quotes Keats as follows: 'I have been endeavouring to discover a better sonnet stanza than we have. The legitimate (i.e. the Petrarchian) does not suit the language over well from the pouncing rhymes; the other kind appears too elegiac, and the couplet at the end of it seldom has a pleasing effect.' With that punctuation, whereby the 'too elegiac' and 'the couplet' are united in contrast to the 'pouncing rhymes', there is only one interpretation, and Mr. Garrod is of course justified in his bracketed equation of 'legitimate' with Petrarchan. He is I think less happy in his explanation of why Keats found the Petrarchan rhymes 'pouncing'. But in any event that is not what Keats wrote, though whether the differences between Keats and Sir Sidney Colvin's amended Keats involve a difference of interpretation will be a matter of opinion. Keats wrote, 'The legitimate does not suit the language over-well from the pouncing rhymes—the other kind appears too elegiac—and the couplet at the end of it has seldom a pleasing effect—I do not pretend to have succeeded—it will explain itself.' Now if that sentence ended at 'effect', and was written by any one but Keats, there could be no doubt of the way to take it; the dashes will mark a parenthesis and we shall have: 'The legitimate does not suit the language over-well from the pouncing rhymes (the other kind appears too elegiac) and the couplet at the end of it has seldom a pleasing effect.' But unfortunately Keats uses the dash as a kind of punctuatory maid-of-all-work, as the latter part of the sentence illustrates. So that all we can be sure of is that there is nothing in the sentence as written to compel us to connect the 'couplet' with the other and 'too elegiac' kind unless we want to do so on other grounds. We can equally well assume that 'the other kind appears too elegiac' is a parenthesis in which Keats is dismissing the Petrarchan form from consideration as he had almost entirely dismissed it from his practice. On general probabilities, what is Keats likely to have meant? Prima facie I should have supposed him a little more likely, in view of his attitude towards Shakespeare, and his adoption of the Shakespearean sonnet form, to have described that form as 'the legitimate', rather than the Petrarchan. 'Elegiac' is a vague word on which to base much of a conclusion. If Keats meant by it 'similar to Gray's Elegy' that of course settles the whole question; but he may as easily have been using a word without any very clear definition to describe the effect which one or the other type of sonnet produced on him, and I should be inclined to feel 'elegiac' a more natural description of the grave and sometimes almost melancholy sonority of the Petrarchan form than of the 'snappier' effect which the alternating rhymes of the Shakespearean quatrains tend to produce. There remain the 'pouncing rhymes'. Mr. Garrod, with his reading of the sentence, has of course no alternative to distract him; he has only to explain why the rhymes of the Petrarchan form are pouncing; which he does as follows:

> 'What he says of the "pouncing rhymes" of the Petrarchian sonnet is directed, I suppose, to the effect of hurry and grab which is sometimes given by the restriction of the octave to two rhymes, and by the fact that, while lines 2–3 and 6–7 are couplet rhymes, 4–5 also make a kind of spurious couplet. A "pouncing" manner, of course, easily results from the bad rhymes to which English is sometimes reduced from want of enough rhyming words to satisfy the demand of a two-rhyme octave.'

Now if we are committed in advance to the presumption

that the 'pouncing' rhymes are those of the Petrarchan form, that is as convincing explanation as can be given. But I do not feel that it is wholly satisfactory, nor that Mr. Garrod is too happy about it himself. In the first place no doubt English is sometimes, from paucity of rhyming words, reduced to bad rhymes; but I am not clear that it is of the nature of bad rhymes to produce an effect that can be called 'pouncing', or indeed any effect but that of irritating anti-climax. Next, what precisely is this effect of 'hurry and grab' which Mr. Garrod says is sometimes given by the restriction of the octave to two rhymes, and by the incidence of those rhymes? This is purely a matter of opinion, and I should be disposed to trust Mr. Garrod's ear at least as readily as my own; but I feel myself a kind of insinuating suavity in the interlocking chime of the Petrarchan octave which is about as far removed as anything can be from hurry and grab. Finally, the 'hurry and grab' and the bad rhymes are, even on Mr. Garrod's showing, only 'sometimes' present. No form is immune from faults when handled by an incompetent artist; but Keats' whole argument surely implies that he is worried by, and proposes to reform, defects which are not incidental to but inherent in the form, defects which either cannot (like the final couplet) or can hardly (like these pouncing rhymes) be avoided, not defects which may sometimes by ineptitude be introduced. Now it is beyond question that the Shakespearean form does with the required inevitability produce a particular effect, however that effect may be described, and I should have thought that the rapid *tick-tack*, *tick-tack*, *tock-tuck*, *tock-tuck* of the alternating rhymes, often emphasized by the monosyllabic rhyme words, was more naturally described as 'pouncing' than the interlacing of the Petrarchan form. It seems then at least possible that the only specific objection which Keats makes to the Petrarchan sonnet is that it is too elegiac (whatever that means), that the Shakespearean form is the 'legitimate', and that it is this form which suffers from the pouncing rhymes, as it is certainly this form which is marked by the final couplet. As against this it must be noticed that in his experiments, in the three sonnets we have examined, in the *Ode to Psyche*, and in the finished stanza form of the other Odes, the one thing which Keats seems resolute to discard is the Petrarchan octave, while he admits, except in the *Andromeda* sonnet, the Shakespearean quatrain, though he never, except once in the *Ode to Psyche*, has more than two quatrains in succession, and in the other Odes not even two.

However, it is clear that, for whatever respective reasons, Keats was dissatisfied with both sonnet forms, and that his experiments, whether in single sonnets, or in an Ode which may be regarded as a loosely connected series of variously reformed sonnets, have not hitherto been very encouraging. The *Fame* and *Sleep* sonnets were awkward; the *Ode to Psyche*, having neither the free irregularity of the 'Pindaric' ode, nor the finished regularity of Keats' own Odes that are to follow, fell unhappily between two stools and gave an uneasy impression of trying to be recurrent and failing; while the *Andromeda* sonnet, in a serious attempt to find out 'sandals more interwoven and complete', did little more than set the naked foot of poesy shuffling in ill-shapen and indeterminate carpet-slippers.

It looks as though from this time on Keats abandoned the sonnet as incorrigible; but he did not at all abandon his search for a verse form which should satisfy him, a stanza form which, while capable of that structural strength which comes from the correspondence of stanza with stanza, should yet avoid monotony, and should offer reasonable freedom of movement within the stanza. And this form, from the experience of his sonneteering experiments, he triumphantly created. All the four great Odes which follow that to Psyche have a stanza which consists of a Shakespearean quatrain followed by a Petrarchan sestet. The only variations are that in the *Nightingale* Ode one line in the sestet is shortened, and that there is some diversity on the rhyme-scheme of the sestets. The *Nightingale* Ode is the only one which holds steadily to one scheme throughout, the scheme being the straightforward *c d e c d e*; the *Ode on Indolence* holds the same scheme for four stanzas, but in the fifth has *c d e d c e*, and in the last *c d e c e d* (one of the only two cases in the Odes in which the final rhyme is not the *e* rhyme); the *Ode on Melancholy* holds it for two stanzas and then breaks in the last to *c d e d c e*; while the *Ode on a Grecian Urn* cannot settle down to any one scheme; it has the *c d e d c e* in the first and last stanzas, the 'normal' *c d e c d e* in the third and fourth, and the unusual *c d e c e d* in the second.[1]

The creation of this stanza was a noteworthy technical achievement. It gave Keats just what he wanted as a vehicle of expression, avoiding the defects which he felt in the two sonnet forms. In whichever form he found 'pouncing' rhymes he is rid of them, since he has discarded the Petrarchan octave and all but one of the Shakespearean quatrains; by the same stroke he is rid of the 'too elegiac' character; and he has discarded the final couplet. Let us set out one of the stanzas and examine its effect:

> Who are these coming to the sacrifice?
>   To what green altar, O mysterious priest,
> Lead'st thou that heifer lowing at the skies,
>   And all her silken flanks with garlands drest?
> What little town by river or sea shore,
>   Or mountain-built with peaceful citadel,
>   Is emptied of this folk, this pious morn?
> And, little town, thy streets for evermore
>   Will silent be; and not a soul to tell
>   Why thou art desolate, can e'er return.

There is no question about the first four lines; they have the neatness, concision and completeness which belong to any quatrain. But the effect of the remainder of the stanza is more subtle, and more interesting. If we are

[1] Mr. Garrod here makes one of his very rare errors, and in so doing obscures the variety of the sestets. He says that three of the four Odes hold to *c d e c d e*, except for a slip in the last stanza of *Melancholy*, while the *Ode on a Grecian Urn* holds to *c d e d c e*.

considering the stanza in isolation, and not as one of a series of a known form, we cannot tell when we reach the end of the sixth line whether we are merely in the middle of a second quatrain. But when we reach the end of the seventh line we get a very pleasant disappointment of the half-expectation with which we were rather uneasily awaiting the rhyme to the fifth line, and we get also a sense of space. We know that whatever happens there must be at least three more lines to come before the stanza can be rounded off, and our ear is led to expect the rounding off to be that of the sestet; and the expectation is pleasantly fulfilled. Here then is the stanza which Keats developed from the two sonnet forms; and we can observe with admiration how he contrives to make the best of both worlds. By shortening his stanza to ten lines, and employing the sestet, he gets rid at one stroke of the repetitive monotony of three successive quatrains and the over-clinching effect of the final couplet. On the other hand, in the Petrarchan sonnet the sestet tends to be over-weighted by the octave, and the beauty of its rhyme-scheme tends to lose emphasis since it has too near a resemblance to the scheme of the octave. But in Keats' stanza the quatrain leads on to the fuller movement of the sestet, and the snap of the rhymes of the quatrain is a piquant contrast to and preparation for the slide of the rhymes of the sestet. And when we see the sestet thus more isolated than in the sonnet we become more aware of one of its peculiar beauties, the combined certainty and smoothness of the conclusion. The couplet jars to a halt with the brakes grinding; the sestet, with the foreseen second recurrence of the third rhyme, swings gently up into the wind and picks up its buoy.

This stanza Keats invented, and used in four of his six great Odes, with certain variations, all of them I think deliberate, and not accidental slips, in the rhyme-scheme of the sestet, and the shortening of one of the lines in each stanza of the *Ode to a Nightingale*. When it has once been done, it looks, like many other notable inventions, obvious enough. How considerable a technical achievement it was we realize, I think, more clearly by seeing what happens when an inferior technician tries his hand at a somewhat similar experiment. For *The Scholar Gipsy* and *Thyrsis* Matthew Arnold adopted a stanza which also consists of quatrain and sestet, but both are Petrarchan, and the sestet precedes the quatrain. The result is a curiously invertebrate stanza. The sestet, in the first place, overweights the quatrain, much in the same way as the octave is apt to overweight the sestet in the full Petrarchan sonnet, and in the second place the rhyme-scheme of the Petrarchan quatrain unfits it for a conclusion. The stanzas do not come to an end which the ear expects and with which it is satisfied; they merely drift uneasily to a standstill. It looks as though Matthew Arnold became aware of the awkward balance between sestet and quatrain; but his remedy is worse than the disease. In fourteen of the twenty-five stanzas of *The Scholar Gipsy* he has a heavier break at the end of the fifth line than at the end of the sixth. That is, in those stanzas he is not writing sestet-quatrain at all, but two quintets, rather feebly and awkwardly linked by the sixth line repeating the rhyme of the first. This stanza form has some merits; it has a certain easy and pensive fluency and from the very indecisiveness of the conclusion there is an easy slide from stanza to stanza. But it is a flaccid thing beside the firm and strongly articulated stanza of Keats. Here is an example of it:

Here, where the reaper was at work of late,
In this high field's dark corner, where he leaves
His coat, his basket, and his earthen cruise,
And in the sun all morning binds the sheaves,
Then here, at noon, comes back his stores to use;
Here will I sit and wait,
While to my ear from uplands far away
The bleating of the folded flocks is borne,
With distant cries of reapers in the corn—
All the live murmur of a summer's day.

And here, to set against it, is Keats. Let us take the type that also has the shortened line, which Keats, with his sure instinct, uses where it is most telling, but which he evidently thought an unnecessary and restless variation, since he uses it only in the *Nightingale* of the five 'regular' Odes.

> Darkling I listen; and for many a time
>   I have been half in love with easeful Death,
> Call'd him soft names in many a mused rhyme,
>   To take into the air my quiet breath;
> Now more than ever seems it rich to die,
>   To cease upon the midnight with no pain,
>   While thou art pouring forth thy soul abroad
>   In such an ecstasy!
>   Still wouldst thou sing, and I have ears in vain—
>   To thy high requiem become a sod.

One would have supposed that that stanza was achievement enough for any craftsman however exacting, for any critic of his own work however severe. But it did not satisfy Keats, and we find him four months later, in the poem *To Autumn*, adding the final touch which turned excellence into perfection. The firm opening quatrain is the same, with the strong break at the end of it. And we continue as before till the fifth line of the 'sestet' which now becomes a septet, since the sixth line, which we have learned to expect to conclude the stanza, does not give us the concluding rhyme, but rhymes with the fifth; and this slight disappointment of expectation, this slight suspense which is created by a couplet which we know cannot be the conclusion, leads us with an even more complete satisfaction, like that at the resolution of a discord, to the serene finality of the concluding rhyme.

> Who hath not seen thee oft amid thy store?
>   Sometimes whoever seeks abroad may find
> Thee sitting careless on a granary floor,
>   Thy hair soft-lifted by the winnowing wind;

Or on a half-reap'd furrow sound asleep,
Drows'd with the fume of poppies, while thy hook
Spares the next swath and all its twined flowers;
And sometimes like a gleaner thou dost keep
Steady thy laden head across a brook;
Or by a cyder-press, with patient look,
Thou watchest the last oozings hours by hours.

ODE TO A NIGHTINGALE

Before we come to an examination of the *Nightingale* Ode, and the light it throws upon Keats' methods of composition, it seems necessary to look for a moment at the status of what is accepted as the 'first draft' of the poem. There are two half-sheets of paper in the Houghton-Crewe collection[1] on which, in Keats' writing, is the Ode, very nearly as printed, but containing a number of alterations, three or four of them of great interest. There is an article by Sir Sidney Colvin in the Keats memorial volume[2] in which he states categorically of this document, 'that we have in it Keats's true and original draft is certain'. And Professor de Sélincourt says[3] that 'Mr. Colvin proves conclusively that the Keats MS. which he reproduces is the original draft, written while the main and essential work of composition was going on in the poet's brain'. It is of course infinitely tempting to regard these two sheets as the first draft; in any case they are of interest, but if they are the first draft they are of first-rate interest and importance. But we ought not to be tempted to disregard evidence or the absence of it. What then could be regarded as evidence that any document was the first draft of a poem? Of external evidence we might have first the poet's own assurance recorded on the document itself. This would, I suppose, be the only absolutely convincing evidence. Or we might have a description by the poet or by some one else of the first draft, and find that the document before us corresponded to the description in such salient particulars that there was no reasonable

[1] Now in the Fitzwilliam Museum at Cambridge.
[2] MV, 65–73.
[3] de S, 473.

doubt of its identity. As to internal evidence there is none that can be regarded as proof. The most that internal evidence can do is to establish probabilities. Heavy correction implies earliness. If the corrections are not merely of isolated words but are a matter of false starts immediately corrected, and recastings of material, the presumption is that we are dealing with a very early draft. No one, for example, who looks at the manuscript of Milton's *At a Solemn Musick* in the library of Trinity College, Cambridge, has any doubt that there we see the development of that poem from somewhere at least very near the stage of the rough block of marble to the finished statue; and few people I imagine have much doubt, remembering Keats' own account of his methods, that the holograph of *The Eve of St. Agnes* is the first draft, since the corrections are heavy, heavier than Keats is likely to have made except while composing; a great number of them are of a kind that could only have been made, by Keats or any one else, while actually composing; and, finally, the physical characteristics of the document correspond to Keats' description of the paper he took down to Bedhampton. But whatever the probabilities, and however strong, it would be a bold man who would say that there was conclusive *evidence* that either of the two holographs is the first draft. On the other hand, the absence of heavy correcting does not prove much. If the writer is one who, where we can watch him at work elsewhere, corrects freely, a draft with only light corrections is likely to be late. But it is a mere matter of probability. It may be merely that he was in an unusually fluent mood, or had done more work than usual in his head, or what not.

Now the only external evidence that there is about this draft of the *Ode to a Nightingale* is some remarks of Brown, who says this:

> 'In the spring of 1819 a nightingale had built her nest near my house. Keats felt a tranquil and continual joy in her song; and one morning he took his chair from the breakfast table to the grass-plot under a plum-tree, where he sat for two or three hours.

When he came into the house, I perceived he had some scraps of paper in his hand, and these he was quietly thrusting behind the books. On inquiry, I found those scraps, four or five in number, contained his poetic feeling on the song of our nightingale. The writing was not well legible; and it was difficult to arrange the stanzas on so many scraps. With his assistance I succeeded, and this was his *Ode to a Nightingale.*'

Sir Sidney Colvin, assuming from internal evidence that the document before us is the first draft, says that we can use it to check the accuracy of Brown's recollections,[1] and comes to the heroic conclusion that Brown recollected 'accurately in the main, though not in all particulars'. What are the facts? Brown speaks of four or five scraps; the document consists of two sheets of note-paper of ordinary size. Brown speaks of the difficulty of arranging the stanzas on so many scraps. Sir Sidney Colvin explains Brown's difficulty as follows:

'The order of the stanzas, as Brown indicates, is puzzling at first sight: not, however, because of the number of the scraps on which they are written, but because of their odd in-and-out arrangement on the two scraps': [we may notice in passing that the sheets have now become scraps]. 'It seems clear that Keats did not know how long his poem was going to be, and only took out these two half-sheets with him under the tree. Having made on one of them (leaf 2 of the facsimile) the false start above noted, he puts aside that and begins again on leaf 1: writes on it the first two and a half stanzas of the poem; then goes to leaf 2 (turning it upside down to avoid confusion with the false start) and continues on it down to the end of the fifth stanza; then goes back to the verso of leaf 1, on which he adds stanzas six and seven; and then to the verso of leaf 2, where he finishes the poem with stanza eight.'

That all sounds very complicated and technical with versos and turnings upside down. Let us for a moment examine the two sheets and the way Keats wrote on them. The 'false start' mentioned is the words 'Small, winged

[1] But the accuracy or inaccuracy of Brown's recollections is of no importance at all in itself (except to a biographer of Brown); it is only of importance if we are going to use it as evidence with regard to something else.

Dryad', written at the head of one of the sheets. It is not certain that it was written at the same time as the rest, or in any case was a 'false start' rather than a jotting or memorandum of a phrase, since when Keats does start the poem on the other sheet he does not write first any words of the poem, but the title. In any case, as the phrase is being neglected, that sheet is for practical purposes a blank sheet and there is no question of upside down or right side up. Keats starts on one sheet and writes the first two stanzas and six lines of the third. Then (whether, as seems likely, for lack of means of blotting the last line or two, or for whatever reason) he writes on the second sheet to the end of stanza v. Then he lays this aside (? to dry) and goes to the blank side of his first sheet, fills that, and finishes off on the blank side of the other sheet. Suppose that the two half-sheets had been the two leaves of an ordinary doubled sheet: Keats wrote his poem exactly as many people still write their letters, in order of 'pages' 1, 3, 2, 4; or as a man naturally writes on single sheets if either he can't blot them, or finds that he unexpectedly has to write on both sides of them. So much for the 'oddity' of the 'in-and-out arrangement'. Now about Brown's 'difficulty in arranging the stanzas on so many scraps'. He had (if he had this document) two sheets in front of him. There is no doubt where the poem begins, since it has a title. He cannot run off the rails till he finds himself at the end of the sixth line of the third stanza; he now has three other sides to choose from. Apart from rhymed words, and the repeated 'where', only one of those three sides carries on in the middle of a stanza, so that there is only Hobson's choice for him and he arrives safely at the end of the fifth stanza and the first side of sheet 2. He now has two sides left; but as one of these contains two stanzas and the other only one it is not a very daring conjecture that the single stanza is the last of the poem, and that the other two are the sixth and seventh. (It is worth noticing that if the four sides had each contained two complete stanzas, the kind of arrangement that his account implies, he would have been in difficulty, since the only side of whose order he would have been sure is that with the title at the head.) That is to say, there is only one possible way in which the poem, as written on these two half-sheets, can be read, and it is hard to believe that it would need more than a few seconds to reveal this to a person of Brown's reasonable intelligence.

Finally, as to the legibility, it is equally hard to believe that any one with Brown's acquaintance with Keats' writing would have had the smallest difficulty in reading the draft that we have. It is about as legible as most of Keats' letters (which present only the most occasional difficulties) or as, say, the copy of *To Autumn* in the letter to Woodhouse. It is not quite so legible as some of Keats' most carefully written fair copies, and infinitely more legible than the holograph of *The Eve of St. Agnes*.

Thus in Brown's account we find 'scraps', 'four or five', or 'so many', in number; there is difficulty in arranging the stanzas; and the writing is not well legible: in the document before us we find that there are two pieces of paper; that they are not scraps; that there could be no difficulty in arranging the stanzas that would give any one more than a few seconds' pause (certainly not that would require the poet's assistance); and that the writing is very reasonably legible. To say that Brown's account, as descriptive of the document before us, is 'accurate in the main though not in all particulars' seems to me much as though we were to attribute a similar design of accuracy to the statement that the first draft of *The Eve of St. Agnes* is written in a copper-plate hand on thick paper in red ink. If what we have in front of us is the first draft, all that Brown is accurate about is that Keats wrote the first draft of the *Nightingale* on paper—which we knew without Brown to tell us.

In brief, then, we can do one of two things. We can assume on internal evidence that the 'document' is the first draft, and use it to check Brown's account, with the result that we dismiss Brown's account as hopelessly inaccurate and forget all about it (and indeed if we are determined that the document is the first draft the less we say about Brown's account the better); or we can use Brown's account as some sort of evidence to help us in determining the earliness of the document. But we cannot have it both ways; we cannot say, what is of course the thing we want to say, 'Here is what looks like the first draft; Brown has an account of that first draft; his description corresponds closely enough with what we have in front of us to strengthen our belief that this is the first draft.'

Suppose for a moment that we had no document in front of us and only Brown's account, and were conjecturing what the draft, if ever it came to light, would be like. What should we expect to see? To that question there can I think be only one answer. We should expect four scraps of paper, each with a stanza on each side, rather ill-written, and probably heavily corrected. We should expect, that is, exactly what we should have if the missing first sheet of *The Eve of St. Agnes* holograph, divided into stanzas by Severn's scissors, should ever come to light.

H. Buxton Forman makes a characteristically wise and temperate comment on the 'document':[1] 'This draft clearly shows Keats in the act of composition—or *re*composition; but I do not think Professor Colvin proves conclusively that those two leaves were the very scraps Brown saw Keats bring in and hide', and he goes on with a conjecture; 'it is quite conceivable that the poet, after hiding—perhaps forgetting where he hid—the scraps, found himself in the mood to give one of the Reynoldses a copy of the ode, sat down, and recomposed it, mainly, of course, from memory.' This supposition accounts for certain curious features in the draft; it has not enough corrections to make one at all confident that it is the first draft; on the other hand it has three or four corrections which do appear to have been made during composition and were certainly made during a period of continuous

[1] In the introduction to the Oxford *Keats*, p. xlviii.

writing. But there is a difficulty about it, if we are to attach any weight to Brown. On Brown's account the 'scraps' never were hidden; he forestalled Keats in the act of hiding them, extracted them, and pieced them together. As we are now in the region of conjecture I will add yet another, which is indeed pure supposition but would make sense of Brown's account and also of the peculiarities of the draft. Suppose Keats, when he went into the garden, armed with more than our two sheets. He uses say three sheets for the real first draft, with his usual false starts, corrections, and so on. He then, still in the garden, takes our two sheets and writes the whole poem out again, with one or two false starts and some improvements as he writes. He then comes into the house with the five sheets and begins to put them away. Brown rescues them, the two fair copy sheets are sorted from the others, and the others are destroyed. I do not pretend that this is wholly satisfactory since Keats' assistance would not be in 'piecing together' but would amount to selecting the two fair-copy sheets from the jumble and giving them to Brown; but it is perhaps no more unsatisfactory than any other supposition.

However, dismissing Brown from consideration and concentrating on the draft as we have it, what do we find? Sir Sidney Colvin's general account of it is as follows: 'There are many vital corrections and alterations; with frequent signs, in the shape of dropped words and letters, unaccustomed mis-spellings and slips of the pen, that while the hand wrote the mind was too much occupied with the act of composition to guide it with strict care.' In fact there are eleven cases of omitted letters (seven of which are *r*, which is always liable to drop out with Keats) and four of unwanted letters; of mis-spellings there are three, 'told' and 'feaver' both immediately corrected, and 'Emperour' (if that is a mis-spelling); there are fourteen verbal corrections of which ten are just Woodhouse's 'word here or there preferable to an expression already used'. Of the remaining four, two, because they involve rhyme words, and two because of the way in which they were made, were evidently made in the process of 'composition or recomposition', and there are six false starts. It is impossible to find any seven consecutive stanzas, or for that matter any seven stanzas at all, in the holograph of *The Eve of St. Agnes* which show so low a proportion of corrections made in the act of composition. A mere glance at the two documents would convince any one that they probably belong to different stages in composition. However, let us take the draft as we have it, and assume either that it is the first draft (in which case I think that it is a miracle, and a miracle quite different in the methods of its wizardry from Keats' usual methods where we can see them) or that it is an early draft, probably a re-writing of the first rough draft at a very short interval after the composition of that rough draft while the poem was still partially fluid, and let us go on to what is I believe in all the Odes a much more interesting study than their 'carpentry', namely the process of what one may call 'distillation' whereby many 'flowers' that we find scattered about in Keats' own earlier work, and in the work of others, together with impressions made upon his senses, are made to yield their concentrated essence. One caveat should perhaps be entered at once. In this region it is impossible to produce any evidence. We know the goal, and we are pursuing a highly conjectural backward trail; occasionally we come on a blaze which seems to be unmistakable, but even so it is no more than an encouragement to proceed on what is to some readers a fascinating adventure, and to others the merest waste of time. 'Why', they will say, changing the metaphor, 'trouble our heads as to what odd lumps of ore went into the crucible when we know how pure the gold is that came out?'

His dramatic sense prevents Keats starting with the nightingale; the stage must be set, however briefly, and he sets it by a description of his own sensations, his heart-ache and a painful numbness. It is the same feeling perhaps that he has described to Bailey in a letter of the preceding year: 'I have this morning such a Lethargy that I cannot write . . . and yet it is an unpleasant numbness it does not take away the pain of existence.'[1] The first line read originally I think

> Heart aches and a painful numbness fall

(*Aches* being Shakespeareanly a dissyllable) and then

> My heart aches and a drowsy numbness falls

and then, with the transference of the idea of pain into the verb, the line as we now have it

> My heart aches and a drowsy numbness pains

The change may have been due to no more than trouble with rhyme, but it is observable that both *ache* and *numbness* seem to have been associated in Keats' mind with the notion of *drowsy*. In stanza XXXI of *The Eve of St. Agnes* we have

> Or I shall drowse beside thee, so my soul doth ache

and in the *Ode to Indolence*

> Ripe was the drowsy hour;
> The blissful cloud of summer-indolence
> Benumb'd my eyes (st. II)

(where also in stanza III we have *ach'd for wings*).

At any rate, the first line surmounted, the stanza moves unhaltingly to its close, with one correction, that of *hence* to *past* in the fourth line, a probable reminiscence of *Britannia's Pastorals*,[2] 'Sweet *Philomela*; . . . I doe not envy thy sweet carolling', and the use of one phrase of which the sound seems to have been running in Keats' head, since in *Endymion* we find *beechen wreath*,[3] *beechen tree*,[4] and *wreathed green*.[5] Part of the effect of this stanza depends on the reiterated *um* and *un* sound, three of the recurrences of which (*some* twice and *one* once) we tend to miss, from our inveterate habit of reading by the eye and not by the ear.

[1] MBF, 63 (159). [2] I. iii. 164. [3] *End.* i. 159.
[4] Ib. iv. 767. [5] Ib. ii. 516.

In the second stanza Keats wants a draught of something which is different both in itself and in its effects from the hemlock of the first stanza, and something, perhaps the link of the *beechen wreath* and *wreathed green* phrases, takes him back to *Endymion*. Here is the material. A passage in a letter of the month before: 'And, please heaven, a little claret-wine cool out of a cellar a mile deep . . . a strawberry bed to say your prayers to Flora in';[1]

> Here is wine,
> Alive with *sparkles*—never, I aver,
> Since Ariadne was a *vintager*,
> So *cool* a *purple* (*End.* ii. 441)

> the rills
> Into the wide stream came of *purple* hue
> . . . .
> Like to a moving *vintage* down they came,
> Crown'd with green leaves (*End.* iv. 194)

possibly two passages in *Endymion* in which sparkling wine is in contiguity though not connexion with the *beechen wreath* phrases;[2] the title of an early poem *A Draught of Sunshine* and a line from the same poem,

> My wine *overbrims* a whole summer

another three lines from *Endymion*,

> Each having a white wicker *over brimm'd*
> With April's tender younglings: next, well trimm'd,
> A crowd of shepherds with as *sunburnt* looks. . . .
> (*End.* i. 137)

perhaps the *low delved tomb* in Milton's *On the Death of a Fair Infant*;[3] and perhaps various descriptions of Provençal country feasts and dances from Mrs. Radcliffe.[4]

[1] MBF, 113 (315–16).

[2] *End.* i. 153–61; ii. 511–17.

[3] st. v. 1. 4.

[4] E.g. the 'dance of the vintage' in *The Mysteries of Udolpho* (vol. iii, p. 433 (c. xxxviii, p. 80)): 'the festivity of the peasants. The scene was in a glade, where the trees, opening, formed a circle round the turf they highly overshadowed; between their branches, vines, loaded with ripe clusters, were hung in gay festoons; and, beneath, were tables, with fruit, wine, cheese and other rural fare. . . . At a little distance, were benches for the elder peasants, few of whom, however, could forbear to join the jocund dance.'

There are the fragments, and from them Keats creates this stanza, redolent of the country, warm with the sunshine of the South:

O for a draught of vintage that has been
Cooling an age in the deep-delved earth
Tasting of Flora, and the country green
~~And~~Dance and p[r]ovencal song and sunburnt mirth
O for a Beaker full of the warm South,
Full of the true and blushful Hippocrene
With cluster'd bubbles winking at the brim
And pu[r]ple stained mouth,
That I might drink and leave the world unseen
And with thee fade away into the forest dim.

He changed *Cooling an age* to *Cooled a long age* in the draft. In the printed version, apart from one or two minor changes, the *cluster'd* bubbles become *beaded*. This last alteration is clearly because of the *cluster'd* in stanza IV, which he there deletes as a repetition of the word here, but finally decides to leave standing there, where indeed it is more appropriate, and so is driven to the felicitous emendation in this stanza.

He starts his next stanza with a repetition which he had already used in *Endymion*, *fade, and fade away*,[1] and the tone of the poem changes as he thinks of leaving the world. There is here the expression of his own longing for release that comes out so poignantly elsewhere; he wants to *dissolve* like the Spirit in *Isabella* (XLI. 1) or perhaps recalls the wish that this too too solid flesh would melt, Thaw and resolve itself into a dew, and that so he could escape from the sorrows of the world. Here I think is just the vivid expression of his own feelings; he knows the weariness and fever and fret; he has watched youth grow pale and spectre-thin and die five months before; he knows the lustrous eyes of beauty and guesses that even the barren ecstasy of pining at them cannot be his beyond tomorrow. This stanza comes so clearly from the tortured heart that I do not know that we need look for the material of it

[1] *End.* iii. 177.

otherwhere than in his experience. We can if we like turn to *Tintern Abbey*, and find

> the fretful stir
> Unprofitable, and the fever of the world

and notice the '*leaden* looks' of the sullen day in *Endymion*, i. 686, 'The *lustrous* passion from a falcon *eye*' in the Song to Sorrow, and three other lines in *Endymion*,

> My fever'd parchings up, my scathing dread
> Met palsy half way: soon these limbs became
> Gaunt, wither'd, sapless, feeble, cramp'd and lame
> (iii. 636)

This stanza gave more trouble in the actual writing. It moves so far easily enough.

> Fade far away, dissolve and quite forget
> What thou among the leaves hast never known
> The weariness, the fever and the fret
> Here, where Men sit and hear each other groan
> Where palsy shakes a few sad last grey hairs
> Where youth grows pale and thin and old and dies

But that is monotonous in rhythm and not too vivid in imagery, so it is strengthened to

> Where youth grows pale and spectre-thin, and dies

For the last four lines I suspect an earlier stage in which there was a rhyme for the *grief* which appears cancelled in the draft, and no *new* before *Love*. Keats then in copying wrote:

> Where but to think is to be full of grief
> And leaden eyed despairs—
> Where Beauty cannot keep her lustrous eyes
> Or Love pine at them

and then stopped, changed *grief* to *sorrow* (for which, after the Song to Sorrow, the rhyme was familiar), inserted *new* and wrote *beyond tomorrow*.[1]

In the fourth stanza the determination to escape

[1] There was clearly a pause in the writing after *them*; though this may have been due not to a need for reflection, but to a need for ink, since his pen appears to have run dry on the last stroke of *them*.

becomes yet more urgent, but the agency of the second stanza is rejected, and the escape is to be on the only wings of a dove on which he knew that he could fly away and be at rest, the wings of poetry, and by the fifth line the escape is achieved, and he is with the Nightingale in the depths of the forest, a forest so dark that even the presence of the throned moon is conjectural. And in this stanza I think one can see that the use of the words *fade away* and *dissolve* has set a whole new chime ringing in his head:

thou(the moon)didst *fade, and fade away*
Yet not entirely; no, thy *starry sway* . . . (*End.* iii. 177)

Dissolve the frozen purity of air
. . . make more bright
The *Star-Queen's* crescent on her marriage night
(*End.* iv. 586 *et seqq.*)

but rather tie
Large wings upon my shoulders, . . .
. . . . . . by all the stars
That tend thy bidding, I do think the bars
That kept my spirit in are burst—that I
Am sailing with thee through the dizzy sky!
(*End.* ii. 177–87)

Add to these perhaps Titian's picture of Bacchus and Ariadne (though the pards of Bacchus are such a commonplace that I doubt whether the picture is very relevant), and probably a passage in Coleridge's *The Nightingale* (a poem which by the way seems to have influenced a passage in *Endymion* shortly before one of those quoted above):

You see the glimmer of the stream beneath,
But hear no *murmuring*; it flows silently,
O'er its soft bed of verdure. All is still
A balmy night. . . . (ll. 5–8)

And so comes the stanza, with that remarkable piece of imagination at the end which feels the light as blown by the breezes, one of those characteristic sudden flashes with which Keats fires the most ordinary material.

Away—Away—for I will fly with thee

but *with* which was appropriate in the *Endymion* passage is not appropriate here and is altered to *to*:

> Away—Away—for I will fly to thee
> Not charioted by Bacchus and his Pards
> But on the viewless wings of Poesy
> Though the dull brain perplexes and retards—

(O for a life of Sensations rather than of Thoughts)

> Already with thee! tender is the night
> And haply the Queen-moon is on her throne
> ~~Clusted~~ around by all her starry fays—
> But here there is no light
> Save what from heaven is with the breezes blown
> Sidelong

One imagines that the line originally ran either

> Sidelong through verdurous glooms and mossy ways

or

> Sidelong through verdurous glooms and winding ways.

But in writing this draft *Sidelong* is cancelled as soon as written. It is a favourite word with Keats[1] and he may have been resisting the temptation to overwork it, but it may be doubted whether this excision was for the better; the word gives so clear a picture of a forest so dense overhead that the only light which penetrates comes sideways from the outskirts. Anyway for good or ill the correction was made, and the line ran

> Th[r]ough ve[r]du[r]ous glooms and winding mossy ways.

And lastly *Clusted* was deleted as a repetition and nothing substituted. For the printed version, as has been pointed out, it was here reinstated and the earlier *Cluster'd* changed to *beaded*.

The next stanza runs very easily, at least at this stage,

[1] 'The sidelong view of swelling leafiness' (*Cal.* 34); 'Nymph of the downward smile and sidelong glance' (*Sonnet to G.A.W.*, 1); 'sidelong aisles' (*End.* ii. 264); 'sidelong laughing' (*End.* iv. 211); 'sidelong fix'd her eye on Saturn's face' (*Hyp.* ii. 91).

and is a piece of pure description, a distillation of many previous descriptions of which the following are typical:

there blew
Soft *breezes* from the myrtle vale below;
And brought in faintness, solemn, sweet, and slow
A hymn from Dian's temple; while upswelling,
The *incense* went to her own *starry* dwelling
('*I stood tiptoe . . .*' 195)

Softly the *breezes* from the forest came
Softly they blew aside the taper's flame;
Clear was the song from *Philomel's* far bower;
Grateful the *incense* from the lime-tree *flower*
(*Cal.* 152)

What is more tranquil than a *musk-rose* blowing
In a green island, far from all men's knowing?
More healthful than the leafiness of dales?
More secret than a nest of *nightingales*?
(*Sleep and Poetry*, 5)

(And perhaps a passage from *The Mysteries of Udolpho*, 'illumined only by moon-beams, which the open casement admitted . . . cool and balmy air, that lightly waved the embowering honeysuckles, and wafted their sweet breath into the apartment';[1] if any reader feels that, while Mrs. Radcliffe may be reluctantly admitted as a possible source of *The Eve of St. Agnes*, to connect her with the *Ode to a Nightingale* is a kind of desecration, there is worse to come.)

I cannot see what flowers are at my feet
Nor what blooms

altered at once to the far better

Nor what soft insence hangs upon the boughs
But in embalmed darkness guess each sweet
~~With with~~

immediately deleted, and the point is a trivial one enough, but worth indicating since it is so characteristic of Keats in a hurry or careless. He has either in his mind or on paper *With which*, and begins to write it, when it occurs

[1] *MU*, vol. i, p. 178 (c. vi, pp. 35, 36).

to him that *Wherewith* will be better, and the second *with* is a jumble of *which* and *with*:

> Wherewith the seasonable month endows
> The grass the thicket and the fruit tree wild
> White Hawthorn and the pastoral eglantine
> Fast fading violets covered up in leaves
> And midmay's eldest child
> The coming muskrose full of sweetest wine
> The murmurous ha[u]nt of flies on summer eves

In the printed version *sweetest* is altered to *dewy*, a change full of interest, when we watch the progression of which it was the last step. In *I stood tiptoe* . . . he speaks of *dewy roses* and perhaps the whole passage is not without interest, for here too is the withdrawal from the world, there is one familiar phrase, and another which may account for the false start of *blooms*:

> Fair *dewy roses* brush against our faces,
> And flowering laurels spring from diamond vases;
> O'er head we see the jasmine and sweet briar,
> And *bloomy* grapes laughing from green attire;
> While *at our feet* . . . . (133–7)

In *Endymion*, ii. 983, we find *dewy balm* and ten lines lower 'I roam in pleasant *darkness*' and 'where we might Be *incense*-pillow'd every summer night'; in *Isabella* '*dewy rhyme*' (of interest only as showing how his ear was caught by the vowel slide from *ew* to long *i*); then in *Meg Merrilies* the last stage but one,

> Her *wine* was *dew* of the wild white rose (st. II)

and so to the stanza before us.

The next stanza resembles the third in that it is a record of Keats' own experience and his mind at the time. We have the line of a sonnet (*Why did I laugh* . . . MBF, 114 (343)),

> Yet would I on this very *midnight cease*

and the conclusion of the same sonnet,

> Death is Life's high meed

There is a kind of link between the two stanzas in the sonnet to Sleep:

> O soft *embalmer* of the still *midnight*
> Shutting with careful fingers and benign
> Our gloom-pleas'd eyes embowered from the light

The spirit is that in which he writes to Fanny Brawne two months later, 'I have two luxuries to brood over in my walks, your Loveliness and the hour of my death'.[1] But the idea of the richness of death has been with him ever since *Sleep and Poetry*:

> That I may die a death
> Of luxury (58)

the idea of its quietness since *Endymion*, ii. 159, 'How *quiet* death is' and both ideas together since

> with a *balmy* power
> Medicined death to a lengthy *drowsiness*:
> The which she fills with visions, and doth dress
> In all this *quiet luxury* (*End.* ii. 483–6)

> Darkling I listen, and for many a time
> I have been half in love with easeful death
> Call'd him soft names in many a mused rhyme,
> To take into the air my painless breath
> Now, more than ever seems it rich to die
> To cease upon the midnight with no pain
> While thou(gh) art pouring thus thy soul abroad
> In such an Extacy—
> Still would thou sing and I have ~~y~~ea[r]s in vain
> ~~But requiem'd~~

The cancellation of these last two words suggests a change in the thought. It looks as though in the first conception there had been a hint of consolation,

> But(nevertheless) requiem'd by thy song, even though a sod

The revised version is more unsparing,

> ~~For~~To thy high requiem, become a sod.

And now for the great stanza in which the glowing imagination is fanned to yet whiter heat, the stanza that

[1] MBF, 130 (393).

would, I suppose, by common consent be taken, along with *Kubla Khan*, as offering us the distilled sorceries of 'Romanticism', the stanza that contains those two lines, of which, along with three from *Kubla Khan*, it has been said, 'Remember that in all the millions permitted there are no more than five—five little lines—of which one can say: "These are the pure Magic. These are the clear Vision. The rest is only poetry".'[1]

We get a hint of the same backward-throwing imagination in an early letter, where he has been looking at less poetic birds at Carisbrooke: 'I dare say I have seen many a descendant of some old cawer who peeped through the Bars at Charles the First',[2] but here he carries the imagination to its limits; the song is the same and deathless through the years, even though it were the ancestor of this particular nightingale that sang to Emperours. And there is a hint perhaps of the generations in *The Excursion*:

> While man *grows old* and withers and decays
> And countless *generations* of mankind
> Depart and leave no vestige where they trod
>
> (iv. 760)

We need hardly look for a more recondite source for Ruth than the obvious one in the Bible. And the casements? Keats had all his life a love of windows. One of his fellow students is recorded as saying, 'In a room he was always at the window peering into space so that the window seat was spoken of by his comrades as Keats's place'. We find the love of windows opening over water in the letters, 'the Window opening upon Winander mere',[3] and 'I should like the window to open onto the Lake of Geneva';[4] and his poetry is full of casements, as in the famous stanza of *The Eve of St. Agnes*, and the 'casement ope' of the *Ode to Psyche*, and the open casement of the *Ode to Indolence*. It has been held that the genesis of the picture of the two famous lines as revised, with the casements *magic* and the seas *perilous*, was Claude's picture of *The Enchanted*

[1] Kipling, 'Wireless'.
[2] MBF, 12 (19).
[3] Ib. 89 (261).
[4] Ib. 108 (309).

Castle.[1] But what are the salient features of this picture? A castle by the sea, with plenty of casements (and *ex hypothesi* from the title of the picture, though apart from the title one would hardly guess it, magic casements); the sea is gently ruffled; in the middle distance is a boat, quietly rowing towards the castle; in the foreground is the placidly contemplative figure of a woman, and several equally placid deer. Any scene less perilous it would be hard to imagine. And we know precisely what impression it produced on Keats from his letter to Reynolds.[2]

> You know the Enchanted Castle it doth stand
> Upon a Rock on the Border of a Lake
> Nested in Trees, which all do seem to shake
> From some old Magic like Urganda's Sword.
> O Phoebus that I had thy sacred word
> To shew this Castle in fair dreaming wise
> Unto my friend, while sick and ill he lies.
>   You know it well enough, where it doth seem
> A mossy place, a Merlin's Hall, a dream.
> You know the clear Lake, and the little Isles,
>
> . . . .
>
>   The doors all look as if they oped themselves,
> The windows as if latch'd by fays and elves—
>
> . . . .
>
>   See what is coming from the distance dim!
> A golden galley all in silken trim!

There no doubt is the magic; but there, equally no doubt, are not the perilous seas. The verbal picture is just that of the original, a picture of dreaming peace. Here is another description, from a writer whose works elsewhere are full of casements, and of casements opening on the sea;[3] 'a room, the windows of which looked upon the sea. The wind burst in sudden squalls over the deep, and

[1] de S, 475; SC, 291 n., and more explicitly in a note to letter xlvi (in his edition). [2] MBF, 55 (135, 136).

[3] E.g. 'the windows opened upon the sea' (*SR*, vol. i, c. ii, p. 60); 'Blanche withdrew to a window, the lower panes of which, being without painting, allowed her to observe the progress of the storm over the Mediterranean, whose dark waves, that had so lately slept, now came boldly swelling, in long succession, to the shore, where they burst in white foam' (*MU*, vol. iii, p. 390 (c. xxxvi, p. 73)).

dashed the foaming waves against the rocks with inconceivable fury. The spray, notwithstanding the high situation of the castle, flew up with violence against the windows. . . . The moon shone faintly by intervals, through broken clouds upon the waters, illuming the white foam which burst around.'[1] That, whether we like it or not, is Mrs. Radcliffe; and if we transport Claude's castle with its atmosphere of magic to the setting of Mrs. Radcliffe's castle of Athlin, we have the picture complete. What we have not is the magic of the presentation, which is Keats' alone.

I do not believe that any reader who has watched Keats at work on the more exquisitely finished of the stanzas in *The Eve of St. Agnes*, and seen this craftsman slowly elaborating and refining, will ever believe that this perfect stanza was achieved with the easy fluency with which, in the draft we have, it was obviously written down. All we can here see is the last two masterly touches.

> Thou wast not born for death, immortal Bird
>   No hungry generations tread thee down,
> The voice I hear this passing night was heard
>   In ancient days by Emperour and Clown
> Perhaps the selfsame ~~voice~~song that found a path
> Th[r]ough the sad heart of Ruth, when sick for home
> She stood in tears amid the alien corn—
> The same that oftimes hath
> Cha[r]med the wide casements opening on the foam
> Of

and then there was trouble over the epithet for *seas*, and trouble ever since for the decipherers of the first attempt. There stands after *Of* a heavily deleted word, of which the accepted reading has been *keelless*. But Mr. Garrod is, and I have no doubt rightly, dubious about *keelless*. He says ' "keelless" certainly does not correspond with the *ductus litterarum*—and I could wish that a good palaeographer should re-examine the MS.'[2] I have no pretensions to being the good palaeographer that Mr. Garrod (and I) would wish for. But I think it is clear that there

[1] *AD*, c. ix, p. 185.

[2] *Keats*, p. 117 n.

were two stages of this word, not one, and that one of these was, or was going to be, *keelless*. Otherwise it is impossible to account for a vertical stroke at the beginning of the word, which is not part of the deletion, and even less part of the *r* that appears to be there. On the other hand, there is an unmistakable *t* before the loop of what has been taken to be the first *l* of *keelless*. What then was the word? Before we hurry into conjecture it may be as well to find out what the indefatigable Woodhouse thought about it. And it does not seem to have been observed that Woodhouse had no doubt what the cancelled word had been. He may have known from Keats himself, in which case his evidence is decisive; or he may have been merely making the best he could of it, in which case his reading has as much or as little authority as any one else's. But at least it should go on record. In his second book of transcripts there is a transcript of the poem in its final form, and in the margin Woodhouse has noted in his neat shorthand (Mavor's) all the important cancelled readings of the draft; and opposite this cancelled word he has written Λ/, i.e. 'rthless' (presumably 'ruthless'). This does correspond with the *ductus litterarum*, with one small exception; it gives the required *t* and makes the loop the loop of the *h* of *ruthless*, not of the *l* of *keelless*. I suggest that the sequence was first *keelless* perhaps not fully written out; then *ruthless*. But *ruthless* with its echo of the immediately preceding *Ruth* is clearly impossible; and the first synonym for it that occurs also suggests the sound of the far better word which then occurs to Keats and which he writes down, the last crowning touch to his stanza; and with the alteration of the rather insignificant *the wide*, we have the lines

> Charm'd magic casements opening on the foam
> Of perilous seas in fairy lands fo[r]lorn[1]

[1] The reading *folorn* has exercised critics who wonder sadly whether Keats so pronounced the word. It is true enough that he more often than not wrote it so (e.g. *Eve of St. Agnes*, st. XXXVII, and *Isabella*, st. LXIII). But it is also true that *r* is the letter he is most careless about, and it is perpetually dropping out in his writing. So that we may suppose that Keats' pronunciation was better than his writing.

The last stanza is something of an anticlimax. The poetic ecstasy is over and the poet comes back wearily to reality. Something of the same idea has occurred in *Endymion*, though in a different relation:

> There, where new wonders ceas'd to float before,
> And thoughts of *self* came on, how crude and sore
> The journey homeward to *habitual self*!
> A mad-pursuing of the fog-born *elf*,
> Whose flitting lantern, through rude nettle-briar,
> *Cheats* us . . . . . .   (ii. 274)

and I am not sure that memories of the ubiquitous Mrs. Radcliffe's *Romance of the Forest* are not traceable, memories of the phrases 'I fell into a sort of *waking dream*'.[1] 'Is this a vision?',[2] not to mention 'the plantive sweetness of the nightingale' and 'the plantive accents of your voice'.[3]

> Fo[r]lorn! the very wor(l)d is like a bell

(his ear catches the coming alliteration too soon)

> To toll me back from thee unto myself
> Adieux! the fancy cannot cheat so well
> As she is fam'd to do, deceit~~ful~~ving elf!
> Adieu! Adieu! thy plaintive Anthem fades
> Past the near meadows, over the still stream,
> Up the hill side, and now 'tis buried deep
> In the next vally'~~s~~ glades.
> Was it a vision real or waking dream?
> Fled is that Music—do I wake or sleep?

ODE TO MELANCHOLY

As we have no original manuscript of this Ode we cannot follow the stages by which it came to its final form; nor are the reminiscences in it of earlier work by any means either so numerous or so interesting as in certain others of the

[1] *RF*, vol. i, c. iii, p. 66 (c. iii, p. 51).

[2] *RF*, vol. ii, c. ix, p. 56 (c. ix, p. 158).

[3] *MU*, vol. i, p. 408 (c. xiv, p. 76). And perhaps we may add to these, 'the nearer forest and the valley's stream' (*RF*, vol. i, p. 208 (c. v, p. 100)); and notice in comparison with stanza v the 'balmy sweets' and the 'wild musk-rose' of the sonnet on Sunrise in *The Romance of the Forest* (vol. iii, c. xvii, p. 145 (c. xviii, p. 333)).

Odes. But it offers itself readily to another type of analysis, which is worth sometimes conducting, if it does no more than make our ears more sensitive in the rest of our reading, an analysis of its 'harmonies'. There are readers who feel that any technical analysis of the sound values of a poem is a kind of desecration, and detracts from the true aesthetic enjoyment of the poem. They regard it as a mechanical process and beneath their notice. I think that it will usually be found that such readers read their poetry with less attention of the ear than any great poem merits, and, by so reading, miss part of the legitimate pleasure which poetry has to give. For part of the appeal of poetry is a musical appeal. A poem has not only to be understood; it has also to be heard. That sounds the poorest kind of commonplace, and so in a sense no doubt it is; but it is a commonplace to which we pay much too little attention. In these days, when we all read so much, we inevitably take in the sense of the greater part of our reading through the eye; we do not hear it at all, we only see it. And through long practice in taking in the sense of whole blocks of words at a glance we have dulled our aural perceptions to the point at which it has become a serious conscious effort to 'hear' anything that we read. We can still listen to music; but the 'music of words', except on the far too rare occasions when we have the chance of listening to a great reader reading aloud, is something to which we are for the most part wholly or partly deaf. But the deafness is curable, and by the expenditure occasionally of a little pains we can as it were re-sensitize our ears, so that all the exquisite harmonies which the great poets can elicit from their instrument no longer slide past us unheard. The process is no doubt in itself mechanical; and if it ended with itself would no doubt be nearly valueless. But the value of the process does not come to us while it is being conducted; while we are going through a poem line by line to see what the sounds in it are, and how they blend and recur, and how again and again our eye is betraying us into supposing that there is a sound which there is not, or that there is not a sound which there is, then no one will suppose that we are appreciating the poem. But when we have finished with this detailed analysis, then we can go back, and read the poem as a whole, and probably for the first time hear the full beauties of its elaborate music. And I do not think that any reader who has tried this experiment on a poem which he thought he 'knew', and found how astonishingly richer a thing it is than he had ever supposed, will think time so spent time wasted. Here are two brief examples which may illustrate at least one of these points, the disastrous domination of the eye. Milton writes:

> the gilded Car of Day,
> His glowing Axle doth allay
> In the steep *Atlantick* stream.[1]

The alliteration on *g* and *d* and *l* in the first two lines, and on *st* in the third, is obvious to the eye, and therefore to the ear. The assonance in the third line on long *e* is partially obscured by the *ee* and *ea* spellings but is so strong that it is probably heard. But there is an alliteration on *k* in the first two lines which is very apt to escape notice, since the first *k* is the hard *c* of *car* and the second is masquerading as the first half of the *x* of *axle*. Or take the last four lines of the second stanza of *To Autumn*:

> And sometimes like a gleaner thou dost keep
> Steady thy laden head across a brook;
> Or by a cyder-press, with patient look,
> Thou watchest the last oozings hours by hours.

Consider first the vowels. In the first two lines there are three *ea's*; but their values are not the same. The first is the long *e* which is repeated in *keep*, whereas the other two are the short *e* which is repeated in *press*. The ringing long *i* of the first line is picked up two lines lower in the two *y*'s. It is also easy, though not so excusable, to miss the assonance, which is in fact on short *u* not on short *o*, in *sometimes* and *dost*. The only assonance that is completely

[1] *Comus*, 95–7.

above-board is that of *laden* and *patient*. And then, for consonants, observe the last line. How easy it is to miss the full somnolence of that line. The eye sees and therefore the ear is awake to (or asleep to) the *z* of *oozings*. But the ear is very liable to miss the fact that the sound is given not once but four times in that one line, since the three final *s*'s are all *z*'s.

And now for the *Ode to Melancholy*. Here is the first stanza:

> No, no, go not to Lethe, neither twist
> Wolf's-bane, tight-rooted, for its poisonous wine;
> Nor suffer thy pale forehead to be kiss'd
> By nightshade, ruby grape of Proserpine;
> Make not your rosary of yew-berries,
> Nor let the beetle, nor the death-moth be
> Your mournful Psyche, nor the downy owl
> A partner in your sorrow's mysteries;
> For shade to shade will come too drowsily,
> And drown the wakeful anguish of the soul.

The first thing, I suppose, that strikes the ear on the most cursory examination, is the slow, almost heavy, movement of the stanza, and when we examine more closely we find that this is due to an unusually high proportion of long vowels. There is no particular subtlety about the first line; there is the abrupt attack with the hammer-strokes on long *o* in the first three words, followed by either two long *e*'s and a long *i*, or by three long *e*'s, according to Keats' pronunciation of *neither*. I should be inclined to guess at the pronunciation with long *e* since this heightens the effect of the alliteration[1] on the hard and soft *th* which is going to be repeated even more decisively five lines lower. There is also a strong and obvious alliteration on *n* and *t*. The rest of the quatrain is more interesting. The long *o* is entirely discarded and the long *e* occurs only once. There is considerable variety of vowel sounds, with a preponderance of long *a* and long *i*, of

[1] 'Alliteration' is used in the remainder of the chapter to include what is more properly described as 'assonance'.

which the latter becomes more and more dominant till the fourth line which it both opens and closes. The second line is a good example of the effect of a particular arrangement of alliteration, which, when one observes it, is singularly effective, what might be called 'looking-glass' alliteration. A simple case of it is Milton's 'Jousted in *Aspramont* or *Montalban*'[1] where the second proper name repeats the whole of one syllable, and the vowels of the other two syllables, of the first name, but in the reverse order. In the line now before us the *w-s-n* of the first word is repeated in the *n-s-w-*(*n*) of the last two words, and in the middle comes a rather too obvious repetition of quickly recurring *t*'s. There is little to be said of the third line except that it 'announces' the *p* and *d* and *b* of the fourth. (There is no alliteration on *d* since the *d* of *kiss'd* is a *t*.) The fourth line repeats the form of the second with variations. The *n-i* of the second word is repeated in the *i-n* of the last, and between come a pleasantly unobtrusive repeated *r* and a strongly marked, but equally pleasant, repeated *p*, which leads the line to its strong close. And this alliteration at the end of the line is prepared for by the repeated *b* at the beginning. In the fifth line the *r* of the preceding line is brought into much greater prominence, being three times repeated, and there are alliterations on the *oo* of *your* and *yew*, and the *z* (not *s*) of *rosary* and *berries*. In the sixth line two previous alliterations are repeated, both times in a stronger form; that on *b* is thrown into prominence because the letter is both times initial, and also because it is followed both times by the same vowel sound; and the alliteration of the first line on the two *th*'s is emphasized because the hard *th* is repeated twice in rapid succession, and also because, whereas in the first line the long *e*'s take a good deal of the weight, in this line the shortness of the preceding vowels throws the whole emphasis on to the consonantal sound. The seventh line opens with a very obvious alliteration on the *oo* already announced two lines earlier (assuming the allitera-

[1] *Paradise Lost*, i. 583.

tive pronunciation of *mournful*), and closes with an equally obvious alliteration on *ow*. The two are linked by the repetition of the *n-l* of *mournful* in the last two words of the line. There is little to notice in the next line except that the rhyme of the first and third lines is picked up in the first syllable of *mysteries*, and that the last syllable of *sorrow's* is not, in spite of appearances, a recurrence of the *ow* alliteration of the preceding line, which is about to be repeated so emphatically in the last two lines. The last two lines must be considered together and are highly interesting. In the first place the long *a* which was prominent earlier, but has been in abeyance for three lines, comes back in full force, three times repeated. In the second place the *ow* alliteration which was used somewhat too obviously in the seventh line is repeated with an obviousness which is made almost blatant by the repetition of the preceding consonants (*drowsily* and *drown*). And the *oo* and *o* of preceding lines recur. Then there are alliterations on *d* (quadruple), *l* (quadruple), *sh* (triple), and *w* (triple, not double, since there is a *w* in the middle of *anguish*), and *n* (triple, though not strongly marked). It is worth noticing that this *w-n* alliteration takes us back to the opening two lines.

I hope that any reader who has had the patience to follow this analysis will now think it worth while to have the stanza put before him again in its entirety, so that he can read it straight through, no longer dissecting, but with his ears, I hope, readier to hear its full and intricate harmonies.

No, no, go not to Lethe, neither twist
  Wolf's-bane, tight-rooted, for its poisonous wine;
Nor suffer thy pale forehead to be kiss'd
  By nightshade, ruby grape of Proserpine;
Make not your rosary of yew-berries,
  Nor let the beetle, nor the death-moth be
    Your mournful Psyche, nor the downy owl
A partner in your sorrow's mysteries;
  For shade to shade will come too drowsily,
    And drown the wakeful anguish of the soul.

The second stanza forms a kind of interlude. It opens with a line in which the only long vowel is that of the rhyming word, and throughout, till the last line, the much lower proportion of long vowels gives it a much lighter and more rapid movement.[1] We can perhaps examine it more cursorily than the first:

> But when the melancholy fit shall fall
> Sudden from heaven like a weeping cloud,
> That fosters the droop-headed flowers all,
> And hides the green hill in an April shroud;
> Then glut thy sorrow on a morning rose,
> Or on the rainbow of the salt sand-wave,
> Or on the wealth of globed peonies;
> Or if thy mistress some rich anger shows,
> Emprison her soft hand, and let her rave,
> And feed deep, deep upon her peerless eyes.

The main recurrent sounds throughout the stanza are *l*, which occurs in every line but one, opening very strongly in the first line, and then decreasing in insistence; *r*, which occurs in every line except the first and increases in insistence; and *n* which also occurs in every line but one, and rises to its maximum in the middle of the stanza.[2] *k* is carried over from the last two lines of the preceding stanza and repeated once in the first line and twice in the second, then fading out. *f* and *h*, which hardly were heard in the first stanza at all, are comparatively prominent. *d* and *p* are quietly kept in the background throughout, in readiness for their very strong emergence in the last two lines. Most important of all, *v*, which occurred in the first stanza only twice, in two unemphatic *of*'s, but which is going to dominate the beginning of the next stanza, is here quite firmly though not obtrusively sounded in the rhyme words of lines 6 and 9, as well as in two *of*'s. The whole of this stanza with its delicate movement is leading up to the strong deliberate emphasis of the monosyllables

[1] The actual figures of long and short vowels are 41 to 60 in the first stanza, 27 to 73 in the second.

[2] The incidences, by lines, are as follows: *l*, 4, 2, 2, 2, 1, 1, 2, 0, 1, 1; *r*, 0, 1, 3, 3, 3, 2, 1, 4, 3, 2; *n*, 2, 2, 0, 4, 3, 3, 2, 1, 3, 2.

of the last line, which quite simply, almost barely, repeats one vowel and two consonants four times each, and culminates in a second strong vowel which is made all the stronger because it has been only weakly foreshadowed by the preceding rhyme word.

The third stanza is slower in movement than the second, though neither so slow nor so heavy as the first; and owing to the arrangement of the long vowels and their recurrences it has a very strongly marked and indeed almost staccato rhythm. And its general effect is one of strong simplicity.

> She dwells with Beauty—Beauty that must die;
> And Joy, whose hand is ever at his lips
> Bidding adieu; and aching Pleasure nigh,
> Turning to Poison while the bee-mouth sips:
> Ay, in the very temple of delight
> Veil'd Melancholy has her sovran shrine,
> Though seen of none save him whose strenuous tongue
> Can burst Joy's grape against his palate fine;
> His soul shall taste the sadness of her might,
> And be among her cloudy trophies hung.

In the first two and a half lines there is an insistence on a sound which was recurrent in the first stanza, but occurred only once in the second, *oo*. Thereafter for six and a half lines there is an even more marked insistence on long *a* and long *i*, which are the only long vowels in two of the lines, and preponderant in two more. The alliteration on the two *th*'s is repeated twice, in the first and fourth lines. There is a steady undercurrent, much obscured by spelling, of *z*, which occurs (once in the *zh* form) once in every line but the third, and twice in the eighth. A good deal is made of *st* in the seventh, eighth, and ninth lines, where it increases the staccato effect which is running counter to the *z*'s. The seventh and tenth lines are linked not only by their rhyme but by the repetition of the rhyme internally, partially in *none* and completely in *among*. And there are the ordinary recurrences of *d* and *n*. But the most interesting feature of the stanza, apart from the limitation of the vowels, is the use of *v*. It occurs in an almost perfectly regular rise and fall. It does not occur in the first line; it is announced in the second, and disappears in the third and fourth; in the fifth it is sounded quite definitely, but, because of the words in which it occurs, not prominently; it is completely dominant in the sixth; in the seventh its two occurrences are still quietly audible; in the eighth it does not occur; and in the ninth we can just hear it dying away. There is one other point which is perhaps worth mention. It has been supposed that the shift in the rhyme scheme of the sestet in this last stanza (from *c d e c d e* to *c d e d c e*) is a mere slip or carelessness on Keats' part. But an artist of Keats' calibre does not, I think, permit himself slips of that kind. He may indeed have found that the demands of the sense as he wanted to write it would not easily allow him to maintain the scheme of the first two stanzas, and so acquiesced in an irregularity; but at least he did not write so from mere inadvertence. But I think that a closer examination will suggest that the shift is a matter of design and not of acquiescence. After the *c d e* of the first three lines of the sestet the ear has been led to expect the run of the corresponding triplet which will not arrive at its culmination till the end of the last line. But when it arrives at the end of the eighth line this expectation is disappointed, and the *d* rhyme coming a line earlier than it should produces a kind of pseudo-culmination, which increases the effect of the semicolon in leaving the last two lines in isolation. These two lines are in any case a kind of couplet in sense, though not a couplet in rhyme; and their conclusive effect is by this isolation greatly heightened. This will become clearer when we look back at the sestet of the first stanza, where the run of the second triplet tends to carry us over the stop after *mysteries*.

Before we leave this technical examination I should like to guard against a possible misapprehension. No one in his senses supposes that Keats or any other poet has these considerations in his mind while he is writing. He does not for example say to himself at the end of the second stanza of this ode, 'Now I must find an epithet for *eyes* that will repeat the *ee* and the *p* of *deep*'. Nor does he say at the beginning of the third stanza, 'Now we will have an exercise on *v*'. But he does know that certain sounds satisfy his ear and certain others do not. And it is not at all I believe the wild-goose chase that it may at first appear for his readers, if they will do him the justice of being also his students, to attempt to discover why some sounds satisfied him and others did not. What we are attempting, not indeed during such technical analysis, but as a result of it, is to hear the poem, as nearly as may be, as Keats himself heard it. And even partially to succeed in that attempt is worth some pains.

VI. *LAMIA*

AFTER completing all the Odes except *To Autumn* Keats began his work with Brown on *Otho* and apparently at the same time reverted to narrative. Exactly when *Lamia* was begun we have no data to determine, but on the 12th of July he writes that in the interval between finishing the first act and beginning the second of *Otho* he has completed the first part of *Lamia*,[1] and by the 5th of September he had finished both *Otho* and *Lamia* and was occupied with the revision of *The Eve of St. Agnes*.[2] The work of this summer marks a very clear stage in Keats' poetic development, and a very significant change in his temper and outlook. And of the two pieces of work on which he was engaged *Lamia* is not only better worth study than *Otho*, as being the piece at which he was working independently, but is also intrinsically worth more careful study than it sometimes receives, not least because Keats himself, in opposition to the judgement of the majority of his critics, rated it very definitely above either *Isabella* or *The Eve of St. Agnes*. Why he did so, and how he expressed himself about it, we shall see later when we come to examine the changed temper and method of narration which the poem exhibits. But at the outset it will not be without interest to examine the metre which he chose for his reversion to narrative, since the metre itself is at once a reversion and a development. Since *Endymion* he has used *ottava rima*, Spenserian stanza, and the stanza which he invented for the Odes (apart from the blank verse of *Hyperion*, which is in a class by itself). None of these perhaps can be called elaborate metres, but they are at any rate stanzaic and have a certain complication. He now returns to the simplicity of the heroic couplet; but not to the heroic couplet of either *Endymion* or of the early poems. There has been a kind of conspiracy of the critics from Woodhouse onwards to persuade us that

[1] MBF, 128 (388). [2] Ib. 140 (414).

Keats did nothing more original than imitate the type of heroic couplet which Dryden used in the *Fables*. The typical comments are such as these: 'The metre is Drydenian heroic, with many triplets and many Alexandrines.' 'The versification is closely modelled upon the *Fables* of Dryden from which Keats learnt how to relate his metre with his sentence structure and to use both the triplet and the Alexandrine with striking success.' 'For his model in Lamia he turned to the *Fables* of Dryden, the best modern example of the use of the heroic couplet in narrative verse. The versification and style of *Lamia* give clear evidence that he had made a careful study of Dryden. In contrast with the earlier couplets of the 1817 volume and of *Endymion* his employment of the run-on line and the feminine and weak endings is now carefully controlled and he trusts to a careful use of the triplet and the Alexandrine to give his verse the necessary variety.' Nothing could be much more plainly or decisively stated; if we accept these statements we shall expect to find in *Lamia* a close resemblance to the metre of the *Fables*, and an equally wide divergence from the earlier poems, not only in the matter of feminine endings but also in the proportion of run-on lines. But before we accept the statements it will perhaps be as well to examine the facts.

In the first place it is necessary to distinguish four different types of 'run-on', which differ widely both in the strength and the nature of their influence on the general effect of the metre. There are first two types in which the run-on is within the couplet:

1. The type in which the opening of the second line, though it carries on the sense of the first and is not separated from it by any punctuation, is yet not essential to the completion of the sense; with the result that even if the passage were being read as prose some slight pause would be admissible, and often natural.

> Frighted away the Dryads and the Fauns
> From rushes green, and brakes, and cowslip'd lawns.

2. The type in which, though still within the confines of the couplet, the sense of the first line is not complete without the second, the commonest case being that in which the verb is in one line and its subject or object in the other.

> For somewhere in that sacred island dwelt
> A nymph, to whom the hoofed Satyrs knelt;
> At whose white feet the languid Tritons poured
> Pearls, while on land they wither'd and adored.

And then two types which are the same as the first two except that the run-on is not within the limits of the couplet but between the second line of one couplet and the first line of the next:

3. The God, dove-footed, glided silently
Round bush and tree, soft-brushing, in his speed,
The taller grasses. . . .

4. Such as once heard, in gentle heart, destroys
All pain but pity: thus the lone voice spake:

Here is a passage which illustrates all the types:

> And by my power is her beauty veil'd   1
> To keep it unaffronted, unassail'd   3
> By the love-glances of unlovely eyes,
> Of Satyrs, Fauns, and blear'd Silenus' sighs.
> Pale grew her immortality, for woe   2
> Of all these lovers, and she grieved so   3
> I took compassion on her, bade her steep   2
> Her hair in weïrd syrops, that would keep   4
> Her loveliness invisible, yet free   1
> To wander as she loves, in liberty.

These types are arranged in ascending order of their effect in breaking down the staccato and disjointed effect of the satiric heroic couplet as used in its most rigid and telling form by Pope, and creating an impression of continuity. An absence, or comparative absence, of any run-on at all forces upon the reader an impression first of a series of single lines and secondly of a series of couplets, sharply marked off from one another. The admission of a reasonable number of type 2 of run-on makes the couplet and not the single line the unit, but if anything marks off the couplets from one another with even more precision. But the moment that types 3 and 4 are admitted in any considerable proportion the metre not only becomes more flexible but in fact entirely changes its character. Becoming legato instead of staccato it becomes more suitable for narrative; but it is also in danger of becoming a trifle invertebrate. At its worst it becomes blank verse with a jingling obbligato of rhyme, which it would be much better without, since the writers are liable to rely upon the rhyme to save them from the necessity of knitting their verse together, which in true blank verse can only be done by the exercise of the skilled craftsmanship of the pause. I suppose that the flaccid heroic couplet is about the easiest of all English metres to write at a barely tolerable level.

Now suppose that we take Dryden's *Fables*, and select, as presumably typical, the first 100 lines of the short *Character of a Good Parson* and the first and last 100 lines of each of the others; we shall have some 1,900 lines for our examination; let us work out the percentage of run-on lines. Then to make sure that we are playing fair let us select the four fables with the highest proportion of run-on lines and work out the figures for them; and then let us work out the same figures for *Lamia*. Here are the results:

	All Fables	*Select Fables*	*Lamia*
Type 1	4·0	4·5	11·6
" 2	6·2	8·1	8·2
" 3	. .	. .	4·2
" 4	0·6	0·9	9·2
Total . . .	10·8	13·5	33·2

That is to say, *Lamia* has proportionately three times as many run-on lines as the *Fables* as a whole, and two and a half times as many as even the four *Fables* that have the highest proportion of run-on lines. But what is much more significant, *Lamia* has at the lowest estimate a ten times higher proportion than the *Fables* of that type of run-on which is the most potent in its effect on the character of the metre. In face of this the statement that Keats modelled his metre for *Lamia* upon the *Fables* seems to me quite untenable. What in fact he did, as we shall see, and very characteristically did, was to adopt from Dryden certain points of technique which modified as he wished the other and looser type of heroic couplet.

And now what about the contrast between *Lamia* and the 1817 poems? When we come to examine this we are met at first with some surprising results. Every reader is aware of a complete difference between the effect of, let us say, the epistle to George Keats, or of *Calidore*, and the effect of *Lamia*. And we tend vaguely and uncritically, though no doubt naturally, to suppose that this difference depends on a difference in the proportion of run-on lines. But when we come from supposition to examination, this will not do at all. In the matter of run-on lines the 1817 poems and *Lamia* are almost absurdly and quite disconcertingly similar. The actual figures are:

	1817	*Lamia*
Type 1 . . .	11·9	11·6
„ 2 . . .	8·5	8·2
„ 3 . . .	5·6	4·2
„ 4 . . .	6·2	9·2
Total . .	32·2	33·2[1]

It is clear then that we have to look elsewhere for the cause of that difference in effect which is so apparent. There are, I think, two main causes. The first is the difference in the proportions of feminine rhymes. The feminine ending in blank verse, when used occasionally for variety, is, or may be, a grateful relief to the ear. When used frequently, as by Fletcher, it results in a kind of sloppy and nerveless monotony. But when used frequently in heroic couplets the effect is even worse, and it results oxymoronically in a sort of feeble emphasis. Now the contrast between the 1817 poems and *Lamia* in this

[1] For the purposes of this analysis I have excluded *Sleep and Poetry* from the 1817 poems, since, as will appear later, it has metrically much closer affinities with *Endymion* than with the other poems in its own volume.

matter of the feminine rhyme is violent. In the 1817 poems this rhyme is not an occasional variant. It is an integral part of the style. Exactly 20 per cent. of the rhymes in these poems are feminine. In *Lamia*, with the possible exception of one 'heaven-given', there is no feminine rhyme at all. And just how important this absence is may be seen by comparing the metre of *Lamia* not only with the 1817 poems but also with the other example of Keats' use of the heroic couplet, *Endymion*. In *Sleep and Poetry*, which is a transitional poem, the proportion of run-on lines rises from the 32 per cent. of the other 1817 poems to 50 per cent., but the percentage of feminine rhymes drops from 20 to 14. In the first book of *Endymion* the percentage of run-on lines remains at this new level, but that of feminine rhymes drops further to 8. In the remaining three books the percentage of run-on lines drops slightly, but that of feminine rhymes very markedly to 4.[1]

The significance of the comparison lies in this, that a typical passage of *Endymion*, in spite of the higher proportion of run-on lines, does yet, because of the much lower proportion of feminine rhymes, resemble much more closely a typical passage from *Lamia* than does any typical passage from the 1817 poems, particularly if we select from *Lamia* a passage which does not illustrate the new element which Keats introduced, which we have still to examine. Let us set three passages against one another.

Was heard no more
For clamour, when the golden palace door
Opened again, and from without, in shone
A new magnificence. On oozy throne
Smooth-moving came Oceanus the old,
To take a latest glimpse at his sheep-fold,
Before he went into his quiet cave
To muse for ever—Then a lucid wave,
Scoop'd from its trembling sisters of mid-sea,
Afloat, and pillowing up the majesty

[1] The detailed figures for this and the other points are given in *Note J* (*page* 305).

Of Doris, and the Aegean seer, her spouse—
Next, on a dolphin, clad in laurel boughs,
Theban Amphion leaning on his lute:
His fingers went across it—All were mute
To gaze on Amphitrite, queen of pearls,
And Thetis pearly too.—[1]

One, who, of late, had ta'en sweet forest walks
With him who elegantly chats, and talks—
The wrong'd Libertas,—who has told you stories
Of laurel chaplets, and Apollo's glories;
Of troops chivalrous prancing through a city,
And tearful ladies made for love, and pity:
With many else which I have never known.
Thus have I thought; and days on days have flown
Slowly, or rapidly—unwilling still
For you to try my dull, unlearned quill.
Nor should I now, but that I've known you long;
That you first taught me all the sweets of song:
The grand, the sweet, the terse, the free, the fine;
What swell'd with pathos, and what right divine:
Spenserian vowels that elope with ease,
And float along like birds o'er summer seas;[2]

Jove heard his vows, and better'd his desire;
For by some freakful chance he made retire
From his companions, and set forth to walk,
Perhaps grown wearied of their Corinth talk:
Over the solitary hills he fared,
Thoughtless at first, but ere eve's star appeared
His phantasy was lost, where reason fades,
In the calm'd twilight of Platonic shades.
Lamia beheld him coming, near, more near—
Close to her passing, in indifference drear,
His silent sandals swept the mossy green;
So neighbour'd to him, and yet so unseen
She stood: he pass'd, shut up in mysteries,
His mind wrapp'd like his mantle, while her eyes
Follow'd his steps, and her neck regal white
Turn'd—syllabling thus. . . .[3]

[1] *End.* iii. 990–1005.
[2] *To Charles Cowden Clarke*, 42–57.
[3] *Lamia*, i. 229–44.

So far we have seen the metre of *Lamia* standing midway between that of the 1817 poems and the *Fables*. On the one hand it is in strong contrast to the *Fables* in the matter of run-on lines, in which it resembles the 1817 poems. On the other hand it breaks away entirely from the 1817 poems in the matter of feminine rhyme, and here it resembles the *Fables*, in the selected passages of which there is only one certain feminine rhyme (in an odd couplet of *The Cock and the Fox*) and two doubtful ones (of the 'heav'n-driv'n' type). But this is not the end of the story. There is no doubt that Keats had studied Dryden; no one can read *Lamia* with the least degree of attention and fail to be convinced of that. What I am trying to show is that his study did not lead him along the easy path of lazy imitation, as has been supposed, but that rather he selected from Dryden, and learned to use, what he wanted for his own purposes, without allowing himself to be lured into a thoughtless copying of what he did not want. He learned two things from Dryden. In the first place he learned how to use the end-stopped couplet when he wanted it, though as we have seen he seldom did want it, and the use of it after the manner of Dryden would have destroyed the effect at which Keats was aiming. But there are a few isolated passages, and effective passages, in *Lamia* when for eight or ten lines there is a run of thoroughly Drydenian couplets.[1] But the chief lesson that he learned from Dryden was the use of the Alexandrine and the triplet, particularly the former. In the 1817 poems there are a few triplets. In *Endymion* there are none. And even his study of Dryden does not seem to have made Keats much fonder of this technical trick, since even in *Lamia* the proportion is considerably less than half that in the *Fables*. But he learned from his study of Dryden to admire the right use of the Alexandrine. Neither in the 1817 poems nor in *Endymion* are there any Alexandrines at all. But in *Lamia* there is a very considerable number (between 5 and 6 per cent. of the

[1] E.g. ii. 86–97; i. 169–80, 257–64.

total number of lines), and indeed a considerably higher proportion than in the *Fables* themselves. Keats saw that the Alexandrine was going to give him something that he particularly needed. The effect of the Alexandrine is much more specific than that of a merely pleasant variation. The end of the ordinary closed heroic couplet is simply a dead stop with no particular expectation of anything to follow. The end of the Alexandrine is just as definite a pause, but with this difference, that it is an expectant pause. It has much the effect of a *ritardando* in music. The ear is waiting for the resumption of the ordinary beat of the rhythm; and therefore, which is the important point, the attention is also waiting for the continuation of the train of thought. The Alexandrine gives a firm articulation, avoiding a shapeless fluency on the one hand and the disjointedness of too heavy end-stopping on the other.

In brief, Keats is doing here, in another metrical region, exactly what we have just seen him doing with the stanza form of the Odes; namely making the best of both worlds. Neither of the two orthodox sonnet forms satisfied him, and so he invented a verse form which incorporates the advantages of both and the disadvantages of neither. So, we may reasonably suppose, neither of the forms of the heroic couplet satisfied him for his narrative purpose. The closed form, even in the much freer than satiric shape to which Dryden had developed it, still seemed to him too staccato and too little continuous for narrative. The freer form, which he had himself used earlier, had a dangerous tendency towards fluent monotony. It might serve for a familiar letter, but he had seen, when his eyes were opened, from the lamentable example of the *Story of Rimini*, how it sagged under the stress of narrative. And even in *Endymion*, though he had managed to use a modified and greatly improved form of it for four thousand lines, he was yet aware of its weaknesses. Its progress was not the kind of progress that he wanted. It was serpentine, not the movement of firm steps, at once connected and distinct. He keeps therefore the freedom of the run-on couplet, as against the abruptness of Dryden; but he stiffens the whole structure by the absolute veto on the feminine rhyme, and by occasional passages of end-stopping; and he articulates it by the skilful use of the Alexandrine. And in the upshot the metre of *Lamia* is not the least of Keats' technical achievements.

Equipped then with this metre, what did Keats do with it. He took as the source for his story a passage in Burton's *Anatomy of Melancholy*:

> 'Philostratus, in his fourth book *de Vita Apollonii*, hath a memorable instance in this kind, which I may not omit, of one Menippus Lycius, a young man twenty-five years of age, that going between Cenchreas and Corinth, met such a phantasm in the habit of a fair gentlewoman, which, taking him by the hand, carried him home to her house, in the suburbs of Corinth, and told him she was a Phoenician by birth, and if he would tarry with her, he should hear her sing and play, and drink such wine as never any drank, and no man should molest him; but she, being fair and lovely, would live and die with him, that was fair and lovely to behold. The young man, a philosopher, otherwise staid and discreet, able to moderate his passions, though not this of love, tarried with her a while to his great content, and at last married her, to whose wedding, amongst other guests, came Apollonius; who, by some probable conjectures, found her out to be a serpent, a lamia; and that all her furniture was, like Tantalus' gold, described by Homer, no substance but mere illusions. When she saw herself descried, she wept, and desired Apollonius to be silent, but he would not be moved, and thereupon she, plate, house, and all that was in it, vanished in an instant: many thousands took notice of this fact, for it was done in the midst of Greece.'[1]

There are the bare bones. Now to clothe them. Or rather, on more carefully examining it, to rearticulate the skeleton. The poem is going to be called *Lamia*, and there is to be no doubt in the reader's mind from the outset as to the nature of the 'phantasm in the form of a fair gentlewoman'. No doubt by this method something will be

[1] Part III, Sect. 2, Memb. 1, Subs. 1.

lost; there will be less chance of 'suggestion' and the eerie; but something will also be gained, in clearness of line and in 'irony'. Keats is quite deliberately discarding the method of *Christabel*, and considers that the gain will more than counterbalance the loss. The contrast between the two poems, both dealing with a serpent-woman, is most illuminating. Coleridge, having used in *The Ancient Mariner* with brilliant effect the direct matter-of-fact method of describing the supernatural, the method of the old ballad, changes his technique entirely in *Christabel* and uses the suggestive method throughout. We are being subtly prepared for some revelation of horror at which we can only guess. And there is a certain trickiness about Coleridge's use of this method which sometimes becomes irritating.

> I guess, 'twas frightful there to see
> A lady so richly clad as she—
> Beautiful exceedingly! (66–8)

says Coleridge. And we wonder why he guesses anything of the kind except that he wants artificially to create an 'atmosphere'. The appearance of a beautiful lady beautifully clothed may be surprising, but is not on the face of it frightful. When we come to the behaviour of the mastiff bitch we are aware that a trick is being played on us, and not too well played. And the clearest glimpse of Coleridge at work is given in a suppressed line. We read in the text:

> Behold! her bosom and half her side——
> A sight to dream of, not to tell!
> O shield her! shield sweet Christabel! (252–4)

And we think, as we were intended to think, that the revelation which we are not allowed to see must have been something too horrible for description. And then we find that as Coleridge wrote the passage there was nothing more horrific than

> Behold! her bosom and half her side
> Are lean and old and foul of hue.

Startling, no doubt, but hardly blood-curdling. But Coleridge is bound that he will make our flesh creep, and thinks that he can do it by an aposiopesis and a comment.

The Keats of *The Eve of St. Agnes* might have attempted this method, though one may doubt whether his defining and etching imagination would easily have succeeded. But the Keats of *Lamia* will have none of it. He is going to delineate, not suggest; everything is to stand clear in the bright hard sunlight of the south. His work is to be a Velazquez, not a Corot.[1] And so he is going to begin, not merely by telling us that the woman of his poem is a snake-woman, but by showing her as a snake, so that we know from the outset exactly where we are, and what the revelation is to be. But with his usual dramatic instinct he is going first to set the stage, and he does this with great beauty, though at perhaps unnecessary length, in the description of Hermes which occupies the first forty odd lines of the poem. And then, after the 'lone voice' has spoken, we come with Hermes, round bush and tree, full on the gordian shape of the snake. It is easy, particularly if we are reading fast for the sake of the story and with slackened attention, to get from those lines little but a rather indiscriminate impression of brilliant colour, and wholly to miss the astonishing compression and vividness of them. There is a wealth of colour, but there is line too, defining the outlines of the colours, and movement, as the colours shift in iridescent interplay with the snake's breathing. The colours are vermilion, gold, green, blue, crimson, silver, and they are set against a dark background; the shapes are stripes, freckles, eyes, bars, and moons. The snake is coiled (*cirque-couchant* and *gordian*) and in movement (*palpitating*). And there is one bit of craftsmanship which is worth noticing; after four strong, balanced, and Drydenian heroic couplets, at the point where it will most effectively reinforce the sense, comes an equally strong

[1] I do not know whether it has been observed how fond Keats is of 'line', particularly of slanting line.

run-on at the end of the fourth couplet in *interwreathed Their lustres*. Here is the passage complete:

> he found a palpitating snake,
> Bright, and cirque-couchant in a dusky brake.
> She was a gordian shape of dazzling hue,
> Vermilion-spotted, golden, green, and blue;
> Striped like a zebra, freckled like a pard,
> Eyed like a peacock, and all crimson barr'd;
> And full of silver moons, that, as she breathed,
> Dissolv'd, or brighter shone, or interwreathed
> Their lustres with the gloomier tapestries— (45–53)

There is the accomplished craftsman enjoying himself in the sure exercise of his craft.

In the long passage which follows, down to line 145, there is little to remark. There is an echo or two of Milton, like

> the star of Lethe not delay'd. (81)

There are two or three reminiscences of *The Eve of St. Agnes*; *mission'd* appears to have pleased Keats, and he repeats it here in the *mission'd phoebean dart* of the manuscript which had to yield, in the interests of correct quantity, to *bright Phoebean dart*; *about these thornless wilds* sounds like an adaptation of *about these thorny ways*; and the picture of the rose shutting to a bud seems to repeat itself in

> self-folding like a flower
> That faints into itself at evening hour. (138)

And there is plenty of interest from the metrical point of view, particularly the frequency of the Alexandrine, which was even more frequent in the first draft, since the straight triplet of lines 112–14, a device of which Keats was not fond, was originally a triplet ending with an Alexandrine.

In line 145 we see the last of the introductory and scene-setting Hermes, and float out into the main stream of the story. And it moves with smooth power from the transformation of Lamia from serpent to woman, through the meeting with Lycius, to their entry into Corinth. Of the opulence of this passage it would be idle to attempt a detailed inventory of the items. They must be allowed to produce their own cumulative effect. But one may perhaps draw attention to a few points: the power of sudden contrast, for example between the violence of the transformation scene and the gentleness which succeeds it; the vividness of the picture of the waiting Lamia, standing out against the background of the wood and the sloping green; the compression of a whole picture into one word, as in 'the *moth-time* of that evening dim', or (though less happy) 'their *Corinth* talk', or '*tress-lifting* waves'; most of all perhaps the power over the great single line, which yet does not overpower its context but is led up to and supported by it, of which the finest instance is probably

> A song of love, too sweet for earthly lyres,
> While, like held breath, the stars drew in their panting fires. (299)

But these rich incidental beauties never for a moment impede the orderly forward movement of the narrative; rather they enhance and vitalize it. And in nothing I think is Keats' development as an artist more clearly shown than in this sense of proportion, the subordination of parts to whole. *Isabella* was ill-proportioned, overloaded with an ill-devised and sentimentally diffuse beginning; even in *The Eve of St. Agnes* there are beauties, which, ill though we could spare them, are irrelevant to the narrative, and indeed distract our attention from it; notably the elaboration of the description of the casement, and the feast of fruits. But in *Lamia* nothing is more remarkable than the well-proportioned and close-knit articulation of the structure, and the nervous strength of its movement, which make it easy for it to carry lightly the richness of its adornment.

Where the narrative halts or moves awkwardly it is not from over-elaboration but from the intrusion of reflection or generalized comment which Keats had not yet learned to manage and control. In the passage now under consideration there are two such unfortunate interludes; the first follows most disconcertingly on the perfect description of Lamia,

> a maid
> More beautiful than ever twisted braid,
> Or sigh'd, or blush'd, or on spring-flowered lea
> Spread a green kirtle to the minstrelsy: (185–8)

The next two lines are a trifle ominous:

> A virgin purest lipp'd, yet in the lore
> Of love deep learned to the red heart's core:

but if Keats had stopped there, there would be little to quarrel with. However, he goes on to write six lines which have a specious appearance of reflective profundity, and in fact mean as nearly as may be exactly nothing; and adds as a kind of ill-connected postscript three lines of a feeble and diffusely irrelevant conceit.

> Not one hour old, yet of sciential brain
> To unperplex bliss from its neighbour pain;
> Define their pettish limits, and estrange
> Their points of contact, and swift counterchange;
> Intrigue with the specious chaos, and dispart
> Its most ambiguous atoms with sure art;
> As though in Cupid's college she had spent
> Sweet days a lovely graduate, still unshent,
> And kept his rosy terms in idle languishment.

How the spending of sweet days, or even the keeping of rosy terms, in idle languishment, even though the course was one of post-graduate research, would equip any student with sciential lore is as obscure as whether the mysterious state of being unshent is an advantage or a handicap or merely a peculiarity.

But if this passage is unfortunate, the second is actively disastrous. The description of Lamia's solicitation has twice shaved the rocks of tastelessness which from the very start of his career have been Keats' most serious peril; but each time he has maintained enough control to hold his craft off and into deep water again. Both *Her soft look growing coy* and *He, sick to lose The amorous promise of her lone complain* have given us a moment of apprehension, but no serious damage has been done. And then quite suddenly, when we feel that the danger is over, Keats with perfect deliberation wrenches his helm hard up and runs straight before the wind full on the reef.

> And every word she spake entic'd him on
> To unperplex'd delight and pleasure known.
> Let the mad poets say whate'er they please
> Of the sweets of Faeries, Peris, Goddesses,
> There is not such a treat among them all,
> Haunters of cavern, lake, and waterfall,
> As a real woman, (326–32)

Much has been said of the unhappy influence of Leigh Hunt on Keats; but one has regretfully to admit a kind of blind spot in Keats which made him react easily to the influence. And Leigh Hunt even at his worst never achieved such a piece of trivial vulgarity as that.

And then, just as suddenly as the disaster occurred, Keats recovers himself and becomes the great poet again. Within twenty lines of the shipwreck Lamia and Lycius have entered the gates of the city of Corinth. The curtain falls and is to rise again at once for the second scene of the first act. But first the new scene must be set, the scene of a great city at night. And this is how Keats does it:

> As men talk in a dream, so Corinth all,
> Throughout her palaces imperial,
> And all her populous streets and temples lewd,
> Mutter'd, like tempest in the distance brew'd,
> To the wide-spreaded night above her towers.
> Men, women, rich and poor, in the cool hours,
> Shuffled their sandals o'er the pavement white,
> Companion'd or alone; while many a light
> Flared, here and there, from wealthy festivals,
> And threw their moving shadows on the walls,
> Or found them cluster'd in the corniced shade
> Of some arch'd temple door, or dusky colonnade. (350–61)

That passage needs no comment; but it merits the most careful study that we can give it if we want to realize what kind of an artist Keats has become. The Keats of *Endymion* would have taken fifty meandering and mellifluous lines to draw his picture, and left it vaguer and less detailed in the end; the Keats even of six months ago, of *The Eve of St. Agnes*, though he would have seen his picture clearly, had not yet learned the power of riding his expression ruthlessly on the curb, of saying just what is needed and not one syllable more, which makes of this passage, in its trenchancy and economy, a miniature masterpiece with few rivals in English.

Across the stage thus set passes rapidly the grave, and to Lycius sinister, figure of the third main actor, and as the two enter the doors of Lamia's house the curtain falls on the first Act, to the accompaniment of the ominous last four lines. It is interesting to notice Keats' strong sense of the theatre again operative. What is described fully is just what the theatre audience would see and hear, and no more. The door is vividly described, and it opens to the sound of music; but as the figures disappear at the back of the stage the open door discloses nothing but a vague space.

At the end of the first Part we can for the first time in this poem see something of Keats at work. The manuscript which H. Buxton Forman collated and from which the majority of the variant readings which he records were taken is described by him as a carefully finished manuscript finally revised for the press, and we need therefore less regret the fact that since it was sold in 1897 it seems to have disappeared. But for certain parts of the poem we have an earlier stage than that represented by this manuscript. There is in the Amy Lowell collection at Harvard a fragment containing the last eleven and a half lines of this first part, and belonging I should guess to a second draft of the poem.[1] The first six and a half lines are written out

[1] The fair-copy condition of the first six lines of the fragment makes it more or less certain that it did not belong to the first draft. On the other hand, it belonged to a draft which contained eight more lines than the printed text, and four more therefore than the 'finished' manuscript (which has four lines not printed), since it numbers our line 392 as 400.

with no correction, and correspond to the printed text except for one or two spellings, and the reading of *Ever* for *Some time* in line 389 and *some few* for *a few* in the next line. But the remaining lines are re-written three times. Keats first wrote:

> the most curious
> Who strove to trace them homeward to their house
> Were foild they knew not how—but what can foil
> The winged muse? What poesy not win

but this does not even rhyme, so the last line is deleted and this substituted—

> The humblest Muse unweried of her toil?

and *trace* in the second line is altered to the awkward *maze*. But Keats is evidently attached to the word *win*, perhaps having it in front of him in the first draft, since under *her toil*, as though it was the end of a line to be completed later, he writes

> and what can win
> The scret

At this point, however, he deletes everything from *Were foild* onwards, and starts again:

> Were foil'd they knew not how, they could not tell
> And

Then he deletes that, and tries it, seeing whether a little punctuation will help matters at all, as

> Were foild, but how it was they knew not well

then tries *and* instead of *but*; then deletes both *foild* and *and* and writes in *puzzled*, so that the line runs

> Were puzzled, how it was they knew not well

and though it is not very satisfactory he cannot bring himself to tinker with this unimportant line any further for the moment and goes on

> ~~Perpaps this~~
> This flitter-winged verse perhaps might tell
> If it durt speak, what it should dare to speak

(which seems about as feeble as a line can be, but Keats goes on, as it were with the obstinacy of desperation)

> But ~~this~~ now is Poesy's long ember week
> And against fashion folly 'tis to sin,
> Tho over Lamia's head the faery Muse flew in

These lamentable lines are, naturally enough, not subjected to any minor emendations, but scratched out bodily, and Keats wearily writes down for the fourth time

> Were foil'd

and reverts to the first continuation

> they knew not how.

Then it occurs to him that this feeble ending to the line may as well disappear altogether, so he puts a full stop at *foil'd.*, scratches out *they knew not how*, and starts a new sentence, so that the line stands

> Were foil'd. And, but this

but then, foreseeing I think that on this basis he is going to find himself at the end of a line with *verse* which he does not want, he deletes what he has written, goes back to the last of the undeleted lines at the top of the page (*Who strove to maze . . .*), cuts that out also, and incorporates its substance in the line he is now at work on, and continues:

> Were foild, who strove to maze them to their house
> And, (but the flitter winged verse must tell
> ~~What woe~~
> For truth's sake, what woe afterwards befel,)
> 'Twould humour many a heart to close the door
> Upon their happy days, incredulous of more.

In the 'finished' manuscript Keats copied the last line but one as above as far as *close*, and then, to avoid the weak ending *of more*, put the idea of closing the door into the one word *shut* in the next line, and wrote his final couplet as

> 'Twould humour many a heart to leave them thus,
> Shut from the busy world of more incredulous.

But the fragment makes clear the intended meaning of the

last line, which, in the absence of a comma after world, is naturally interpreted to mean 'the busy world of more incredulous people'. The study of this passage, trivial enough though it is in itself, is of some significance as showing how Keats only arrived at even the more pedestrian portions of Lamia in the sweat of his brow and with a deal of vexation.

Part II of the poem opens with another unhappy piece of generalized reflection, but after ten lines of this, and five further lines of a vigorous but somewhat incomprehensible description of Love behaving like a monstrous and hornet-like glow-worm, the narrative gets under way again, and begins with a piece of lovely description, two lines of which are so characteristic of the bright sunlight and clean-cut outlines of *Lamia*, as contrasted with the faery moonlight of *The Eve of St. Agnes*, that they are worth quoting:

> and let appear
> Unveil'd the summer heaven, blue and clear
> Between two marble shafts. (20–2)

But after this Keats has to wander for a while in a region in which he is never happy. It is unfortunately necessary that Lycius and Lamia should have a conversation in which the climax is prepared for, and while Keats is seldom successful with a conversation of any kind he is almost invariably at his bad worst when the exchanges are between two lovers. And for all the pains that he took over this passage, and he took many, he could not raise it to within measurable distance of the rest of the poem. It is as though a kind of languor overtook him, his only escape from which was into a febrile over-emphasis.

To realize the efforts which Keats made to render this passage adequate we have only to glance at H. Buxton Forman's edition, in which the apparatus criticus takes up more room than the text; and the passage from line 82 to line 105 is of particular interest, since for it we have three different states. There is the Houghton fragment, which shows the usual signs of the preliminary rough work; then we have readings of the 'finished' manuscript as recorded by Buxton Forman; but this differs much more widely from the printed text than it does in the rest of the poem, and it is clear that Keats worked over the whole passage again, greatly to its improvement. But after the time spent in examining the close of the last book the detailed examination of this passage had better perhaps be relegated to the notes.[1]

After we have hurried through this unsatisfactory passage, delaying just long enough to appreciate the few gems that stand out from the unworthy setting, such as

> Fine was the mitigated fury, like
> Apollo's presence when in act to strike
> The serpent— (78–80)

we come back with relief to Lamia alone, the promise of the wedding feast given, setting herself

> high-thoughted, how to dress
> The misery in fit magnificence. (115)

and the poem rises again to its true level. The description of the glowing banquet room, magically created, is vivid and superbly rich. But just as we are beginning to wonder whether Keats is not becoming, as he used too easily to be, intoxicated by the mere pleasure of gorgeous description, we find that it is all only a background for the central figure.

> Lamia, regal drest,
> Silently paced about, and as she went,
> In pale contented sort of discontent,
> Mission'd

(Keats is determined to get his favourite word in somewhere)

> Mission'd her viewless servants to enrich
> The fretted splendour of each nook and niche (133–7)

And from this point on the poem moves strongly, with hardly a false step, to its conclusion. There is the coming of the rout of guests, and among them the fatal sage; the

[1] *See Note K* (*page* 304).

yet fuller and more lavish description of the banquet hall and the growing fervour and clamour of the feast (which was only arrived at by the most rigorous treatment of an unhappy earlier draft).[1] There follows the last of the reflective or choric interludes, but even this, though probably longer than it need have been, is carried by the urgency of the approaching climax, and also contains in it the kernel of the 'meaning' of the whole story:

> Do not all charms fly
> At the mere touch of cold philosophy (229)

and after this the tension steadily increases as Lamia pales into insensibility and the music dies away into a deadly silence as the guests watch the voiceless contest between Apollonius and the bride. One has to admit that the last forty lines or so hardly maintain this level, and are almost anticlimactic. The troubles, as usual, begin with conversation, and the interchange between Lycius' denunciation of the sage and the latter's reply 'Gruff with contempt', which is meant no doubt to be realistic, is not in the least convincing, and then the tension cannot be restored, even by the startlingly effective

> Then Lamia breath'd death breath;

in time to have us in the right mood for the climax

> no sooner said,
> Than with a frightful scream she vanished:

One cannot escape the impression that Keats was tiring, that he has, as it were, run himself out twenty yards from the tape, and has to finish not as he would but as best he can.

And he might well be tired. It is not only that *Lamia* is part of a very hard summer's work, and of hard work conducted under the almost intolerable strain of a passionate love which distracted him from the very work through success in which alone lay any hope of its consummation. It is that *Lamia* drew for its 'fire' relentlessly on the strength of its creator. We are aware of a tensity

[1] *See Note L (page* 307).

and a passion behind it of which we are aware I think in no other poem at all which Keats wrote, except (if he wrote it) the small fragment *This living hand* . . ., but of which we are all too painfully aware in all his later letters to Fanny Brawne. The *Ode to a Nightingale* and *The Eve of St. Agnes* are both 'poems of escape'. In the one he leaves the world together; in the other he takes refuge in an imagined realization in the world of phantasy which the actual world does not appear to offer. But by the time he came to write *Lamia* he was finished with such evasions; he had turned to face things as he saw them, and the prospect was a pretty daunting one. But just because he knew that at last he had turned, and knew that in *Lamia*, for all that it was a fairy tale, he yet had a firmer grip upon essential realities than ever he had in the milder beauties of all that had gone before, he rated *Lamia* as he did. The contrast between Keats' own judgement and that of his critics is one of the most significant curiosities of criticism. Lamb greatly preferred *Isabella* on the surprising grounds that he preferred an ounce of 'feeling' to a pound of 'fancy'.[1] Sir Sidney Colvin, though admitting that it is a work of genius, would yet put it lowest of the three tales, partly on the grounds of the incidental flaws, but mainly on the grounds of the 'one fundamental flaw' of the moral, by which he means, as he explains, not any crude moral lesson but 'the bewilderment in which it leaves us as to the effect intended to be made on our imaginative sympathies'. And later, in reference to the lines beginning 'What wreath for Lamia?', he makes the significant comment, 'These lines to my mind have not only the fault of breaking the story at a critical point and anticipating its issue, but challenge the mind to untimely questionings and reflections'.[2] Even Professor de Sélincourt, having written, 'It is a masterpiece of narrative, in construction not equalled elsewhere by Keats, whilst the conflict of emotion between the worship of beauty and

[1] In a notice contributed to the *New Times*; see *The Works of Charles and Mary Lamb*, ed. E. V. Lucas, vol. i, pp. 200, 470.

[2] SC, 408.

the calls of higher reason gives a passionate force to the whole', which seems to me a just summary, and one of far more insight than the other two, yet goes on to single out for special praise certain passages in *Lamia* which are more characteristic of the earlier Keats, and continues 'These qualities find their fullest and most unfettered expression where Keats is freest from external restrictions of style and method, in the treatment of romantic themes drawn from mediaeval sources—in *Isabella*, in *The Eve of St. Agnes*, in the fragmentary *Eve of St. Mark* and in *La Belle Dame sans Merci*'.[1] Keats himself does not say a great deal about it, but what he does say is decisive enough. He told Woodhouse that he thought *Isabella* mawkish,[2] and writing to him ten days later he compares the three tales. 'Isabella is what I should call were I a reviewer "A weak-sided Poem" with an amusing sober-sadness about it. . . . There is no objection of this kind to Lamia—A good deal to St. Agnes Eve—only not so glaring.'[3] And writing to George and Georgiana Keats a few days earlier he said, 'I have been reading over a part of a short poem I have composed lately call'd "Lamia"—and I am certain there is that sort of fire in it which must take hold of people in some way—give them either pleasant or unpleasant sensation'.[4]

The truth is, I think, that Keats realized, what some of his critics do not, that *Lamia* is not only different from the other two tales, but something wholly different, in kind, not merely in degree. Those therefore who rate *Lamia* the lowest, or for that matter the highest, of 'the three tales' appear to start with a misconception which is bound to vitiate their conclusions. And those who rate it lowest are, in brief, expressing their regret that Keats was growing up. They see him, in *The Eve of St. Agnes*, moving with perfect felicity and security in a world that is at most only partly real; and if they could they would keep him there; when he begins to emerge into the real

[1] de S, liii, liv.
[2] See p. 170.
[3] MBF, 143 (426).
[4] Ib. 147 (438, 439).

world, the world of the 'agonies and strife of human hearts', learning from his own bitter experience and trying to express his new knowledge, they dislike it. It is surely significant that Sir Sidney Colvin, who rates *Lamia* so low, is also always trying, so far as his dominant honesty will permit him, to avert his eyes from the letters to Fanny Brawne. But if we are to understand *Lamia*, and to realize the gulf, across which there was no path of return, which separates it from *The Eve of St. Agnes*, we must read those letters.

I have stressed this point, perhaps unduly, because I think that in studying *Lamia* we are watching something far more fundamental than a technical advance. That we no doubt are watching; there are passages in *Lamia*, as we have seen, which have a strength and power of compression which is new; and the whole poem shows a growing command of structure and balance. We are watching the artist develop. But we are watching too something of a much more painful interest, the boy of happy genius growing into the man of shadowed experience.

VII. *THE FALL OF HYPERION*

I HAVE suggested that Keats when he was writing *Lamia* was developing not only as artist but as man. Let him put the nature of the change in his own words:

> 'We no sooner get into the second Chamber, which I shall call the Chamber of Maiden-Thought, than we become intoxicated with the light and the atmosphere, we see nothing but pleasant wonders, and think of delaying there for ever in delight. However among the effects this breathing is father of is that tremendous one of sharpening one's vision into the heart and nature of Man—of convincing one's nerves that the world is full of Misery and Heartbreak, Pain, Sickness and oppression—whereby this Chamber of Maiden Thought becomes gradually darken'd and at the same time on all sides of it many doors are set open—but all dark—all leading to dark passages. We see not the ballance of good and evil.'[1]

In that sentence lies, I think, the answer to Sir Sidney Colvin's difficulty about the 'moral' of *Lamia*. Keats does not take sides; he is propounding a problem, not solving it. Lamia is lovely, but a serpent and a phantasm; Apollonius is far from lovely, but he is reality; Lycius must be saved from the phantasm, even though the salvation kills him. Keats is wandering down one of the dark passages.

And in this same temper, I think, he turned to explore another of the passages, or perhaps to amplify, in the light of more experience, what he had so brilliantly outlined a year earlier in the passage quoted above, the idea of the darkening of the whole Chamber of Maiden Thought. All through his life, as we see both in poems and letters, he has been exercised about the true function and qualities of the poet; and perhaps it occurred to him that Apollo in *Hyperion*, though the process is differently described, experienced just this darkening of the Chamber, and only so came to his full godhead, which with the poet-god is the same as saying to full poetic stature. This

[1] MBF, 61 (156).

recollection may have urged Keats, as well as the dislike of leaving a piece of work half-finished, to take up *Hyperion* again and see how far it could be incorporated in the new poem in which he hopes to embody his fresh ideas which are demanding expression. I have said 'new' since I believe that we get nowhere at all in the examination of *The Fall of Hyperion*, and miss the greater part of its significance, if we persist in regarding it as a rather feeble recast of an earlier work. I do not believe that the feeling in Keats' mind was just 'Now I must try to finish *Hyperion*'; I think that it was much more nearly 'Now the ideas to which I gave only dim expression at the end of *Hyperion* have become more clearly defined; the kind of problem which they propose I cannot leave without an attempt to solve, and to express the solution; and to do this I must write a new poem; but in it I can use some of what I wrote before'. At any rate, whatever was in Keats' mind, he did write a new poem, and a new poem which is great enough to be studied and judged on its own merits, and not by a comparison with the earlier one, with the implication that where the new poem differs from the earlier it is likely to differ for the worse. And if we start in this way I think that we may easily find ourselves being led to an unexpected critical conclusion.

The poem begins with what Keats described as 'a kind of induction', which, in verse which is somewhat obscure mainly from the amount which it is trying to say in small compass, distinguishes the two types of dreams, states the relation between Imagination and the Poetry without which Imagination is dumb, emphasizes the fact that visions are no prerogative of a special class, and ends with the finely humble, but I think confident, leaving of his poem to the judgement of posterity

> Whether the dream now purposed to rehearse
> Be Poet's or Fanatics will be known
> When this warm scribe my hand is in the grave.[1]

The dream proper then begins, with the description of the

[1] The passages are quoted as they occur in Woodhouse's transcript.

woodland scene, the fruits of which he eats, the draught of cool transparent juice of which he drinks, and his waking in a far different scene. I do not feel by any means as convinced as does Professor de Sélincourt that 'It is clear that in the garden, the temple, and the shrine, are presented to us those three stages in the poet's development towards the attainment of his ideal which Keats had dwelt upon in *Sleep and Poetry* and in the letter to Reynolds'.[1] Since Moneta is to be a Priestess, the dreamer must be got into a temple, and the food followed by the draught which produces trance seems little more than a conventional opening to a dream, not improbably suggested by *The Arabian Nights*.[2] I feel myself reluctant to make the assumption, with which Professor de Sélincourt starts, that the whole opening passage is an allegory; and an allegory of such detailed elaboration as he goes on to indicate. But if his assumption is correct his reading of the allegory is as satisfactory as we have any right to expect; it is in any case extremely interesting, and many readers will find it convincing. But quite apart from any possible allegory, what of the descriptions in themselves? In the description of the 'feast of summer fruits', as was almost inevitable, seeing that it seemed refuse of a meal

> By Angel tasted, or our Mother Eve

there are strong Miltonic reminiscences. But even in that passage, and oddly enough just where another name which was to Keats' ear Miltonic is mentioned, Proserpine, there is a most un-Miltonic cadence

> For proserpine return'd to her own fields,
> Where the white heifers low.

And for the rest, it is surely as certain that this is great blank verse as it is doubtful whence its cadences are derived. Omitting, lovely though it is, the opening description of

[1] de S, 516.

[2] e.g. Scott, vol. iv, p. 44 (*History of Ganem*) or 213 (*Story of Abou Hassan, or the sleeper Awakened*).

the woodland with its sounds and scents, let us go on to the description of the sanctuary:

> I look'd around upon the carved sides
> Of an old sanctuary with roof august,
> Builded so high, it seem'd that filmed clouds
> Might spread beneath, as o'er the stars of heaven;
> So old the place was, I remembered none
> The like upon the Earth: what I had seen
> Of grey Cathedrals, buttress'd walls, rent towers,
> The superannuations of sunk realms,
> Or nature's Rocks toil'd hard in waves and winds,
> Seem'd but the faulture of decrepit things
> To that eternal domed Monument.

I am not clear that it is easy to parallel that in English. It is stronger than Shakespeare's earlier style and smoother than his later; nor is the manner Elizabethan; it is 'paragraphic', built up by the shift of the pauses to the wholly satisfying conclusion of the last two inevitable lines; but yet it is not Miltonic; it is far too natural in its movement for that. Milton achieves his superb and weighty dignity in part at least by what Keats himself called 'a curruption of the language'.[1] But this is as English as it can be. With the exception of *roof august* there is not an inversion or any other trick in it. It says what it has to say with perfect dignity and a kind of strong and controlled fluency. I believe that we are here watching Keats achieving the last of his great technical triumphs, the creation of his own blank verse rhythm, at once flexible and powerful and sonorous, in which he could write as he felt. And if we are to find a parallel I think that we must go outside English to find it. I do not know whether the suggestion will seem fantastic, but to my ear that passage, with others like it in *The Fall of Hyperion*, has more of the right Virgilian ring than all but a very few in our language. And one line in particular, so far as the decasyllable can ever bring back the more fluid

[1] MBF, 147 (465).

movement of the hexameter, irresistibly recalls a famous line in the *Georgics*

> The superannuations of sunk realms,
> Fluminaque antiquos subterlabentia muros.[1]

On this passage there follows a curious catalogue of miscellaneous objects, which we can allegorize as we choose (and in which, by the way, there has been some quite unnecessary trouble about a reading),[2] and then a further description of the sanctuary, with the black gates to the east and the great image to the west, whose altar is to be approached by innumerable steps. By the altar stands 'one minist'ring' and from it pour clouds of Maian incense.

Before we go on from this point to consider the real essence of the poem, it may be worth while to stop for a moment and consider what 'sources' we may suppose Keats to have used. The *old sanctuary* itself, though not the description of it, we may reasonably guess was carried over from a rejected reading in line 243 of the first book of *Hyperion*, which read *Even here, in my old sanctuary*. . . . But what of the description of it? We saw some reason to guess that Keats had read *Vathek* with attention and a retentive memory. Here are some passages from that peculiar novel which seem not without significance: 'a place, which, though roofed with a vaulted ceiling, was so spacious and lofty, that, at first, they took it for an immeasurable plain',[3] 'the lofty columns which reached from the terrace almost to the clouds',[4] 'They reached, at length, a hall of great extent, and covered with a lofty dome',[5] 'a staircase of polished marble',[6] 'ascending the steps of a vast staircase',[7] 'they descended the fifteen hundred stairs'.[8] And 'portals of ebony' occur *passim*.[9]

[1] *Geor.* ii. 157.

[2] Woodhouse put a *qy. correct* against *so*, *in some*, *distinct* (76), and SC suggested (see de S, 520) the reading of *zone* for *some*. But the meaning is surely quite clear, though the order is a trifle awkward. The linen was so white, and where it had been embroidered the imageries were so distinct, that it must have been of asbestos or . . . &c.

[3] *Vathek* (1816 edn.), p. 206.

[4] Ib., p. 202.

[5] Ib., p. 211.

[6] Ib., p. 204.

[7] Ib., p. 202.

[8] Ib., p. 69.

[9] E.g. ib., pp. 47, 166, 205.

There at any rate, for what they are worth, are the lofty roof, the columns, the dome, the stairs, the marble, and the black gates.

But the stairs, I suspect, came from Dante. It would be strange if the only book which he took with him on the Scotch tour, particularly when the book was as close an imitation of Milton's style as its author could contrive, had not influenced the first *Hyperion*; and some passages from Cary's *Dante* which appear to be parallels to passages in *Hyperion*, will be found in the notes. But it is difficult to resist the impression that *The Fall of Hyperion* owed more to Dante than a few phrases. The whole conception of the dream is that of Dante, though no doubt plenty of poets have written visions. But the difficult ascent of the fourth canto of the *Purgatorio*, and the steps at the threshold in the ninth (the lowest being marble) suggest a direct influence; and even more perhaps the account of the climbing of the stairs at the end of the twelfth and beginning of the thirteenth cantos:

> We climb the holy stairs:
> And lighter to myself by far I seem'd
> Than on the plain before; whence thus I spake:
> 'Say, master, of what heavy thing have I
> Been lighten'd; that scarce aught the sense of toil
> Affects me journeying. . . .
> We reach'd the summit of the scale, and stood
> Upon the second buttress of that mount
> Which healeth him who climbs.
>
> (*Purg*. xii. 107–12; xiii. 1–3)

> my iced foot touch'd
> The lowest stair; and as it touch'd, life seem'd
> To pour in at the toes: I mounted up,
> As once fair Angels on a ladder flew
> From the green turf to heaven.
>
> (*Fall of Hyperion*, i. 132–6)

and the prayer *Purge off, Benign, if so it please thee, my mind's film* may well be a reminiscence of *purging as they go The world's gross darkness off* (*Purg*. xi. 29).

The identification of Mnemosyne with Moneta is undoubtedly due, as Sir Sidney Colvin pointed out,[1] to a passage in the notes to Hyginus in *Auctores Mythographi Latini*, a copy of which Keats owned. Here we are told 'Certe Moneta eadem est, quae Mnemosyne, nam auctor infra dicet matrem esse Musarum Monetam quae a Pindaro . . . Mnemosyne dicitur'.[2]

And now as the dreamer arrives, after his long ascent, at the altar and the lofty sacrificial fire and the clouds of incense, he hears a voice, and in the next hundred lines, in the interchange between the dreamer and Moneta, is contained Keats' attempt to put into words all that his mind has been turning, this way and that, and without I think finding a solution, about his own work, and the position in the world of 'the poet' in general, and the distinction between the poet and the man of action on the one hand and the poet and the dreamer on the other. I shall make no attempt to summarize the dialogue. Of all futilities of misdirected energy, paraphrases of poetry are I believe the idlest. A poet can express himself, if at all, only in his own words and his own idiom; and not indeed always then. But if he cannot express himself in his own poetry, he certainly cannot be made to express himself in some one else's prose. I should like, however, to say this, that any student of Keats who is a sincere student, who wants not only to appreciate justly Keats' artistry, but also to understand truly the workings of the mind behind it, must read that hundred lines, and re-read them, and read them again, until he has made up his mind what Keats was trying to say. Perhaps also one may venture to suggest that what we are watching here is not the logical

[1] SC, 447 n.

[2] Since the above was written Mr. J. L. N. O'Loughlin has pointed out to me another quite unmistakable and most interesting source, Coleridge's *Allegoric Vision*, written in 1795, published in *The Courier* of August 31, 1811, and adapted and affixed to the Introduction of *A Lay Sermon: Addressed to the Higher and Middle Class*, 1817. Mr. O'Loughlin is presenting the details of his find in a paper shortly to appear, and I need not therefore anticipate this by an inadequate summary.

exposition of a train of thought to a foreseen conclusion which is by the exposition to be proved, but rather that process which Keats himself, as we have seen, earlier described as the 'stepping of the Imagination towards a Truth';[1] and we may well be right if we conclude that the steps as we see them do not arrive at the goal, that Keats knew that he had not solved his problem. We also have to come to a decision about lines 187–210. Woodhouse in his transcript erased them in pencil and added a note that Keats seemed to have intended to erase them. Mr. Middleton Murry insists with a vigour almost amounting to violence that they must be omitted.[2] Professor de Sélincourt meets Mr. Murry on his own ground and demolishes his arguments, and gives further arguments, both in the notes to his edition of Keats' poems,[3] and even more cogently in a passage of the most penetrating and illuminating criticism in the introduction to Woodhouse's transcript,[4] for the retention of the lines. One difficulty indeed he seems to me to dismiss too lightly. That is the repetition of lines 194–98 in lines 216–20. This repetition does strongly suggest that Keats had in mind the rejection of the disputed passage, but salvaged from it, as was his habit, what was too good to lose, and used it for the introduction to a quite different subject. But the difficulty may perhaps be met by supposing that Keats intended in recasting the passage to omit the description of the tall shade, feeling that it was more appropriate not as a break in the dialogue, but as the introduction to a new section of the poem. Apart from this there can be no doubt that, as Professor de Sélincourt says, not indeed this passage as it stands, but something like it, is badly needed to complete or at any rate carry on the line of thought, which otherwise comes to so abrupt and inconclusive a termination.

With the description of *the tall shade, in drooping linens*

[1] MBF, 39 (98).
[2] *Keats and Shakespeare*, pp. 178–9.
[3] de S, 583, 4.
[4] *Hyperion, a facsimile of Keats's autograph manuscript, with a transliteration of the manuscript of The Fall of Hyperion a Dream*; with introductions and notes; E. de Sélincourt. Clarendon Press, 1905; pp. 26–8 of the second introduction.

veil'd we return to the narrative, and pass through Moneta's promise of the revelation of the past, and her unveiling, to the point at which the earlier poem is to be used. Before we revert to that we may remind ourselves of the new rhythms that Keats had found for himself.

Then saw I a wan face,
Not pin'd by human sorrows, but bright blanch'd
By an immortal sickness which kills not;
It works a constant change, which happy death
Can put no end to; deathwards progressing
To no death was that visage; it had pass'd
The lily and the snow;

The interest of the rest of the poem is almost entirely the technical one of watching a skilled carpenter conducting a very tricky piece of dovetailing. The great opening of *Hyperion* is damaged in the process of transference to its new setting, since it is split into two pieces, and the vale is introduced not as the background for the great figure of Saturn, but as the place in which the dreamer and Moneta are standing. And the *Forest on forest* which hung so grandly about Saturn's head have, for some reason not easy to conjecture, disappeared. But some very interesting things happen to the description of the stillness. If Keats was working from the manuscript as we now have it, and had not been emending it in the interval (and we have no reason to suppose that he had), what he now had in front of him is not, it will be remembered, the reading of the 1820 volume, but

No stir of air was there;
Not so much life as on a Summer's day
Robs not at all the dandelion's fleece

Now it is clear that *air* and *life* are in the wrong order; and that the dandelion, though vivid, is, perhaps by being too specific, a little trivial. So the lines are altered:

No stir of life
Was in this shrouded vale, not so much air
As in the zoning of a summer's day
Robs not one light seed from the feather'd grass,

the only possible flaw in the perfection of which is the uncertainty as to the picture intended by the word *zoning*. For some way after this things proceed smoothly, with no more alteration than is demanded by the different method of narration. *His fallen divinity*, since the figure of Saturn has not yet been properly defined, has to be weakened to *the fallen divinity*; and in the process of defining it *his feet* has to become *old Saturn's feet* which causes a dislocation of the lines, with the unfortunate result that the old right hand has to be overloaded with two extra adjectives in addition to the three it had already. It will be noticed that in line 321 Saturn's feet *rested*. This seems to me to show decisively that the correct reading in *Hyperion* i. 16 is *stay'd*, as Keats wrote in his manuscript and Woodhouse duly transcribed, and not the *stray'd* of the 1820 text. After a short interlude, in which Mnemosyne figures rather incongruously as a kind of showman introducing the new character, the earlier poem is resumed for forty lines. The modifications are mostly slight, apart from the total and significant omission of the Miltonic description of Thea (*Hyp*. i. 26–36). Five *O*'s are got rid of (50, 54, 64, 68), and one of these excisions causes consequential alterations which are interesting from their very unimportance, as showing the care with which Keats was revising. Lines 53–6 of *Hyperion* ran:

> Saturn look up—tho' wherefore poor old King?
> I have no comfort for thee, no not one.
> I cannot say *O wherefore sleepest thou*
> For heaven is parted from thee, and the Earth
> Knows thee not, thus afflicted, for a God

The deletion of *O* results in the recasting of this line as

> I cannot cry, *Wherefore thus sleepest thou*:

but the introduction of *thus* here leads to the alteration of *thus* to *so* two lines lower; and also Keats' attention has been caught by the repetition of *wherefore*, so that the first of the five lines is altered, with the additional strengthening of the epithet, to

> Saturn! look up—and for what, poor lost King?

The repeated *O* of line 64 is drastically dealt with by cutting out the whole line and the two following lines and compressing their sense into the much more effective

> With such remorseless speed still come new woes

The excision of the last of the *O*'s causes the abrupt and unexpected Miltonism of *Me thoughtless*. And the thunder becomes even more personal by being *captious* rather than *conscious*. There are some changes in Thea's hair, and the *natural sculpture in cathedral cavern* gives way to a rather awkward conceit. The chief alteration concerns the famous passage on the tall oaks, and it is full of interest. Here is the passage as it stood:

> As when upon a tranced summer night
> Those green rob'd Senators of mighty woods
> Tall Oaks, branch-charmed by the earnest Stars
> Dream and so dream all night without a stir
> Save from one sudden solitary gust
> Which comes upon the silence and dies off
> As if the ebbing Air had but one wave.

Now that is of course a wonderful picture; but what is it a picture of? Surely of some great trees, motionless at night. The woods are a background to the individual trees, which are made to stand out by their metaphorical description as senators; and the emphasis is on their stillness, in the sense of immobility (without a *stir*, just as in the 'no *stir* of air was there'); the importance of the sudden gust in the picture is not so much that it makes a sound (though this is implied by *upon the silence*) as that it moves the trees, whose hitherto still outline has been stressed by *branch-charmed*. Now in that, as a picture, there is nothing to cavil at and everything to praise. But this picture is a simile, and it is a simile which is to make more vivid the sound of spoken words; *so came these words and went*. And I think it will be found that every modification which Keats made in that passage was made with the sole object of causing it to perform more effectively its function as a simile. The emphasis is to be transferred from the motionless trees to a silence followed by the sound of the wind. So the tall oaks disappear and their place is taken by *forests*; we shall not see their outlines but we shall hear through them the sough of the wind. The change of *without a stir* to *without a noise* has been harshly criticized, but only I think by critics who would not trouble to consider what Keats was doing. From the point of view of euphony the change is obviously deplorable, but Keats is concerned with something more important than euphony, and he has now contrived to say exactly what he wanted and what the simile required. For the same reason the gust becomes *gradual* instead of *sudden*, and the rhythm of the next line is most expressively changed. Here is the passage as re-written:

> As when, upon a tranced Summer Night,
> Forests, branch-charmed by the earnest stars,
> Dream, and so dream all night, without a noise,
> Save from one gradual solitary gust,
> Swelling upon the silence; dying off;
> As if the ebbing air had but one wave;
> So came these words, and went;

This is real craftsman's work. Keats has transformed a lovely ornament into an honest and integral part of the structure which will do its job. He has had to sacrifice one beautiful line and admit one cacophony to do it, but it was worth doing. And it is one of the marks of the great artist that he will never hesitate to exchange one kind of beauty for the other, the irrelevant and showy for the organic and harmonious. The examination of those two passages alone, whatever we may think of the quality of the new material in the poem, seems to me to render at once and finally untenable the view that Keats when he came to write *The Fall of Hyperion* was no more than an exhausted man botching earlier and greater work.

The rest of the first canto is a curious, very interesting, and not wholly satisfactory mosaic, consisting of some lines taken over bodily from *Hyperion*, others modified, and others entirely new. Lines 386–7, 400–3, 413–17, and

432–8 correspond to lines 87–8, 89–92, 107–12, and 127–33 of *Hyperion* with the omission of one line and two characteristic alterations, *couchant* giving way to the more ordinary, and for the picture more correct, *bending*, and the Miltonic *Upon the gold clouds metropolitan* (in which, apart from the Miltonism, the last word appears to be sound and fury signifying very little) giving way to *From the gold peaks of Heaven's high-piled clouds*. The lines about the moon,

> One Moon, with alteration slow, had shed
> Her silver seasons four upon the night

is given an altered context, and the Miltonic inversions are got rid of at the expense of an awkward adverbial adjective and a still more awkward participle:

> a whole Moon.
> For by my burning brain I measured sure
> Her silver seasons shedded on the night.

Saturn's speech, where it does not repeat the earlier version, is entirely changed in tone, and becomes far weaker and even querulous. And for some reason he addresses it not to Thea, who is there at his feet, but to the solitary Pan, whom he surprisingly addresses in the plural as *brethren*. The rest of the passage, which is wholly new, consists of one lovely simile, which only just, if at all, comes off, and some rather nerveless narration. These ninety lines are the only part of the poem in which, as I think, one is conscious of a flaccidity of grip, a fumbling of touch. And it is significant that only in this part of the poem is Keats attempting what he is attempting here. In the rest of the poem he is either writing entirely freshly, or he is using large blocks of the earlier work, with certain modifications and with linking passages of new material. But here he is attempting a true recast, a melting down of the old material to combine it with the new in a fresh alloy; and the two refuse to combine.

In the second canto he reverts to the other method. He starts with the introduction which he quoted to

Woodhouse[1] 'on account of a word in the last line of a fine sound':

> 'Mortal, that thou may'st understand aright,
> I humanize my sayings to thine ear,
> Making comparisons of earthly things;
> Or thou might'st better listen to the wind,
> Whose language is to thee a barren noise,
> Though it blows legend-laden through the trees.—

After which all but six of the remaining fifty-five lines are taken almost en bloc from *Hyperion*, with some slight modification. The passage in *Hyperion* is i. 158–220. Of this the portents of eagle's wings and neighing steeds, with their Miltonic repetition, are omitted. So also is the description of the opening of the palace door. Apart from this the *other realms* become *melancholy* realms, and the *mammoth-brood* becomes an *eagle-brood*. The Titans listen not *in sharp pain* but more hopelessly *in their doom*. The gloom-bird's screech is now *Even* rather than *hated*. The simile of the anxious men reverts to its earlier form (cancelled in the MS.) in which the troops were *sad* rather than *panting*. This change has been criticized as a loss in vividness, which no doubt it is; but the same instinct is at work which caused the changes in the simile of the oaks. The vivid touch is also the irrelevant touch, and so it is sacrificed. Finally two Miltonisms are altered: the *omens drear* become *dire prodigies*, and Hyperion, instead of coming *slope upon* is *sloping to*. The great picture of Hyperion advancing down the diamond-paved arcades is kept unchanged (though with a transposition of order) but before he can reach the *great main cupola*, on the words *on he flared*, the great attempt came to an end and *The Fall of Hyperion* was finally abandoned.

What is our judgement on it to be? Are we, after examining the poem even thus cursorily, content to say that the new material is weak, and so overshadowed by the greatness of the earlier work that it fades into insignificance? If we are judging the new and the old, as is I think too

[1] MBF, 143 (422).

often done, by their comparative success as imitations of Milton, that will be no doubt our verdict, and a just one. But if we dismiss this criterion, which we are certainly not obliged to accept, and consider the new work as poetry of some kind, its own kind, are we not drawn towards the conclusion that the new work is great poetry, but of a kind so different that the earlier work, great too in its own way, cannot live with it; that the attempt to combine them was doomed to failure, and that Keats recognized this and abandoned the whole. There is, I believe, between the first two books of *Hyperion* on the one hand, and much of the third book of *Hyperion* and all the first three hundred lines of *The Fall of Hyperion* on the other, the difference between a brilliant artistic exercise and the stuff of great poetry, not yet indeed fully wrought, but the work of a *ποιητής*, a creative maker, not a copyist however talented. If that is at all true we need the less regret that *The Fall of Hyperion* is, apart from one short perfect poem, the last work of Keats with which we need concern ourselves. In it he climbed to a higher point than he had ever reached on the mountain of poetry, even though he stumbled as he climbed, and fell before the top was reached.

VIII. *TO AUTUMN*

WE are nearing the end of our study, since I propose for our final examination a poem which shows Keats I think in the secure exercise of his powers. *To Autumn* has not indeed the Merlin's spell of the *Ode to a Nightingale*, nor the tense ethereal beauty of the *Ode on a Grecian Urn*. But neither has it the weak ending that mars the magic of the one, nor the touch of didacticism that weakens the urgency of the other. The transparency of its rich beauty is unflecked.

The first hint that we have of the poem is, in view of what is to come, frankly comic. Just a fortnight before Keats wrote it he wrote a letter to Taylor about climates and soils suitable for Taylor's health; and in it he says 'the autumn fogs over a rich land is like the steam from cabbage water'.[1] But apart from this lowly domestic parallel, he had from his own earlier work a whole selection of pictures floating in his head of mists, and fruit swelling to ripeness, and bees, of corn reaped and garnered, and wine-presses, of sunsets, and the music of gnats, and sallows by a stream. Let us begin by collecting a few of them.

> but who, of men, can tell
> That flowers would bloom, or that green fruit would swell
> To melting pulp, (*End.* i. 835–7)

> Through sunny meadows, that outskirt the side
> Of thine *enmossed* realms: O thou, to whom
> Broad leaved fig trees even now foredoom
> Their *ripen'd fruitage*; yellow girted bees
> Their golden honeycombs; our village leas
> Their fairest blossom'd beans and poppied corn
> (*End.* i. 250–5)

> every sense
> *Filling* with spiritual *sweets* to plenitude,
> As *bees* gorge full their cells. (*End.* iii. 38–40)

[1] MBF, 140 (413).

together with a host of shorter phrases, *autumn mists* and '*moss'd* oaks' from *Endymion*,[1] '*swelling* apples' from *Sleep and Poetry*,[2] '*swelling* peaches' with bees buzzing round them from *Calidore*,[3] perhaps the lean bat that could *plump* its wintery skin from *Endymion*,[4] and the picture of the receptacle filled to the brim that always so delighted him.[5]

And now for the first stanza, and its distillation. We have two versions of the poem in Keats' own hand. The poem was conceived, as he tells Reynolds,[6] and presumably composed, on Sunday the 19th of September. Either on that day or between then and the 21st he wrote the draft which is now in the Harvard Library; on the 21st he made in a letter to Woodhouse[7] a copy, clearly from this draft, but with one or two interesting alterations. The draft is a somewhat puzzling document since prima facie it appears to be as certainly the 'first' draft of the second stanza as it is certainly not the first draft of the first stanza, and probably not of the last. It almost suggests that as Keats first wrote the poem it had only two stanzas, and that in copying it out he added what is now the second. It is observable, for what it is worth, that the idea which prompted the poem, as he tells Reynolds, and as we shall see, is embodied in the last stanza of the poem. However, the Harvard draft is at all events the earliest that we have for our examination, and in that the first stanza is written with only one correction (and that of spelling), but with a number of errors of spelling, *furuits*, *sweeness* and so on, the type of error that is always liable to overtake any one, and certainly not least Keats, when in a hurry; but in view of the absence of any of the characteristic false starts and emendations it seems clear that the hurry is not the hurry of composition, but the hurry of copying, when he is in haste to get on to the stanza that has to be composed.

[1] *End.* i. 991; ii. 49.
[2] *Sleep and Poetry*, 361.
[3] *Calidore*, 66.
[4] *End.* iv. 377.
[5] 'rich brimm'd goblets' (*Epistle* to *GK*, 39); 'wicker over brimm'd' (*End.* i. 137); 'brimming the water-lilly cups with tears' (*End.* iv. 186).
[6] MBF, 142 (418).
[7] Ib. 143 (421, 2).

Season of Mists and mellow fruitfulness
Close bosom friend of the naturing sun;
Conspiring with him how to load and bless
The Vines with fruit that round the thatch eves run
To bend with apples the most'd Cottage trees
And fill all furuits with sweeness to the core
To swell the gourd, and plump the hazle shells
With a white kernel; to set budding more
And still more later flowers for the bees
Until they think wam days with never cease
For Summer has o'erbrimm'd their clammy cells—

In the copy for Woodhouse most of the mistakes in spelling are corrected, though a new one is introduced; the cells acquire a capital letter, but the Vines and the Cottage are deprived of theirs; the stanza is more or less punctuated, which indeed it badly needed; and the sixth line is changed so that it runs

And fill all fruit with ripeness to the core.

The second stanza presents an entirely different picture in the draft. Here we have again Keats writing as he composes, none too easily. And if we are determined that this document is the first draft we shall remember a remark of Keats about Byron. 'He describes what he sees—I describe what I imagine. Mine is the hardest task.'[1] In the first stanza Keats is describing what he sees. Now he is going to fill in at least a part of his picture from his imagination. For his background he moves from the ripened fruit, and the flowers and the bees, to the ripened corn, and a cider press, and against this background he sets a personified figure of Autumn. Here is some of the material for the background and for the figure:

golden *store*
In Autumn's *sickle* (*End.* iv. 422)

and on
Her voice I hung like fruit among green leaves:
Her lips were all my own, and—ah, ripe sheaves
Of happiness! ye on the *stubble* droop,
But never may be *garner'd*. (*End.* iii. 270-4)

[1] MBF, 147 (452).

Before my pen has *glean'd* my teeming brain,
Before high-piled books, in charactery,
Hold like *rich garners* the full-*ripen'd grain.*
(Sonnet, *When I have fears . . .*)

Then there is '*Sleep* quiet with his *poppy* coronet' in *Sleep and Poetry* (348), and a passage in *Endymion* which is interesting for a probable associative link:

A little onward ran the very stream
By which he took his first soft *poppy* dream;
And on the very bark 'gainst which he leant
A crescent he had carv'd, and round it spent
His skill in little stars. The *teeming* tree
Has swollen and green'd the pious *charactery*. . . .
(*End.* iv. 785–90)

And then a passage which has in it autumn and the harvesters, and sleep, and patient watching, as well as the trees by the river and the wailful gnat which will come in the third stanza:

So she was gently glad to see him laid
Under her favourite bower's quiet shade,
On her own couch, new made of flower leaves,
Dried carefully on the cooler side of sheaves
When last the sun his *autumn tresses* shook,
And the tann'd harvesters rich armfuls took.
Soon was he quieted to slumbrous rest:
But, ere it crept upon him, he had prest
Peona's busy hand against his lips,
And still, a *sleeping*, held her finger-tips
In tender pressure. And as a *willow* keeps
A *patient watch* over the stream that creeps
Windingly by it, so the quiet maid
Held her in peace: so that a whispering blade
Of grass, a *wailful gnat*, a bee bustling
Down in the blue-bells, or a wren light rustling
Among sere leaves and twigs, might all be heard
(*End.* i. 436–52)

And let us add to these

a pure wine
Of happiness, from fairy-*press ooz'd* out (*End.* iii. 801)

and so go on to the stanza.

Who hath not seen thee? for thy haunts are many
 Sometimes whoever seeks for thee may find

but either at once, seeing that *many* is going to be awkward for rhyme, or when he reaches the end of the third line, Keats alters, feeling also no doubt a kind of thin abruptness in the half-line question, and a certain feebleness both of sound and sense in *for thee*:

Who hath not seen thee oft amid thy stores?
 Sometimes whoever seeks abroad may find
Thee sitting careless on a granary floor
 Thy hair soft lifted by the winnowing wing

The final *s* of *stores* is deleted, and *wing* at once changed to the intended *wind*.[1]

However, whatever small points there may have been in the first four lines, they were soon and easily solved. Now the real troubles begin.

husky
While bright the Sun slants through the ^ barn;
 Or sound asleep in a half reaped field
 Dosed with read poppies; while thy reeping hook
 Spares form Some slumbrous

At this point the lines, which have clearly been going from bad to worse, have petered out altogether, and no rhyme for *field* is in sight anyway. The next stage is some minor tinkering. The line about the sun, and the next line, are deleted altogether, and the second re-written as

on on a half reap'd furrow sound asleep

[1] There are various small points here, all pointing to the haste of composition. In line 1 *for* began by being *nor*, or at any rate a word beginning with *n*; in line 2 *may* started as something else, I think *must*, though it got no further than the first stroke of the *u*; *careless* either began as something else or began to be corrected into something else; there is a half-hearted attempt at deleting the *a* before *granary* as though Keats had at one moment intended to keep *stores* plural, and rhyme *floors* with it; and *floors* is certainly not *floors*; it is more like *floorn*, but it might be *floors* with some ill-made mark of punctuation after it. The writing of *wing* is interesting, since it shows conclusively that Keats had no use for that subservience to exactitude of rhyme which mispronounces *wind* to rhyme with *bind*, thereby wholly missing one of the most delicate of those 'half-rhymes' (consonants identical but vowel modified) in the use of which our poets are so skilful.

(i.e. intending not to delete the *Or* and to write *on* once only), then *Some slumbrous* is deleted, and under it written

minutes while wam slumpers creep

So that now he has in front of him

~~husky~~
~~While bright the Sun slants through the barn~~
on on a half reap'd furrow sound asleep
~~Or sound asleep in a half reaped field~~
Dosed with read poppies; while thy reeping hook
Spares form ~~Some slumbrous~~
minutes while wam slumpers creep

That has at least achieved a rhyme; but if the line about the sun is to disappear altogether the rhyme is in the wrong place; none of it is very satisfactory; and the *eep* sound has got out of hand. So Keats cancels the whole passage with some vigorous cross-hatching, and begins all over again, using the re-written sixth line as the fifth, and improving the old seventh for use as the new sixth.

Or on a half reap'd furrow sound asleep
Dos'd with the fume of poppies, while thy hook
Spares for ~~one~~some slumbrous minutes the next swath;

So far, so good; and as any troubles about a rhyme for the unpromising *swath* are still four lines off he goes on his way rejoicing:

And sometimes like a gleans thost dost keep
Steady thy laden head across the brook
Or by a Cyder-press with patent look
Thou . . .

Well, and now what about the swath, waiting four lines above for its rhyme. But the Cyder-press is going as well as can be, so for the moment confound the swath, and finish

watchest the last oozing hours by hours

and now go back and get the rhyme, even if we have to sacrifice in the process the idea of the tenacious *slumpers* which has hung onto existence through two corrections.

Spares the next swath and all its twined flowers;

The copy in the Woodhouse letter omits to notice the cancellation of the *s* of *stores*; corrects some spellings, but writes *Stready* for *Steady*; does some punctuating; reads *a brook* for *the brook*, and *Dased* for *Dos'd*, either an easy misreading of a word so written that it might be either, or a deliberate alteration; and greatly accentuates the opiate *z* sound of the last line by reading *oozings* for *oozing*.

The last stanza contains the picture that was the germ of the whole poem. Keats writes to Reynolds on Tuesday September 21: 'How beautiful the season is now—How fine the air. A temperate sharpness about it. Really, without joking, chaste weather—Dian skies—I never lik'd stubble-fields so much as now—Aye better than the chilly green of the Spring. Somehow a stubble-plain looks warm—in the same way that some pictures look warm. This struck me so much in my Sunday's walk that I composed upon it.'[1] One need not look further for material except to the *wailful gnat* which we have already seen, and perhaps the *sallows* of a *river nook* in *Endymion*, iv. 392, and a 'swift *treble* pipe' in *Endymion*, i. 314. But I cannot courteously conclude without bringing upon the stage, though for 'positively her last appearance', and even though she may be hissed off it, Keats' 'Damosel Radcliffe'. There are in her descriptions of autumn and of sunset-lights some coincidences, not only of phrase but of rhythm, which if they are no more than accidents are curiosities. 'Tinged their snowy summits with a *roseate hue*';[2] the *vapours* of an *autumnal evening*';[3] '*mellowed* with autumnal tints';[4] 'the tranquillity of the scene, which *autumn* now *touched* with her sweetest tints';[5] 'and *touched the forest glades with softer light*';[6] '*the distant landscape, touched with yellow hue*'.[7]

[1] MBF, 142 (418).
[2] *MU*, vol. iii, p. 344 (xxxv, p. 65).
[3] Ib., vol. i, p. 164 (c. vi, p. 33).
[4] Ib., vol. i, p. 154 (ib., p. 31).
[5] *RF*, vol. i, c. vii, p. 250 (c. vii, p. 121).
[6] Ib., vol. i, c. v, p. 207 (c. v, p. 99).
[7] *MU*, vol. iv, p. 214 (c. xlix, p. 121), from an incidental poem *To Autumn*.

The stanza starts easily enough:

> Where are the songs of Sping? Aye where are they?
> Think not of them thou hast thy music too—
> While a gold cloud gilds the soft dying day
> And

at this point he sees that, the cloud still being singular, *And touches* is going to be awkward, so he deletes *And* and writes *Touching the*, and then, I think before completing the line, goes back to the third, which will clearly not do as it is with the redundance of *gilds* and *gold*. First he deletes *a*, makes *cloud* into *clouds* and cancels the *s* of *gilds*, and begins to emend *gold*, possibly to *yellow*, but before getting far with it scratches it out and writes *barred* above. Finally he finds a word which will give him the alliteration that led to the redundance, and cancels *gild* and writes in *bloom*. Then he goes back to the unfinished fourth line, finds that it will now do in its original form and so reverts to that, and we have

> Where are the songs of Sping? Aye where are they?
> Think not of them thou hast thy music too—
> While barred clouds bloom the soft dying day
> And touch the stibble plains with rosy hue—
> Then in a wailful quire the small gnats mourn
> Among the river sallows, ~~on the~~ borne afots
> Or sinking as the light wind lives and dies
> ~~Then~~And full grown Lambs loud bleat from hilly bourn,
> Hedge crickets sing, and now again full soft
> The Redbreast whistles from a garden croft
> And new flock still

the last four words immediately deleted, and below written

> Gathering Swallows twiter in the Skies

and then *And* which I think began as *The* written in before *Gathering* and *Gathering* itself changed to *Gather'd*.

There are a few small points here. *afots* is an amusing word. I imagine that Keats knew that the rhyme was going to be *soft* and the letters of the rhyme word became mixed up with the *aloft* which he was trying to write.

Secondly, though I have retained the accepted reading, *again full* does not at all represent what is before us in the draft. *Agim* followed by a badly written *feble* would more nearly represent it. In view of the reading in the copy in the letter this makes one wonder whether there was not an earlier draft, which even Keats himself could not for the moment read, which already contained *treble*.

In the copy made for Woodhouse, apart from spelling corrections, this is the only alteration of importance; *and now with treble soft* is read for *and now again full soft*.

The poem as printed shows the following variations from the copy in the letter: the transposition of order in *The vines with fruit*; *sweet kernel* for *white kernel*; *Drows'd* for *Das'd*; and the reversion *gathering* for *gather'd*.

We have now reached September of 1819. We started this examination of a great poet's poetic development in February of 1818, with the kind of tentative and transitional introduction of *Isabella*. Since the late autumn or early winter of that year we have been watching and studying what must surely be the most crowded and marvellously fertile twelve months of fiery and unflagging creative energy in the life of any English poet, perhaps of any creative artist. And we cannot I think do better than leave him at this moment, when, in a brief interlude of peace, with all his great achievement behind, and nothing before but the weariness the fever and the fret that ended nearly eighteen months later in Severn's arms in Rome, in this brief space, in the autumn fields round Winchester, for the last time in this world his own free master, he found all his disciplined powers, of observation, of imagination, of craftsmanship, combining in one moment of power to produce the most serenely flawless poem in our language, *To Autumn*:

Season of mists and mellow fruitfulness,
  Close bosom-friend of the maturing sun;
Conspiring with him how to load and bless
  With fruit the vines that round the thatch-eves run;

To bend with apples the moss'd cottage-trees,
  And fill all fruit with ripeness to the core;
    To swell the gourd, and plump the hazel shells
  With a sweet kernel; to set budding more,
And still more, later flowers for the bees,
Until they think warm days will never cease,
    For Summer has o'er-brimm'd their clammy cells.

Who hath not seen thee oft amid thy store?
  Sometimes whoever seeks abroad may find
Thee sitting careless on a granary floor,
  Thy hair soft-lifted by the winnowing wind;
Or on a half-reap'd furrow sound asleep,
  Drows'd with the fume of poppies, while thy hook
    Spares the next swath and all its twined flowers:
And sometimes like a gleaner thou dost keep
  Steady thy laden head across a brook;
  Or by a cyder-press, with patient look,
    Thou watchest the last oozings hours by hours.

Where are the songs of Spring? Ay, where are they?
  Think not of them, thou hast thy music too,—
While barred clouds bloom the soft-dying day,
  And touch the stubble-plains with rosy hue;
Then in a wailful choir the small gnats mourn
  Among the river sallows, borne aloft
    Or sinking as the light wind lives or dies;
And full-grown lambs loud bleat from hilly bourn;
  Hedge-crickets sing; and now with treble soft
  The red-breast whistles from a garden-croft;
    And gathering swallows twitter in the skies.

NOTES

Note A (*page* 14)

All students of Keats owe a debt to Miss Lowell and the enthusiasm which led her to collect in her *John Keats* such a wealth of material, however much they may feel that in her use of it she was led into most possible errors; and these notes of Woodhouse are not the least interesting of the documents which were for the first time made available for study in that book. But it was perhaps unfortunate that having presented them for examination she then went on to depreciate their importance so drastically. It is indeed hard to see why she took the trouble to transcribe them when she was about to explain that they are all nonsense. She thinks, Heaven knows why, that when Keats gave Woodhouse the data for the notes he was pulling Woodhouse's leg. She says, 'That Keats ever said the things here attributed to him, as they stand, it is ridiculous to suppose.... He may have said that on reading a passage over it sometimes struck him as being better than he remembered, he probably did say that he never forced himself to write when not in the mood, but the sentimental tone of awe attributed to him by Woodhouse is absolutely foreign to his habit of thought. And that he wrote his poems out almost as they were to stand and seldom corrected them, is simply not so. Keats corrected and corrected. Not only at the moment of writing, but up to the last proof.'[1]

Suppose that instead of conjecturing what Keats 'may have said' we see what he did say, not in the almost irrelevant passage which Miss Lowell quotes as representing his views but in another. In a letter to Haydon of May 1817 he says, 'I remember your saying that you had notions of a good Genius presiding over you. I have of late had the same thought, for things which I do half at Random are afterwards confirmed by my judgement in a dozen features of Propriety. Is it too daring to fancy Shakespeare this Presider?'[2] This does not seem to be far from the tone of Woodhouse's account. I do not know that we need regard it as a tone of sentimental awe, but some such feeling might be neither so unnatural nor so improper as Miss Lowell seems to think for a young writer of twenty-one who fancies Shakespeare presiding over his work. At any rate I can see no reason why on the evidence of those two passages we should not accept it as a fact that Keats sometimes found himself writing 'unconsciously', nor why, finding Woodhouse square with Keats here, we should be hesitant in accepting, or at least in examining with care, the rest of what he says. (Unless indeed we are to suppose that Keats was also pulling Haydon's leg. But if Miss Lowell finds it ridiculous to suppose that Keats ever said the things which Woodhouse attributes to him, I find it at least as ridiculous to suppose that Keats, high-spirited humorist on some occasions and some subjects though he could be, ever pulled the legs of two of his best friends

[1] AL, i. 502, 3. [2] MBF, 14 (30).

on this subject, the poetry which was his life, and which always in the letters evokes his most serious and thoughtful writing.)

As to the other important point in Woodhouse's account, I think that Miss Lowell is too summary in her treatment of it. Woodhouse was not a fool, and he had seen at least as much of Keats' methods of composition and of the drafts of his poems as any modern critic however confident. It is therefore more prudent, if nothing more, to give what he says a more careful examination than Miss Lowell could trouble to accord it. No doubt the statement, particularly in isolation from its context, that Keats never corrected, except perhaps a word here and there, does, to any one who has looked at drafts of Keats' poems, seem at a superficial glance absurd. And so Miss Lowell hurried to dismiss Woodhouse: 'And that he wrote out his poems almost as they were to stand and seldom corrected them is simply not so. Keats corrected and corrected. Not only at the moment of writing, but up to the last proof.' That is to say, in plain terms, either Woodhouse or Keats is a liar, and probably both. But this dispute arises, like so many others, mainly from a confusion of terms; and arises partly also from a misinterpretation of evidence, as I have tried to indicate in the text. It is perhaps also worth pointing out that Miss Lowell, in her anxiety to demolish Woodhouse, omits a passage from his notes, which I have also omitted as not relevant to Keats' methods, but which quite robs the passage of any tone of sentimental awe, since Woodhouse is at pains to explain that Keats' experience is one that is probably common to any one who ever uses a pen: 'Perhaps every one in the habit of writing verse or prose may have had a somewhat similar feeling, that of the extreme appositeness and happiness (the *curiosa felicitas*) of an idea of the excellence of which he was unaware until he came to read it over. It seems scarcely his own; and he feels that he would never imitate or hit upon it again: and he cannot conceive how it came to him. Such Keats said [reading doubtful] was his sensation of astonishment and pleasure when he had produced the lines "His white melodious &c.—It seemed to come by chance. . . .'

Perhaps I may say here all that I have to say about Miss Lowell's *John Keats*. It is an ungrateful task to criticize adversely the work of so genuine an enthusiast, even though one may think that in this biography the writer showed little sense of perspective and less of scholarship. But one must say something of a book which is on the one hand of real importance to students of Keats, since it offers to them a considerable amount of material not hitherto accessible in print, and on the other is more often than not gravely misleading in its presentation of the material. Miss Lowell's transcriptions of original documents are almost invariably inaccurate, and no student of Keats should accept any reading that he finds in her book without verification. To give three instances: in her analysis of the first draft of *To Autumn* she says that Keats inserted the word 'bushy' before 'barn' (AL, i. 503); whatever a 'bushy barn' may be, that is not what Keats wrote; he wrote 'husky barn'. In the long letter from Woodhouse about the corrections in *The Eve of St. Agnes* (AL, ii. 317–20), apart from some thirty minor errors, including the reading of 'then' for 'thus' and 'declared' for 'confessed', she makes Woodhouse speak of 'the "Don Juan" style of swinging up sentiment and sneering', whereas what Woodhouse said, more intelligibly, was 'mingling up sentiment and sneering'. While in the reproduction of the 'lost' letter to Woodhouse (AL, ii. 332–8), which is announced as 'absolutely correct', as distinct from the transcription contributed to the Keats Memorial Volume, though two of the major errors in that transcription and some forty of the sixty-odd minor ones are corrected, there still remain the readings of 'thoughum' for 'thongum', 'nos' for 'vos', 'line' for 'live', and 'pre-occupatus' for 'per-occupatus'.

For this reason, whereas I have thought it as well to comment on the very rare cases where Buxton Forman seems to be in error, just because as a rule one can rely without question on his almost impeccable accuracy, in dealing with material hitherto only accessible in Miss Lowell's book I have contented myself with making as accurate a transcription as I can from either originals or photostats, without commenting on the divergences from hers.

Note B (*page* 17)

Before we leave the letters for the poems, to watch in them Keats' mind and hand at work, it may be of some interest to spend a few moments in examining one or two passages from the letters themselves, and one or two *obiter dicta* of prose criticism, which not only show Keats' imagination characteristically at work, associating, transmuting, developing, but also show that besides being a poet he was one of the richest executants on the organ of English prose since the Elizabethans.

He is writing, for example, a quite ordinary letter to Jane Reynolds, and he says, 'Believe me, my dear Jane it is a great Happiness to me that you are in this finest part of the year, winning a little enjoyment from the hard World', and then without any sort of warning his imagination kindles, and he goes on, 'in truth the great Elements we know of are no mean Comforters—the open Sky sits upon our senses like a Sapphire Crown—the Air is our Robe of State—the Earth is our throne and the Sea a mighty Minstrell playing before it—able like David's Harp to charm the evil Spirit from such Creatures as I am—able like Ariel's to make such a one as you forget almost the tempest-cares of Life'.[1] Elsewhere in the letters he speaks of his power of association ('chequer work leads us naturally to a Milkmaid, a Milkmaid to Hogarth, Hogarth to Shakespeare, Shakespeare to Hazlitt—Hazlitt to Shakespeare—and thus by merely pulling an apron string we set a pretty peal of Chimes at work'),[2] and it is surely not too fanciful to see in the passage before us the same kind of association

[1] MBF, 19 (43). [2] Ib. 61 (155).

producing another peal of chimes, the World to the Elements, Sky, Air, Earth, Sea, the Sky to a Crown, the Crown to a Robe (?Cleopatra's 'robe and crown'), crown and robe to a King throned, Saul, Saul to David and his harp, the harp to music, music to Ariel, Ariel to the Tempest.

Or again, he walks home with the enigmatic 'lady whom he saw at Hastings', and he describes her room, 'a very tasty sort of place with Books, Pictures a bronze statue of Buonaparte, Music, aeolian Harp; a Parrot, a Linnet, a Case of choice Liquers &c. &c. &c.',[1] and later in the same letter the lady and her room are transmuted, though only, even when so transmuted, to be rejected. 'Though the most beautiful Creature were waiting for me at the end of a Journey or a Walk; though the carpet were of Silk, the Curtains of the morning Clouds; the chairs and Sofa stuffed with Cygnet's down; the food Manna, the Wine beyond Claret, the Window opening on Winander mere, I should not feel—or rather my Happiness would not be so fine, as my Solitude is sublime. Then instead of what I have described, there is a Sublimity to welcome me home. The roaring of the wind is my wife and the Stars through the window pane are my Children'.[2]

Or he is talking about his favourite Claret; 'now I like Claret whenever I can have Claret I must drink it,—'tis the only palate affair that I am at all sensual in. . . . For really 'tis so fine—it fills the mouth one's mouth with a gushing freshness—then goes down cool and feverless';[3] so far no more than vivid, like his explosively unpunctuated comments on the nectarine ('this moment I was writing with one hand, and with the other holding to my Mouth a Nectarine—good god how fine. It went down soft pulpy, slushy, oozy—all its delicious embonpoint melted down my throat like a large beatified Strawberry').[4] But then his imagination takes ship and sets out on its voyage; 'then you do not feel it quarelling with your liver—no it is rather a Peace maker and lies as quiet as it did in the grape;—then it is as fragrant as the Queen Bee; and the more ethereal Part of it mounts into the brain, not assaulting the cerebral apartments like a bully in a bad-house looking for his trull and hurrying from door to door bouncing against the waistcoat: but rather walks like Aladin about his own enchanted palace so gently that you do not feel his step'.[3]

And here lastly are two instances of more serious importance. Keats is reading *A Midsummer Night's Dream*, and he comes to the passage

> And never since the middle Summers spring
> Met we on hill, in dale, forrest, or mead,
> By paved fountaine, or by rushie brooke,
> Or in the beached margent of the sea,
> To dance our ringlets to the whistling Winde.[5]

And he underlines it,[6] and then at the bottom of the page writes this

[1] MBF, 89 (260). [2] Ib. (261). [3] Ib. 114 (323, 324).
[4] Ib. 144 (429). [5] II. i. 82.
[6] In his Folio Shakespeare, now in the Dilke collection at Hampstead.

comment: 'There is something exquisitely rich and luxurious in Titania's saying "since the middle summer's spring" as if bowers were not exuberant and covert enough for fairy sports until their second sprouting—which is surely the most bounteously overwhelming of all Nature's goodnesses. She steps forth benignly in the spring and her conduct is so gracious that by degrees all things are beaming happy under her wings and nestle against her bosom: she feels this love and gratitude too much to remain selfsame, and unable to contain herself buds forth the overflowings of her heart about the middle summer. O Shakespeare thy ways are but just searchable! The thing is a piece of profound verdure.' There is a certain youthful lusciousness about it, but there is surely the creative imagination working at the full stretch of its yet immature power.

And here is an illuminating instance of his 'stepping' imagination. He is struck by these lines in *Troilus and Cressida*:

> the seeded Pride
> That hath to this maturity blowne up
> In ranke *Achilles*[1]

He underlines them, and notes at the bottom of the page, 'Blowne up, &c. One's very breath while leaning over these pages is held for fear of blowing this line away as easily as the gentler breeze Robs dandelions of their fleecy Crowns'. That is interesting enough comment in itself, and we shall meet the dandelions again in connexion with the opening lines of *Hyperion*. But later[2] he is reading *Lear* and he comes to the passage in the first Act[3] in which Goneril and Regan discuss Lear's rejection of Cordelia, and the infirmity of his age and the inconstant starts that they are likely to have from him. Keats underlines the passage; and then there comes back to his mind the phrase from *Troilus* and the picture of the dandelion's wind-blown seeds which it conjured up, and he, like Shakespeare, spurs out, if not to the mighty grapple, at least to poetic creation. 'How finely is the brief of Lear's character sketched in this conference—from this point does Shakespeare spur him out to the mighty grapple. "The seeded pride that hath to this maturity blown up" Shakespeare doth scatter abroad on the wings of passion, where the germs take buoyant root in stormy air, suck lightning sap, and become voiced dragons—self-will and pride and

[1] I. iii. 316.

[2] This 'later' is probable, but hardly provable. It is evident that Keats read *King Lear* frequently. He quotes from it in letters of April and May 1817; he is reading in 'once again' and writing a sonnet preparatory to his reading in January 1818 (MBF, 38 (95)); and it is moderately certain from the note in the margin opposite III. iv. 37 ('Sunday Evening Oct. 14: 1818') that he was reading it again during Tom's last illness. But this tells us nothing as to when he made the critical note here quoted. He had clearly read *Troilus and Cressida* by October 1818 (MBF, 89 (262)). It is at least a reasonable conjecture that both the plays were being read, and the comments made, during this period.

[3] I. i. 289–end.

wrath are taken at the rebound by his giant hand and mounted to the clouds there to remain and thunder evermore.' There is the insight of spiritual kinship. Keats was at least an interpreter of whom his fancied presider had no need to be ashamed.

Note C (page 24)

In the British Museum (Egerton MS. 2780) is a small volume, which belonged to George Keats, containing a number of his brother's poems, some in John Keats' own handwriting and some in transcript. The rectos of the leaves numbered 1–28 are occupied by a fair-copy of *Isabella* in Keats' own hand. As to the date at which this fair-copy was made we can have, I think, no certainty. All that we can be moderately sure of is that it was made earlier than September, 1819, since leaves 33–6 of the same volume are occupied by *The Eve of St. Mark*, also in Keats' own hand, but with a considerable amount of deletion and correction, and the corrections are embodied in the fair-copy which he made for George and Georgiana Keats in his journal letter of September, 1819 (MBF, 147). (The fact that the holograph of *Isabella* precedes that of the *Lines on the Mermaid Tavern* in the British Museum volume does not help us, since the latter is also a fair-copy.) It is no doubt tempting to accept H. Buxton Forman's conjecture that this holograph is the copy which Keats promised to make for Reynolds and send to him by George (see letters of April 27 and May 3, 1818; MBF, 60 and 61); but if so he sent Reynolds the whole book, and not just a manuscript of *Isabella*, since it is clear that this fair-copy was made in the book, and not (as HBF thought) on loose sheets which were afterwards bound into a book. This is apparent because in stanza xxxiv, on leaf 15, the *e* of 'vale' and part of the *d* of 'aloud' have run over on to the edge of leaf 16 with an exactness of coincidence which must have been disturbed in the binding of loose sheets.

In any event what matters for our purposes is not the date when the fair-copy was made but the date of the state of the poem which it represents. And here we are on surer ground. The fair-copy appears to me to represent a stage of the poem intermediate between the completion of the first draft and the final version of the 1820 volume, but very much nearer the former than the latter. For the letter to Reynolds of April 1818 in which three stanzas of Isabella are quoted we have only Woodhouse's transcript. There is no reason to doubt the accuracy of the transcript except the perhaps trifling fact that the punctuation of the stanzas is exactly that of the 1820 text, whereas the punctuation of the holograph is widely different from the 1820 text throughout. The transcript and the holograph are verbally identical with one another and with the 1820 text in the first two stanzas quoted (xii, xiii). In the third quoted stanza (xxx) the letter, the holograph, and the Potts fragment (of which more in a moment) all read *wept* against the 1820 reading *weeps*; but the letter and the Potts fragment read *What might have been too plainly did she see* against the reading in which the holograph and 1820 agree, *His image in the dusk she seem'd to see*. The Potts fragment consists of 'what would seem to be two fragments of the original draft' (HBF) in the possession of Mr. R. A. Potts. They give us stanzas XXX, XXXI, and XXXIII–XL. In these stanzas in the following instances the holograph agrees with 1820 against the fragment—the 1820 readings being given first: XXXIII. 4, *keep; bind*. XXXV. 1, *drowsy; heavy*. XXXVI. 5, *Languor; Passion*. XXXVI. 7, *And; But*. XXXVII. 2, *fear; fears*. XXXVI. 6, *river; Arno*. XL. 2, *rage; rave : spirits; shadows*. On the other hand, in the following instances the holograph agrees with the fragment against 1820—the holograph readings being given first: XXXIII. 5, *Month after Month; Time after time*. XXXVI. 1, *poor; pale*. XXXVIII. 7–8, *Go shed a tear upon my hether bloom And I shall turn a diamond in the* (Potts *my*) *tomb; Go shed one tear upon my heather-bloom And it shall comfort me within the tomb*. XXXIX. 5, *And; While*. While in XL. 3 the Potts fragment reads *Though I forget what pleasure was a kiss*; the holograph *Though I forget the heaven of a kiss*; and 1820 *Though I forget the taste of earthly bliss*. When we compare the holograph of stanzas LX and LXIII with two scraps in Keats' writing in the Harvard Library, which were detached by Severn from an early draft, we find that the holograph makes three minor verbal changes in which it coincides with 1820. On the other hand, there is a number of differences in which the 1820 text differs from the holograph—the holograph readings being given first: I. 6, *each other; the other*. IV. 6, *tongue speak; lips breathe*. V. 8, *worst; least*. VII. 7–8, where the holograph ends the stanza differently and then has an entire stanza absent from 1820. VIII. 7, *Those; Thine*. X. 3, *all; more*. XVII*a*, between stanzas XVII and XVIII there was a stanza in the original draft which is copied in the holograph and then cancelled. XIX. 1, *O Eloquent Boccace of green Arno; O eloquent and famed Boccaccio*. XIX. 7–8, *For venturing one word unseemly mean In such a place, on such a daring theme; For venturing syllables that ill beseem The quiet glooms of such a piteous theme*. XXV. 7–8, the final couplet is not completed in the holograph; and indeed, judging by the ink and the writing, even the end of the seventh line and what there is of the eighth were written in later than the rest. XLVIII. 6, *were they; they labour'd*. L. 1–2, *With duller sliver than the persean sword They cut away no foul Medusa's head; With duller steel than the Persean sword They cut away no formless monster's head*. L. 6, *If ever any piece of Love was dead; If Love impersonate was ever dead*. LI. 5, *single; fringed*. Further, as a matter of interest, there are wide differences of punctuation between the holograph and 1820, that of the holograph being, I think, in almost all cases more effective and vivid, and in a few cases causing a definite difference of sense, notably in stanzas XLIII and LX. The upshot appears to me to be this, that the differences between the holograph and 1820 are wider than those between the holograph and the original draft; where we can check these, we find them to be almost entirely changes of an isolated word such as would be made by the copyist improving as he copied his own work. And since it was, as we have seen, unlike Keats to conduct a continuous process of correction, we can, I think, reasonably conjecture three states of *Isabella*: the first draft, corrected in Keats' usual fashion; the British Museum holograph, made from this first draft in its completed state (and possibly, but not probably, identical with the fair-copy that was promised to Reynolds); and the final state of 1820, the result of a much later revision when he had at last made up his mind to publish the poem.

Note D (page 58)

In the letter to Woodhouse (MBF, 143), in which Keats quotes passages from the second *Hyperion*, he quotes as 'what I had written for a sort of induction' only the first ten and a half lines of the first canto. But the introductory passage as we have it consists of eighteen lines, of which the last is

When this warm scribe my hand is in the grave.

And this is clearly connected with the famous little fragment which begins

This living hand, now warm and capable
Of earnest grasping, would, if it were cold
And in the icy silence of the tomb. . . .

This is written by Keats at the bottom of the sheet on which he wrote stanza 51 of *The Cap and Bells*. It is therefore probable that the completion of the introduction of the second *Hyperion* was made about the time of *The Cap and Bells*. But it is not more than probable, for various reasons connected with the fragment as well as with Keats' methods of work. In the first place I do not think that the fragment was written at the same time as the stanza of *The Cap and Bells* on the same sheet; apart from the fact that it is entirely different in tone, the writing is Keats' at its smallest and neatest, and quite different from that of the stanza. It is also, I think, clear that the fragment was written earlier than the stanza; it is written as it were upside down on the sheet, and if Keats having written the stanza suddenly wished to record the fragment he would naturally have taken another sheet for the purpose. What happened was surely that having written stanzas 49 and 50 on one side of a sheet he turned it over and found the bottom of the other side already occupied by the fragment, so that he could only write one stanza on this side instead of two. On the other hand, the fragment can hardly have been written much earlier, or the sheet with it on would not have been among those on which Keats was writing *The Cap and Bells*. It is also of course possible, though not I think likely, that the line in *Hyperion* suggested the fragment, and not vice versa. I think this unlikely for a thoroughly heretical reason, namely, that I have a strong feeling that the fragment is not by Keats at all, but merely copied out by him. It is so purely dramatic, and so calls out for its dramatic setting and the stage direction at the end of it, that it is hard to believe that it was written as a fragment. It will be remembered that some lines in a letter to Fanny Brawne (MBF, 125 (383)), even though Keats says that he read them, were regarded as possibly his own for over twenty years before it was pointed out that he was quoting with modifications from Massinger. I believe that he read this other fragment also in an Elizabethan play, and noted it down, as being, like the one from Massinger, applicable to his own situation and feelings. And I hope that some scholar of the Elizabethan drama will be able to place it for us.

Note E (*page* 60)

Polymetis, or an Enquiry concerning the Agreement between the Works of the Roman Poets and the Remains of the Ancient Artists, in Ten Books, by the Reverend Mr. Spence; London, 1747. This is a work of considerable learning, with extensive quotations from the classical writers, written by a man genuinely interested in his subject in a somewhat ponderous but eminently readable eighteenth-century style, and above all illustrated with a large number of excellent plates. I think that any one who will glance at Plate XXVI, figure 4, in Spence, will agree that this drawing from 'a medal; of Antoninus Pius; in the Great Duke's collection, at Florence' might have been executed as an illustration for

> the numerous tramplings quiver lightly
> Along a huge cloud's ridge (*Sleep and Poetry*, 129)

while Plate VII, figure 1, of a sardonyx in the same collection, is, apart from the mount, perfectly the 'feather'd lyrist' of *Endymion*, ii. 432. But all this is really part of another investigation. For those who care to pursue it I suggest the following parallels: *End.* iii. 653, *Polym.* 209, note 56; *End.* ii. 424–7, *Polym.* 72, note 59; *End.* iv. 93, *Polym*, 57; *Sleep and Poetry* 170, *Polym.* 51; *Lamia*, i. 218, *Polym.* 48, note 5; *End.* iv, 955, *Polym.* 182 and Plate XXVI, 2; *End.* i. 626, *Polym.* Plate XXX, 3; together with one which is directly relevant to *Hyperion*, *Polym.* 219, where Neptune is described as 'passing over the calm surface of the sea in his chariot drawn by sea horses', cf. *Hyperion*, ii. 234,

> his chariot, foam'd along
> By noble winged creatures he hath made?
> I saw him on the calmed waters scud.

Note F (*page* 76)

Davies tells us that Virgil had studied in the mysticism of Druid lore, and that all the accounts of Orpheus agree with Druidism (pp. 143, 144). Also 'according to our *Bardic* documents, the *Cymry* have preferred their claim to an ancient connection with not only the territories, but the mythology of *Greece*' (176). 'The music, and the nightly dance of *Apollo*, were, perhaps, pageants of *Druidical* device' (192). '*Tydain*, or in more ancient orthography, *Titain Tâd Awen*, *Titan*, *the father of inspiration or genius*, introduced order and method, into the poetry and memorials of the *Cymry*. This personage, who is identified, by *name*, and *character*, with *Titan*, or *Apollo*, of the *Orphic* hymns, and of *Greece*, forms a connecting link, between the mythologies of *eastern* and *western Europe*' (pp. 168, 169).

And this is perhaps as good a place as any to record some of the Egyptian references in Davies. 'We learn from Manetho, the celebrated Egyptian historian . . . that this Thoth lived *before the flood*. For he left his discoveries engraved upon certain columns, in the *sacred Dialect*, and in *Hieroglyphic Letters* . . .' (p. 24). 'The hieroglyphics on the Egyptian obelisks' (p. 37). 'This idea of a mutual intercourse, between the *Sages* of the *east* and the *west*, is countenanced by *Mr. Wilford's* incomparable dissertation, upon *Egypt* and the *Nile*, Asiat. Rec. V. 3' (p. 197). (This is clearly not far from 'When sages look'd to Egypt for their lore'.) I have no wish to press the Egyptian element in Davies; the passages quoted, and several others like them, are less significant than those quoted by Professor de Sélincourt and Miss Darbishire from other sources; but they are perhaps worth observing.

Note G (*page* 82)

Book I, line 13. HBF gives the cancelled MS. reading as *Spreading across it*; it is certainly *Shading across it*. In line 17 the original reading was *And slept without a motion since that time*, and not with the punctuation that both HBF and de S give it; the colon was a later insertion.

Line 81. de S says that *be outspread* is a correction in the MS. of *make spread*, but this does not represent what happened. Keats wrote *make* (as HBF justly notes the remains of a rejected thought, *make a mat*); then deleted *make* and wrote *spread*, still with the same idea of an object to come; and finally wrote in *be out* over the deleted *make*.

Line 111. de S notes that *arts* is clearly written in the MS. But in the *Arches* of line 180 the undoubted *c* is even more like an *r* than the doubtful letter here and I have no doubt that Keats meant *acts*.

Line 112. de S reads a cancelled *lest* as *but*; and the passage then makes no sense.

Line 131. There is a mysterious note in de S '*things* MS. corrected by Woodhouse. The bad writing of *strings* in our MS. accounts for the clerk's mistake'. It should read, I think '*things* in the transcript corrected by Woodhouse', since there is no sign of *things* in the MS.

Line 199. The significant alteration of *sad* to *saddened* almost certainly preceded, rather than, as de S says, followed, the indifferent cancellation of *a*.

Line 205. de S says that the line was originally

As open a Rosebud to a farae's Lute

doth being omitted by accident, and afterwards inserted. But the line is not a line at all, hypermetric or otherwise, with *doth* inserted. There is no doubt I think that HBF is right, and that the stages of the line were

As opes a Rose bud to a farae's Lute
As open Rose buds to a farae's Lute
As doth a Rose bud. . . .
Most like a Rose bud. . . .

Line 220. HBF reads the MS. as *paned*. But Keats often writes his *v* like an *n*, particularly when followed by *e*, and exactly the same combination of letters occurs in the repeated *nave* two lines above, in which the letter which must be a *v* is just as much like an *n* as the letter here in dispute.

Line 243. HBF leaves out one stage in the alterations, namely *in my old sanctuary*, which followed *into my sanctuary*, and so gives a reading which never existed at all.

Line 248. The deleted word is certainly not *seiz*; Keats' writing of *seize* is plain two lines lower, and the word in question ended with either *y* or *g*. It might be the beginning of *range* deleted before the *e* was written.

Line 257. The cancelled reading is certainly *glossy* (so HBF) and not *glassy* (de S).

Line 271. de S reads the cancelled word as *darkest*, HBF as *duskest*; since the second letter is more like *u* than *a* and the third more like *r* than *s* there is not much to choose.

Line 272. de S records only two attempts before *hid* was arrived at; there is clearly a third, which HBF reads as *dun*; I should read it as a badly written *dusk* (which would rather support *duskest* as against *darkest*).

Line 275. For *dark* there were two rejected attempts, of which de S says nothing; and in his edition, though not in the notes to the facsimile, he says that the line passed through the intermediate stage of *glared through* . . . But there is no sign whatever that *glow'd* was ever anything but *glow'd*.

Line 277. By a curious lapse de S transcribes *Up to the Zenith* as *Down to the Zenith*.

Line 284. HBF reads *Possess*. The double *s* is crowded, and the *d* ill-made and faint, but the MS. quite clearly reads *Possessd*.

Line 323. HBF gives the cancelled reading as *hurtled*; it was I think certainly *hurled* (and so de S), though with an extra minim.

Line 353. I think that HBF represents the stages more probably than de S, and that they were

And still they all were the same patient stars
And still he saw the same bright patient stars
And still they were the same bright patient stars.

Book II.

Line 16. HBF fails to decipher one of the cancelled words and gives it as *shoulder(?)*. de S rightly deciphers it as *sharpedg'd*, but by reading *ridged* as *ridge* gets the stages of alteration wrong. They were: *edge of Slate*, *sharpedg'd Slate*, *ridged Slate*, *Slaty ridge*.

Line 23. HBF records the MS. reading as *that keep*; it is certainly *that kept*.

Line 25. I can see no sign that the line was ever in the condition recorded by both HBF and de S, namely

Locked up like Metal veins with cramp and screw

the *t* and *d* being later additions. The stages were I think

Lock up (altered at once to Lock'd up)
Lock'd up like veins of Metal
Lock'd up like Metal veins, with
Lock'd up like veins of Metal, crampt and screw'd

Line 36. *the chill rain* was certainly never *a chill rain* (de S) because of the spacing. What was read as a cancelled *a* is a *c*, presumably the false start of *chill* or *chilly*, immediately written over by *the*.

Line 68. de S records after *lion-thoughted* an illegible word. HBF reads it as *sour'd*. But the second letter is almost certainly not an *o*, and the word is more like *sear'd* or *scar'd* (i.e. for *scarr'd*).

Line 83. HBF and de S both read the cancelled word as *tell*, which is indeed the natural reading, but for the fact that there is a minim too many and an apparent dot of an *i*. If it were not that it seems inconceivable that Keats should here write the word, one would confidently read it as *trill*. It might also be *toil* corrected to *tell*.

Line 136. HBF reads *secretly*; the word was *scantly*, and so de S.

Line 157. HBF reads a cancelled word as *thus*; de S is almost certainly right in reading it as *Alas* though the *A* is very incompletely made.

Line 169. HBF reads *gloom*; it is *glooms*, and so de S.

Line 179. de S does not record the interesting cancelled opening *healthy content*.

Line 209. Both HBF and de S omit the cancelled reading *size* before *form*.

Line 310. There is no justification for the introduction of a comma after *foolish* (de S), and HBF's original conjecture is amply confirmed without it.

Line 366. HBF reads the cancelled word as *shamed*, which in the context barely makes sense; de S, I think certainly rightly, as *showed*. But the pencilled *caught* in the margin can hardly be Keats' own, as de S thinks it may be, since not only is it unlike Keats' writing, but like the pencilled *hateful* four lines lower opposite the misspelt *heateful* it is preceded by *q* (i.e. *query*).

Line 387. HBF reads the last word of the cancelled line as *despair*, de S (numbering the line wrongly 385) as *desp(air?)*. But there is no sign of an *a* and the last letter appears to be *e*. It is more like *despise*, possibly an error for *despite*.

Book III.

Line 57. HBF and de S each leave out one, though not the same, stage. The stages were

These solitudes and seen the grass and flowers
These solitudes seeing the grass and flowers
These grassy solitudes and seen the flowers.

Line 63. The line never existed in the shape indicated by de S (*Didst find a golden lyre by thy side*). Keats got as far as *Didst find a golden Lyre* and then cancelled *golden* and completed the line as in the printed text.

Line 116. Again the line was never in the shape given by de S (*Creations, visage of destroyings and calm peace*, which, even as a record of the words on the page, omits an *s*, an *and*, and a comma). Keats wrote first *Creations, visages of* and then deleted *visages of* and continued *and destroyings, and calm peace* and finally substituted *all at once* for *and calm peace.*

There are various other minor points of doubt which are hardly worth notice. Any reader who studies the facsimile will observe that Professor de Sélincourt has not thought it necessary to reproduce in the transcriptions in his notes either the capitalizations or the punctuation of the MS.

Note H (*page* 97)

Egerton MSS. No. 2780. Some doubts have been expressed as to whether the transcripts in this volume are by George Keats, the suggestion being that they are by Georgiana Keats, on the grounds that the writing is not like that of George Keats. Buxton Forman dismissed both the doubts and the suggestion on the ground that the writing of all but one of the transcripts is unmistakably that of George Keats. This conflict of evidence is a trifle bewildering, and a matter for experts in handwriting. But it is, I think, clear that the transcript of *The Eve of St. Agnes* was made in England; therefore certainly not by Georgiana Keats, and presumably while George Keats was in England, and therefore probably by him. This is, I think, conclusively proved by the fact that in this volume *The Eve of St. Mark*, in Keats' own handwriting, comes in the middle of the transcript of *The Eve of St. Agnes*, the opening stanzas of *St. Agnes* being on leaves 31 and 32, followed by *St. Mark* on leaves 33–6, and the rest of *St. Agnes* on leaves 37–51, while the common watermark throughout the volume and the distribution of the leaves seem to preclude the supposition that George Keats took home with him John Keats' holograph of *St. Mark* and Georgiana Keats completed the transcripts of the other poems. And for our purposes all that matters is that the transcript of *The Eve of St. Agnes* was made (it is immaterial by whom) during George Keats' visit to England.

Note I (*page* 100)

Apart from differences of punctuation, and mere *lapsus calami*, such as *tiard* which the British Museum transcript reads for *tiara*, the differences between Woodhouse's second transcript as corrected and the British Museum transcript are as follows: Stanza I, line 7, W *in*, BM *from* (and omits *pious*); IV. 5, W *The high-lamp'd*, BM *High-lamped*; VI. 3, W *loves*,

BM *love*; vi. 8, W *require*, BM *enquire*; xiii. 3, W *muttered*, BM *uttered*; xiii. 5, W *the*, BM *a*; xiv. 4, W *elfs*, BM *Elves*; xv. 3, W *As*, BM *Like*; xix. 3, W *of such privacy*, BM *if such one there be*; xxiv. 3, W *fruit*, BM *fruits*; xxiv. 6, W *sunset*, BM *damask'd*; xxv. 9, W *knelt*; BM *prayed*; xxvi. 1, W *praying*, BM *vespers*; xxix. 3, W *with care quick* (misreading of *with anguish*), BM *half-anguished*; xxix. 6, W *midnight*, BM *braying*; xxix. 8, W *faintest*, BM *dying*; xxx. 6, W *syrups*, BM *syrup*; xxxi. 2, W *salvers*, BM *dishes*; xxxiii. 1, W *Awaking*, BM *Awakening*; xxxiv. 6, W *moan*, BM *mourn*; xxxv. 5, W *art thou*, BM *thou art*; xxxvi. 2 (rejected version), W *quick*, BM *close*; xlii. 6, W *long*, BM *all*; xlii. 7 (rejected version), W *by the palsy*, BM *with the palsy*.

Note J (*page* 246) [See Opposite]

Note K (*page* 261)

In the Houghton fragment we find:

After the hotest day comes Languidest
The colour'd eve, half-lidded in the west—
So they both look'd, so spake if breathed sound,
That almost silence is, hath ever found
Compare with nature quit. Which lov'd most,
Which had the weakest, strongest heart so lost,
So ruin'd, wreck'd, destroy'd: for certes they
Scarcely could tell if this was misery
Spells are but made to break. ~~said then the Youth~~
Whisper'd the Youth
Sure some sweet name thou hast; though by my truth
I had not ask'd it, ever thinking thee
Not mortal but of heavenly progeny,
~~As now I do~~ As still I do. Hast any mortal name?
Of fit ~~silver~~ sound for this soft ethereal frame

This is incorporated in the finished manuscript (here very far from finished) with the alteration of *lidded* to *hidden*, the cure of the hurried misspellings, and an alteration of the last line. The manuscript at first had the passage following our present line 81 as follows:

She burnt, she lov'd the tyranny,
Became herself a flame—'twas worth an age
Of minor joys to revel in such rage

(where we surely catch an echo of

Or if thy mistress some rich anger shows,
Emprison her soft hand, and let her rave,
And feed deep, deep upon her peerless eyes)

She was persuaded, and she fixt the hour
When he should make a Bride of his fair Paramour.

Note J (page 246)

	Early	SP	E.I	E.II	E.III	E.IV	Dryden All	Dryden High 4	Lamia
1.	11·9	14·8	7·3	5·0	6·0	7·7	4·0	4·5	11·6
2.	8·5	11·1	12·3	14·0	12·0	13·3	6·2	8·1	8·2
3.	5·6	8·9	8·7	9·3	5·0	8·7	..	..	4·2
4.	6·2	15·3	21·7	20·3	16·0	18·3	0·6	0·9	9·2
Total	32·2	50·1	50·0	48·6	39·0	48·0	10·8	13·5	33·2
Trip.	1·0	..	..	..	..	..	4·5	3·8	1·7
Alex.	..	..	..	..	..	..	3·5	3·9	5·7
Dis. Rhyme	20·0	14·8	8·0	2·7	4·7	4·7	..	..	..

After the hotest day comes languidest
The colour'd Eve, half-hidden in the west;
So they both look'd, so spake, if breathed sound,
That almost silence is, hath ever found
Compare with nature's quiet. Which lov'd most,
Which had the weakest, strongest, heart so lost,
So ruin'd, wreck'd, destroy'd: for certes they
Scarcely could tell they could not guess
Whether 'twas misery or happiness.
Spells are but made to break. Whisper'd the Youth
'Sure some sweet name thou hast; though by my truth
'I had not ask'd it, ever thinking thee
'Not mortal but of heavenly progeny,
'As still I do. Hast any mortal name?

And then he likes both *fit* and the deleted *silver* so much that the next line has to become an Alexandrine:

'Fit silver appellation for this dazzling frame?
'Or friends, or kinsfolks on the citied Earth,
'To share our marriage feast and nuptial mirth?'

And then the real difficulties begin:

'I have no friends' said Lamia as you list
~~Seeing it must be~~
~~Do with your own~~
Intreat your many guests. Then all was was wist
She fell asleep, and Lycius to the shade
Of sleep sunk with her ~~dreaming~~ when his fancy stray'd
Into a dream. . . .

The last two lines were cut out, and the next line, continuing from *to the shade* was first started as

Of sleep went

and then written as

Of deep sleep in a moment was betray'd.

Then he went back two lines, cancelled *as you list* and wrote

no not one
My presence in wide Corinth is unknown;

and went on to amplify this:

My parent's bones are in their dusty urns
Sepulchred, where no kindled incense burns,
Seeing all their luckless race are dead, save me,
And I neglect the holy rite for thee.

Then he changes what he has already written about the bidding of the guests:

> Even as you list invite your many guests;
> But if, as now it seems, your vision rests
> With any pleasure on me, summon not
> Old Apollonius. Lycius ignorant what
> Strange thought had led her to an end so blank,
> Made close inquiry; from whose touch she shrank,
> Feigning a sleep; and he to the dull shade
> Of deep sleep in a moment was betray'd.

Then he cancelled the whole passage from *Became herself a flame* and re-wrote it, with a few minor differences (amongst them the retention of *silver* before *appellation*) as we now have it. He cut out, that is to say, ten largely irrelevant lines, and strengthened the others.

Note L (*page* 262)

For parts of the passage which now stands as lines 122–220 we have four different versions, which in order of date are as follows: some Houghton fragments, covering lines 122–47, 191–8; a long quotation in a letter to Taylor of September 5, 1819, covering lines 122–62, and foreshadowing lines 199–220; the finished manuscript; and the 1820 text.

The first three lines stand in all versions. For the next line Keats wrote first the simple

> The carved cedar

and then began to elaborate it; first

> Sweet cedar carv'd there

then

> Fresh Carved Cedar spread a

then

> Fresh Carved Cedar mimicking a glade

This reading was arrived at in the fragment, and persists. In line 133 the letter reads *Teeming a perfume*; in the finished manuscript this was first copied, then deleted and the more elaborate *Teeming wing'd odours* substituted, which in turn gave way to the simple *Teeming with odours* of the text.

In line 134 the fragment reads *silverly* for *silently* and the letter follows it. The manuscript gives the reading of the text.

In line 137 Keats first wrote

> The splendid finish of each nook and niche

in the letter this is changed to

> The splendid cornicing of nook and niche

while the manuscript has the more defined picture

> The fretted splendour of each nook and niche

In line 138 the letter reads *wainscoated*; the manuscript follows this, but then deletes the word and substitutes the *marbled plain* of the text.

In line 140 Keats first wrote the colourless

> Forth tenderer imagery of smaller trees (Fragment)

but at once altered it to the reading of the text.

After line 141 the fragment has four lines which were cancelled before the copy was made in the letter. Two of them are hardly modified repetitions of Part I, 57–8.

> And so till she was sated—then came down
> Soft ligh[t]ing o'er her Brows a brilliant crown

altered to

> Soft lighting on her head a brilliant crown
> Wreathed turban-~~like~~wise of tender wannish fire
> And sprinkled o'er with stars like Ariadne's tiar.

In lines 146–7 the fragment reads

> The day came soon and all the gossip-rout
> O senseless Lycius Dolt! Fool! Madman! Lout!

and this weakly apostrophic reading is repeated in the letter, which continues

> Why would you murder happiness like yours,
> And show to common eyes these secret bowers?

In the manuscript *came soon* is written but changed at once to *appear'd* and the rest of the passage altered to the reading of the text.

In lines 150–3 the letter reads

> The Herd came, and each guest, with buzzy brain,
> Arriving at the Portal, gaz'd amain,
> And enter'd won'dring

The manuscript reads

> The Herd came, and

and then The Herd arriv'd

the *approach'd* of the text not appearing in the manuscript. But the manuscript after giving *wondring* alters it to *marveling*. The passage from line 163 to line 172 does not appear at all except as an addition to the manuscript, where it is written first on the back of the preceding page and then copied out on a separate sheet.

Nor are there any signs in the letter of lines 173–98, but this I think must simply be because Keats was not in the letter quoting continuously, but just giving Taylor samples, since lines 191–8 occur with various readings in the Houghton fragment. But in the letter immediately on line 162 follows a passage which is presumably the first attempt at lines 199–220 of the 1820 text, and it is worth giving in full as showing what Keats could still perpetrate. And we must observe that he evidently did not regard it at all as a rough draft to be worked over, since it comes in the same letter in which he says that he has finished *Lamia*. 'Since I have finished it (Otho) I have finish'd Lamia: and am now occupied in revising St. Agnes' Eve and studying Italian.'

> Soft went the music, and the tables all
> Sparkled beneath the viewless banneral
> Of Magic; and dispos'd in double row
> Seem'd edged Parterres of white bedded snow,
> Adorned along the sides with living flowers
> Conversing, laughing after sunny showers:
> And as the pleasant appetite entic'd,
> Gush came the wine, and sheer the meats were slic'd.
> Soft went the Music; the flat salver sang
> Kiss'd by the emptied goblet—and again it rang:
> Swift bustled by the servants:—here's a health
> Cries one—another—then, as if by stealth,
> A Glutton drains a cup of Helicon,
> Too fast down, down his throat the brief delight is gone.
> 'Where is that Music?' cries a Lady fair.
> 'Aye, where is it my dear? Up in the air?'
> Another whispers. 'Poo!' saith Glutton 'Mum!'
> Then makes his shiny mouth a knapkin for his thumb. &c. &c. &c.

One can only hope that the triple *&c.* did not represent much more in this vein, and wonders whether Woodhouse commented in such a way as to make him alter it. In the same letter in which Woodhouse alarmed Taylor about the alterations in *The Eve of St. Agnes*, he tells him that Keats had read him *Lamia*, and he says 'the friends are invited to the wedding feast—and K. wipes the cits & the low lived ones: of some of whom he says "who make their mouth a napkin to their thumb" in the midst of this Imperial splendour'. So that it is clear that this is the passage that Woodhouse heard, and clear too that though he makes no adverse comment in the letter, the cheap phrase about the napkin had stuck in his mind, as well it might. It is also clear that, if Woodhouse is correct, Lamia was not 'finished' in the sense of being finally copied out, since Woodhouse records that Keats has 'half fair copied' it.

INDEX

References in heavy type are to the main passages in the text relevant to the entry

PRINTED IN GREAT BRITAIN AT THE UNIVERSITY PRESS, OXFORD
BY JOHN JOHNSON, PRINTER TO THE UNIVERSITY